FRANCES IN THE COUNTRY

LIZ GARTON SCANLON

SEAN QUALLS

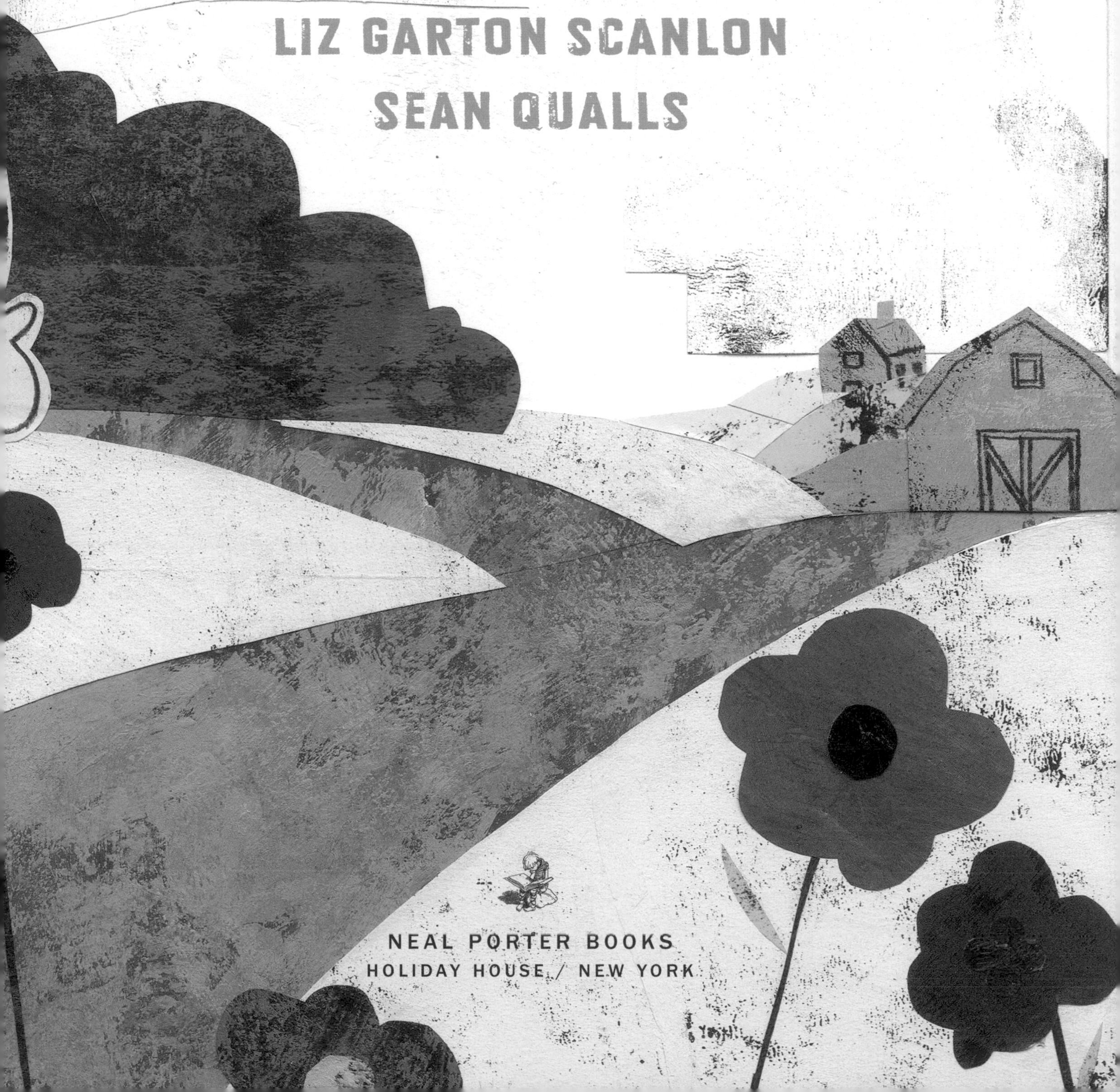

NEAL PORTER BOOKS

HOLIDAY HOUSE / NEW YORK

For VWA and her city kids
—L.G.S.

For Ginger and Czen
—S.Q.

Neal Porter Books

Text copyright © 2022 by Liz Garton Scanlon
Illustrations copyright © 2022 by Sean Qualls
All Rights Reserved
HOLIDAY HOUSE is registered in the U.S. Patent and Trademark Office.
Printed and bound in February 2022 at Toppan Leefung, DongGuan, China.
The artwork for this book was created with acrylic paint, collage, and pencil.
Book design by Jennifer Browne
www.holidayhouse.com
First Edition
1   3   5   7   9   10   8   6   4   2

Library of Congress Cataloging-in-Publication Data

Names: Scanlon, Elizabeth Garton, author. | Qualls, Sean, illustrator.
Title: Frances in the country / by Liz Garton Scanlon ; illustrated by Sean
  Qualls.
Description: First edition. | New York : Holiday House, [2022] | "A Neal
  Porter book" | Audience: Ages 4 to 8 | Audience: Grades K–1 | Summary:
  "A spirited girl visits her cousins in the country for a chance to break
  free from the clamor and crowd of life in the city."—Provided by
  publisher.
Identifiers: LCCN 2021037880 | ISBN 9780823443321 (hardcover)
Subjects: CYAC: City and town life—Fiction. | Conduct of life—Fiction. |
  Cousins—Fiction. | LCGFT: Picture books.
Classification: LCC PZ7.S2798 Fr 2022 | DDC [E]—dc23
LC record available at https://lccn.loc.gov/2021037880

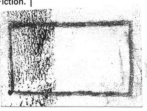

Frances is a city kid, but the city never seems quite right for Frances.

City walls aren't for climbing
and city cats aren't for catching.

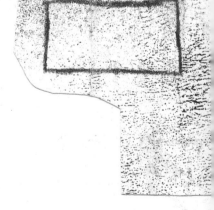

City rooms aren't
for running
and city steps aren't
for sliding down.

City shops are crowded and city parks are, too.

Frances tries to be good, but it's hard when you're not supposed to climb or ride or race or shout. There are so many rules, and Frances can't seem to follow any of them.

That's why city mamas say things like

look out!

hush . . .

come back right this minute!

And city sisters say things like

Frances!!

And
city
lights
just
say

stop.

So Frances visits her
cousins in the country,

where hay is
for hiding.

And cats are for catching.

And roads are for racing down.

(At home, walls and cats and shops sit still.
There is no Frances crossing the street . . .
or skipping rope . . .
or singing.)

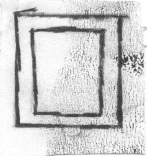

In the country, ladders
are for leaping
and showers are
for splashing

and fields are crowded with creatures
and cowbells and cud.

In the country, Frances gets to
go
go
go.

(In the city, her mama sighs
and her sisters do, too.)

When it's time for Frances to leave,

it isn't easy.

The lake says **Look!**
The horse says **Hush.**
And the cousins say
Come back soon.

Frances says,
Yes, I'll be back!

But then she says,
You could come see me, too.
At home!

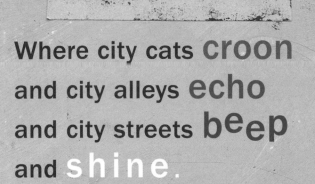

Where city cats **croon**
and city alleys **echo**
and city streets **beep**
and **shine**.

Where city steps **thump**
and city rooms **ring**
and city lights climb
and run and dance
and **zoom**—a little
like Frances!

Where city sisters
say things like
Frances!

Oh, Frances!

And a certain
city mama says,
You're back,
my girl!

Come here,
right this
minute!

And Frances does.

Paul Bosman Architects
302 Main Street, Suite 201
Los Altos, CA   94022

Small Houses for the Next Century

Other McGraw-Hill Books of Interest

Small Houses
for the
Next Century

Second
Edition

___

Duo Dickinson

McGraw-Hill, Inc.
New York   San Francisco   Washington, D.C.   Auckland   Bogotá
Caracas   Lisbon   London   Madrid   Mexico City   Milan
Montreal   New Delhi   San Juan   Singapore
Sydney   Tokyo   Toronto

Library of Congress Cataloging-in-Publication Data

Dickinson, Duo.
    Small houses for the next century / Duo Dickinson.—[2nd ed.]
        p.   cm.
    Updated ed. of: The small house.   c 1986.
    Includes index.
    ISBN 0-07-016828-8
    1. Small houses—United States—Designs and plans.   2. Architect-
designed houses—United States—Designs and plans.   I. Dickinson,
Duo.   Small house.   II. Title.
NA7205.D55   1994
728′.37—dc20   94-23191
                                                                           CIP

    3 4 5 6 7 8 9 0   KGP/KGP   9 0 9 8 7 6

ISBN 0-07-016828-8

The sponsoring editor for this book was Joel Stein, the editing
supervisor was Ruth W. Mannino, and the production supervisor
was Suzanne W. B. Rapcavage. It was designed and set in Adobe
Garamond by Silvers Design.

Previously published under the title *The Small House: An Artful Guide to
Affordable Architectural Design.*

Printed and bound by Quebecor/Kingsport Press.

McGraw-Hill books are available at special quantity discounts to use as premiums
and sales promotions, or for use in corporate training programs. For more information,
please write to the Director of Special Sales, McGraw-Hill, Inc., 11 West 19th Street,
New York, NY 10011. Or contact your local bookstore.

This book is printed on acid-free paper.

For Will and Sam

Contents

Foreword

I wonder about the title of this book, *Small Houses for the Next Century.* If these buildings fulfill the needs of their owners, then they aren't small. They are appropriate. Perhaps all larger dwellings should be called "Big Houses" and this collection, "Houses."

Appropriateness ought to be the measure of any dwelling, but appropriateness to what? The answer can only be: "To the needs of the user (and, for us, of the site)." A description of needs is the necessary starting point for the design of any dwelling. Although any owner and site will always have a unique set of needs to which an architect should respond, I believe these can be divided into three general categories:

1. Physical and spatial needs of a family
2. Physical needs of the place
3. Spiritual needs of the individual

These categories are not hierarchical but must be considered simultaneously.

Just as a garment fits the physical and spatial needs of sheltering the body, so must a house do the same for the institution of family. In order to clothe that institution, one must first understand and measure its anatomy and organize a plan that fits around it. The smaller the garment the more care is needed in sizing it, so that it doesn't pinch here or feel too tight there. When designing a big house (like baggy clothes), inches don't count. In small houses they do.

The designer should strive to create public areas that are open and inviting and private areas that are concealed and have controlled access. The entry should simultaneously invite a guest but keep out a stranger. The garden must join with the interior to connect the occupants with their natural environment. If all of this can be done without individuals bumping into one another, then the house is not only appropriate but efficient. It takes no crystal ball to recognize that efficiency in the use of resources will be both morally and legally a prime determinant of building design in the future.

The notions of appropriateness and efficiency are consistent with a concern for the physical needs of the land on which the house is constructed. Not only does a smaller more efficient building take up less space but its footprint is more easily fit into and molded by the unique circumstances of vegetation and topography.

Flexibility is key in designing a building to fit its surroundings. Over time and through many regrettable misperceptions about the true nature of the profession, we have come to realize that architecture rarely if ever makes the land better (particularly land that is in a natural state). The task, then, is to look for ways to mitigate the damage done to the land.

The value of knowledge gleaned from surveying the contours and location of the vegetation by the designer is immeasurable. Understanding the land can better inform the direction of the design in a way that minimizes damage and facilitates the orchestration of the staging and construction process. Respect for the living systems of the land can to some degree lessen the impact of architecture on nature.

This aspect touches upon the unquantifiable aspects of building a house. If all we need is shelter, we could live in prefabricated utility buildings, put in a kitchen and a toilet, and be satisfied. I would be out of a job, and you wouldn't be reading this book. However, we do need more than simply shelter, and this need involves a comprehension of the dream (and the place) and the ability to conceive of its physical manifestation and then to execute that conception in detail.

Small houses, because of their size and limited elements, allow the designer greater scope in expressing the interpretation of these dreams. Furthermore, because of the more limited number of intersections and detail connections, the necessary construction details can be carefully examined and refined to more thoroughly reinforce the manifestation of these dreams.

In the finality, we are dream spinners. What we really sell are magic beans that grow into livable objects. The pages that follow display built dreams that are appropriate for the present and even more so for the future.

Jim Cutler, FAIA

"I would rather solve the small house problem than build anything else I can think of (except the modern theatre). But where is a better small house to come from while Government housing itself is only perpetuating the old stupidities? I do not believe it will come from current education, from big business or by way of smart advertising experts. It must come from common sense—a pattern for more simple and at the same time more gracious living."

Frank Lloyd Wright,
Architectural Forum, January 1938

Preface

Houses have a unique place in our hearts and minds. They are at once the most familiar and idiosyncratic of buildings. A house consumes the lion's share of our wallet and the sweetest side of our material dreams. Successful houses not only fit their particular occupants but also serve as cultural icons.

Although everyone is an expert about his or her dream house, building or renovating a house is one of the most stressful discretionary acts possible; it empowers and threatens, exhilarates and depresses, and ultimately gives a family its worldly focus.

Because experience is not mandatory in designing a house, young architects often design private residences. Moreover, architect-designed houses can be the height of esoterica. The results can be an ever-widening circle of legendary blunders and insensitivities; it leaks, it rots; you trip, you freeze; doors hit each other; furniture doesn't fit. The client ends up hurt, angry, and broke.

Whether the blind arrogance of an architect or the confused motivations of a client, the lack of proper perspective triggers most design failures. A house, for instance, will not fix a troubled marriage or make children love their parents. On the other hand, if the architect's hidden agenda is to use the project to progress to bigger and better commissions via designing for the camera and publication, the client will be pushed out of the picture with unfortunate results.

Designing a house is inherently pressurized, frightening, and frustrating. Yet, more than any other type of building, a house can convey the quiet power of truth, and, like poetry or music, it can have a resonant meaning that defies explicit analysis.

This book is a sequel to one written in 1985 and published in 1986—*The Small House*. Times have changed, and it is time to take a fresh look at one of the oldest human constructions, the home. The intent of the book is not only to update the state of the art but to apply new thoughts and views evidenced by the quality of the projects received.

Rather than reiterate the abstract architectural tools for effective small-house design, I've opted to focus this book on the benefits that the small-house building type has on the nonarchitectural issues of late twentieth century America. Each of the 35 case studies analyzes the means and methods employed, but glued between these disparate projects is their essential utility in the context of the coming millennium, a time of large cultural evolution and some tough hurdles for those who wish to design and/or build homes.

Methods of collecting materials were similar to the first book. For the period subsequent to the publication of the first book, virtually every residential magazine focusing on house design (whether it was intended for architects or homeowners or both) was reviewed with well over 200 architects contacted by mail. All accredited architecture

schools in the United States were written to, with a broadside included in the mailing. All state and local chapters of the AIA in the United States were written to, also with a broadside included. Personal solicitations were made of nationally known architects, and follow-ups were made on secondary and tertiary referrals from those whose work didn't fit but who had a name or two to offer.

The net result was that over 400 individual houses coming from well over 300 total architects nationwide were reviewed. Criteria used in the process of selection included size, geographic distribution, and stylistic diversity, as well as the intent to mix the work of well-known and established firms with that of new and emerging talent, the latter often using small homes to evidence their "take" on aesthetics and to showcase their practice of the profession of architecture.

Unlike the first book, this project does not have architect sketches or quotes; unfortunately, a significant percentage of both were simply retroactive rationalizations. In their place are two new abstract design criteria that have been introduced and described in the Introduction. Also, in receiving 35 viable built projects for publication, there was no need to have a section devoted to "paper projects."

This book is not intended to provide negative examples. It is hoped that in the broad context of a wide variety of projects, a positive, forward-looking ethic of rigorous and innovative home design can be evidenced. The intention is not to provide examples of what's *wrong* with residential architecture in America today—95 percent of the homes that dominate America's landscape do that job so well that anyone reading this book while looking out of the window will have a healthy contrast by which to gauge the talents of the designers evidenced within its pages.

Duo Dickinson

Acknowledgments

In the formulation of this book I would like to thank Shirley Halstead, my office manager, who typed every word of the manuscript; Ruth Mannino, my editing supervisor, who thoughtfully shepherded the book through every inch of the production process; and especially Joel Stein, Senior Editor, Architecture, who had the enthusiasm and patience to inspire this effort. Lastly, my family bears much in tolerating my life's work; thank you Liz, Will, and Sam.

Introduction

I. Sequel Reasoning

When *The Small House* was written in 1985, America was on the verge of its greatest residential building boom since the 1950s. Millions of baby-boom-generation households were participating in the inevitable "echo boom" of family creation. As in the 1950s, marriage and the birth of children combined with lowering interest rates and widespread employment and prosperity to foster a rising sense of promise and optimism.

Obviously, this book is being fashioned in the 1990s. It is a time when, metaphorically, the exuberance and optimism of childbirth has been replaced by a somewhat somber focus upon a looming awkward adolescence in the American outlook. It seems we will have to work longer to earn less. Even though the cold war is over, we are left with a foreboding sense that the future has a risky, rather than an energizing, countenance.

Most of the projects included in this book have been conceived and built in this more sober mind-set. Several projects that considerably predate the 1990s are included because they evidence inherent virtues and innovations. When businesses feel threatened, overhead costs are analyzed and reduced. So it is and will be in American domestic life as families look to limit the cost of their accommodation. Whereas in the 1980s it was timeless common sense that argued for the reduction in building mass and square footage as a method to both reduce cost and enhance amenity, in the 1990s it has become an economic and environmental necessity to create homes as efficient as any of the high-tech appliances or automobiles that are being reinvented all around us on a daily basis.

Although technological innovations will be addressed within the book's format on a case-by-case basis, the core concept of this book (as with the last edition) is that houses that are relatively smaller than our recent norms serve their occupants best. America has long been the land of the ever-expanding frontier, with a "homesteading" attitude extending into our perception of what makes homes desirable. Most people have felt, and still feel, that when there is a problem of "fit" in a home, the answer is to expand to provide generous elbow room, rather than to rethink the spatial priorities of the building's essential organization. This open-ended expansionist philosophy serves the purposes of designers who do not wish to think deeply about designing homes.

II. Demographics, Mind-Set, and Fit

The single-family home is often seen as emblematic of the family unit or of an American culture based on a suburban utopia. This picturesque vision has seldom had a hard edge of purely functionalist thinking applied to its design principles. At the other end of the spectrum of public consciousness are homes that receive academic acclaim and architect envy. These projects are often designed as esoteric sculptures in which people happen to live.

It is the premise of this book that truly successful homes for the reality-based twenty-first century will have much tougher design criteria to deal with—the idiosyncratic nature of the way each and every family lives within any

home. The nuclear family is ever present, but its subatomic particulates are spiraling into our culture and will soon become a very large portion of the housing market—if they haven't already. It's always tough to design for individuals, but in a culture whose typical family structure is fragmenting into a wide variety of households, the list of occupant design programs widens to include single-parent homes, multigenerational homes, homes that contain offices, homes that harbor empty-nesters, homes for unrelated individuals living together as a family, and on and on. Microdesigning to accommodate the different use patterns of nontraditional households becomes a necessity because the needs of these households preclude a large segment of available housing stock. Levittown does not fit the 1990s. The idea of small, mass-produced identical houses set row upon row cannot accommodate the extraordinary variety of use patterns homes are put to today. What will not change within the next generation in America is that the freestanding, single-family house will almost always be viewed as desirable over mass-produced common living arrangements.

I believe that there is a growing future for the architect-designed American home. Homes almost always represent a family's largest investment, and a growth industry lies in the accommodation of the widespread diversity of familial definitions that will define our culture in the next century. Extraordinary innovation and architectural exploration occur when the idiosyncratic qualities of particular homeowners mesh with the similarly idiosyncratic characteristics of individual architects. There is powerful synergy present when innovative minds get together to form a short-term limited partnership to build something that is inherently unprecedented. It's long been true that many of the most exploratory and exciting movements in architectural history were tested in the conceptual waters of single-family residential design. The individual home has served as a laboratory for many radical ideas—mostly dealing with abstract aesthetic notions that could be applied to any building, perhaps even any object. It is now time to apply the same sort of creativity in the fitting of homes to their occupants that architects have historically used in embracing new technologies and materials.

The unavoidable truth is that the act of architectural design too often exists in a relative vacuum. Its practitioners are often isolated creators looking inward, ignoring environmental or cultural factors that get in the way of aesthetic preconception. Schools have no viable method for utilizing the most important generative aspect of any single-family design, namely, client input. It is almost impossible to find clients in the classrooms of architecture schools. Professors, by necessity, have to set up relatively abstract problems that deal more with hard-edged design criteria such as site limitations and programmatic requirements than with well-understood functions (while eschewing any sense of budgetary constraint). So when any architect (but especially the youthful practitioner) initiates the design process of a single-family home, there is a natural tendency to give client input short shrift and to push a preconceived or thoroughly abstract design product that has been formed "out of the loop" of an open design process. The houses that result from this mind-set often pay only lip service to the accommodation of any client requirements, because these may blunt the spear of an architect's preconceived notion. It's a lot easier to ignore those elements that get in the way of a powerful image. If not a blind eye, then a lazy eye is often cast to integrating clients' "unenlightened" perspectives into the place where they will live.

A secondary value of this book would be to chip away at the conception that architects and clients have an inherently adversarial relationship. Just as a tailor needs to measure an inseam with an accuracy that often creates embarrassment, architects need to gauge and measure a client's heartfelt fantasies and reality-based use patterns to create homes that contour directly to both their personalities and their life-styles.

This extent of deeply personal knowledge can only be conveyed between two open nonjudgmental minds—the client's and the architect's. Having had a prejudicial education and coming into an atmosphere with fewer opportunities for architectural expression, architects today (and in the future) will have to look at house commissions as a growing but slightly daunting area of opportunity. It is rare that the combination of house and occupants is totally successful without direct accommodation of owner input. Whereas in previous generations large quantities of built space compensated for any idiosyncratic use patterns, homes of the present and the future will, by necessity, shrink to fit their occupants, and this customization requires planning and design.

It may be said that the sum total of any architect's experience needs to be brought to bear when incorporating the large number of particular factoids provided by a homeowner. In house design, relatively inarticulate or incoherent musings, dreams, and fears of clients often overlay the entire process, and the designer requires the highest

level of architectural competence and personal confidence to absorb and integrate all these items into a successful home. It might be said that the small home should be the province of our most experienced designers since they possess the tools that allow the most cogent and efficient expression of the personal values of both the architect and the homeowner within the limited palette (and often budget) a single-family home affords. Unfortunately, architects' design fees are always greater than the costs of stock plans or the gratis offering of stock or modified stock plans from a speculative builder. Therefore, the level of service must be worth the cost. And that level of service is directly keyed to the ability of architects to embrace client input.

III. Sizing Up Downsizing

This book displays successful designs that use spatial constriction to their advantage, thus gaining a sense of aesthetic focus that a larger, less rigorously designed building simply does not have.

The adjective *small* is a relative one. Although reviews for the first edition were quite favorable, those who found fault with it could not understand calling a six-bedroom, 3,500-square-foot, house "small." For that reason, this book emphasizes that any home can be deemed to be relatively small as defined by its *total* square footage in relationship to its most essential requirement: bedroom count. A small gymnasium is still a relatively large building. You can have a small six-bedroom home if it contours to a size that is well below expected norms. Therefore, with a few exceptions, acceptance of potential projects for this book has been limited to the following size criteria:

1. One bedroom: less than 1,500 square feet
2. Two bedrooms: less than 2,000 square feet
3. Three bedrooms: less than 2,500 square feet
4. Four or more bedrooms: less than 3,500 square feet

It should be noted that most standard American houses tend to be significantly larger than the sizes given here, and most of the homes presented in this book are far below these maximum square footages.

To emphasize this organizational logic, the projects presented in this book are divided by bedroom count and are presented in order of increasing square-footage. This departure from the first edition of this book responds to the way readers said they used the first book—usually to find an occupancy size that was similar to their own. So, unlike the first edition, this volume mixes full-time occupancy residences with vacation homes, but each project description clearly represents the specific use pattern accommodated.

IV. Limits: Natural and Conspired

More often than not, successful homes plan for their future use as well as their present needs. This often means that master planning at the initiation of the design process will allow for the inclusion of future revisions or expansions. Planning will also have to anticipate that the fossil fuels that we depend on today are at relatively depressed prices and that these prices will increase over the next generation—either because of government-imposed trade sanctions and taxes or because of the vagaries of international politics. Additionally, the relatively accessible fossil fuels we enjoy today will become harder to harvest, and thus inevitably more expensive to develop.

Therefore, it is imperative that beyond the simple act of downsizing to minimize the amount of air mass to be treated, homes of the future (and small homes in particular) will need to embrace the available natural elements that help heat and cool buildings—wind, sun, shade, and the thermal mass of the earth itself—and to aggressively utilize the ongoing development of microprocessor-assisted energy efficiency as well as the material breakthroughs that enhance thermal resistance.

Beyond the undeniable logic of size reduction to enhance efficiency and ongoing maintenance, the nature of available building sites is an ever-increasing influence for the minimizing of a home's footprint. As mentioned in the first edition, sites that are available in and around our major urban centers are typically steeply sloped, wet, or rocky (or all three!). Often, prime sites in urban areas already have a house set upon them that is simply not worth saving

because of its condition or its irrevocably misfitting nature; "teardowns" have become common in coastal areas and will be an ever larger portion of the sites used for new construction.

In the last decade, a large range of zoning and engineering limitations have served to limit the buildable area available on many sites. Chief among these are septic requirements, because municipalities all across the country have realized that the shrinking supply of groundwater cannot tolerate ineffective septic systems nor can the potability of the water table be maintained with full coverage of all available land with developed sites that discharge effluent and increase runoff on an ongoing basis. So in many (if not most) communities, "100 percent reserve" septic designs not only provide for all the area that is required for a fully functional septic system but also segregate a backup area of the site equivalent to the area of the installed septic system to be set aside and not built upon. This area is required as both a backup system location in case the one in place fails and as a de facto method of the reduction in site development density, thus serving to limit septic loads and runoff. The practical reality of this imposition is that the space left on the site for building shrinks.

Additionally, towns around major urban centers have seen their infrastructure stressed out by large-sized homes on small-sized lots (even if common sewer systems and common water distribution networks are present). In response, some towns are now employing *floor area ratio,* or *FAR,* site limitations, where the size of the *total floor area of the house* is keyed to the size of the lot. This zoning limitation is almost exclusively applied in commercial or industrial districts and is often used to limit the size of a skyscraper's projection into the available three-dimensional building envelope provided in most city's zoning codes.

Beyond that, for coastal and wetlands sites many municipalities have enhanced or increased limitations in terms of setbacks, definitions of wetlands and watercourses, and restrictions on site disturbance as well as the area of the site to be built upon. All these trends combine with a defensive posture many highly developed towns assume when they have been "burned" by for-profit, high-density developments. This attitude preempts flexibility in interpreting the "as-of-right" siting criteria—thus causing many sites to have restrictive limitations on their buildable area, once again necessitating expertise in small house design.

When these code regulations are seen in conjunction with the natural limitations of "leftover" sites of dubious perimeter configurations, topographical variation, or subsoil viability, the nonaesthetic, nonethical, nonfiscal realities of the late twentieth century are trending to compel America's homes to diminish in size.

This book presents exemplars of homes that respond to all of these criteria and hopefully point to the viability of enhanced amenity despite shrinking expectations.

Small Houses for the Next Century

The Concept of "Fit"

IN the previous edition, the concept of "perceived space" was described in general, and the results of the computations executed for each project were offered. That standard will be applied to this book as well (see the Appendix for the definitional aspects of this concept). Perceived space deals with the idea that homes can feel bigger than they are dimensionally, but there was no abstract method employed by the first edition by which efficiency can be gauged.

If overall sizing were the only criterion, a sleeping bag would win any efficiency contest. If the occupant-per-square-foot ratio were the best way to gauge efficacy, then prisons and academic dormitories would be paradigms of efficiency. These building forms do not contour to the classic American ideal of a single-family home with its own land and sense of personal empowerment. The prototypic aspirational path of most homeowners is to diverge (at least at the middling years) from the tight communal aspects of condominium or apartment house living. Therefore, there needs to be a way to describe the way any house, big or small (by anyone's definitions), can be gauged to be efficacious in the way it harbors people.

The projects selected for this book show that there can be another perspective used to evidence the efficacy of small house design, namely, "fit." There are two ratios that I think are important and can serve as a gauge by which the concept of "fit" can be applied. Before describing the arithmatic derivation of these ratios, it is necessary to define what my personal vision of fit is.

"Fit" is a word that has one common definition: that what is offered contours to what is to be accommodated. In off-the-rack clothing or automobiles, there is very little adjustment that can be made other than getting a different product to fit your body. In homes, it's hoped (and advocated in this book) that architects will be sensitive to what will make a house fit a client. After all, fit is the bottom-line practical reality that can make a smaller than normal house truly work for its tenants.

Fit can be said to be that aspect of a house which makes living in it effortless. If a pair of pants is too loose, hems drag and hands tug to keep them up; when too tight, every movement becomes a reminder of the misfit. So it is with houses. The problematic aspect of a universal definition of the concept of fit lies in the fact that there are millions of idiosyncratic definitions of "fit." This book proposes to offer two quick measures of the fit within the four walls of any house.

If the desire is to make a home efficient, then what areas of it should shrink to fit? For most people the only areas that would not be universally missed if they were diminished are spaces solely given over to circulation (hallways, entryways, and so on) and large spaces given over to sleeping. How can those areas be gauged as functioning efficiently within the context of a house? As with any arithmetic analysis of an absolutely personal design problem, there will be projects where these measurements are simply not applicable or are incalculable. But all comparisons have some odious aspects, so in the desire to be consistent when cross-referencing so many diverse projects, these two methods will be employed.

I. Circulation-to-Total-Area Ratio

By measuring the square feet allowed for circulation and applying that figure against the square footage of the entire house, it's relatively easy to determine how much area is given solely to circulation. Note that no area will be counted as circulation if it serves as part of the perceived space of any room; it will be counted as circulation only if it is defined by two walls as a place for paths only. Space counted as circulation must provide access between habitable spaces; it cannot be habitable space as addressed by most building codes.

The simple logic is that the less space given over solely to circulation, the better the fit makes sense in and of itself. Obviously, this calculation can often be counterbalanced by the application of the perceived-space construct, where ceremonial entries and hallways often enhance the perceived space of the house. But for the vast majority of houses, especially ones that are designed to be smaller than normal, less circulation space means a more efficient, and thus more desirable, house.

Hence, the lower the ratio of circulation to total areas, the better the fit.

II. Bedroom-Space-to-Total-Area Ratio

This arithmetic construct is also somewhat arbitrary, but it establishes the fact that in most contexts small houses use bedrooms as places for beds and dressing and little else; thus if more space is given over to these functions than is necessary, efficiency is compromised. This construct can fly in the face of somebody's dream of what constitutes a perfect dwelling if he or she wishes to live in a house that is virtually a huge master bedroom suite with a kitchen. But that use pattern is so seldom found that this ratio does seem to make sense as a way to gauge fit between the public and private parts of a house. The use pattern that generated the concept of "bedroom as second home" was not encountered in any of the 35 houses included in this book.

Simply put, the square footage solely given over to sleeping spaces (the hybrid den/guest bedroom and closet space will not be counted) will be applied against the total square footage of a house to derive a ratio: the smaller the percentage, the greater the likelihood the house maximizes its sense of spaciousness, efficacy, and fit.

The Small House Expanded

To provide an in-depth description of the ways in which *any* small house can be designed to fit problematic sites and reflect an occupant's life-style, the first edition of this book focused on the design and construction of my house in Madison, Connecticut.

When the original home was built, it was intended that it would harbor two full-time professionals who were creating their first home—a 1,100-square-foot, single-bedroom house. The idea of expansion was a glimmer on the horizon, and was conceptually accommodated with a pocket of space available to the east of the house.

Any thoughts of our home's expansion were beset by the same limitations that were in effect when we built it in 1984:

1. *Wetlands.* Set adjacent to a salt marsh, the available land to build upon was restricted beyond the normal, town-required setback off the property line, and the regulations mandated that the level of the first-floor framing had to be set far above the existing contours of the landscape.
2. *Deed restrictions.* The sellers of the lot were also the neighbors to the south, and their home looked out over our lot to the salt marsh; part of the covenants of the land transaction was that our house could *not* be extended to the west as it would impinge on a sight-line restriction as defined in our deed.
3. *Septic capacity.* Given the proximity to wetlands, the size of our lot, and the new 100 percent reserve capacity provisions of the septic system code (briefly described in the Introduction), we simply could not move the septic from its present westerly location, nor could we build a home that was ultimately larger than three bedrooms.
4. *Vehicular access.* Given our sloped site and the nature of our driveway, which was set along a right-of-way, we simply could not change any configuration or destination of our driveway access.
5. *Existing trees.* Directly east of the house is a 200-year-old white oak whose presence was a beloved aspect of the original home's siting; therefore, eastwardly expansion was limited beyond the normal zoning code set-backs.
6. *Budget.* As with the original home, financial constraints did play a part in how we approached any addition, especially given the fact that renovating or adding onto any structure is almost always more costly per square foot than building from scratch.
7. *Timing.* This construction project had a short and undeniable deadline, as described below.

Consequently, there was but one place to go—east—and that area was limited by our sacred tree. The original design had placed the cross-axial entry and second-floor hall orienting to the east, setting up an easy, direct point of attachment.

Despite these limitations to adding onto our little home, any homeowner's life has changes, with the most unalterable and highly impactive life change being the advent of children. Fortunately, given the highly structured and planned life-styles of two-income childless couples, the advent of children is (more often than not) not only a planned experience but also a heavily anticipated one. Such was the case with our family, and we knew within a month of conception that we were going to have a child. This left eight months for the design and construction of an addition to our little house intended to harbor our child, a live-in caregiver, and (we hoped) a second child.

Photos © Mick Hales. Drawings by the architect.

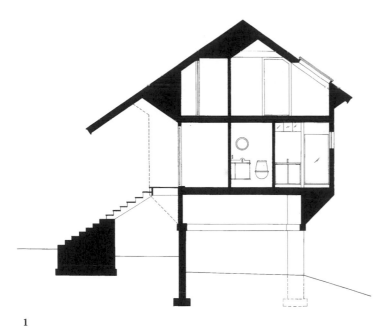

1

Within the eight months allocated to us, we proceeded to add a 700-square-foot addition that had the following characteristics:

1. *Two bedrooms.* Upstairs for children, downstairs for caregiver
2. *A nursery.* An open area for a crib and changing table
3. *A new bathroom.* Shower and vanity were solely intended for the downstairs bedroom, with a separate toilet as part of an adjacent powder room (five years of a walk-up single bath came to an end)
4. *Storage.* A mud room area off the entry, deep walk-in closets on the second floor, and large closets in both new bedrooms
5. *A new entryway.* A replacement for the poetic (nonchild-proof) open millwork construction in the original home.

The original home involved the architecture of open interconnected spaces and axial vistas. However, with infants and unrelated people living within the confines of an 1,800-square-foot, three-bedroom house, there needed to be some sense of aural and visual separation. Thus—and not surprisingly—there are more doors present in the addition than there were in the entire original home. Similarly, our original home had five distinct spaces: living-dining-kitchen, study-office, bedroom-closet, bathroom, and mechanical room. Even though our addition was only two-thirds the size of the original house, it had six distinct spaces: entry/mud room, au pair bedroom, bathroom, powder room, children's bedroom, and nursery.

The planning of the addition was extraordinarily simple. Given the location of the existing front door, it was clearly evident where our new entry had to orient, and given the location of our waste-line access to the septic system, the new bathroom had to orient directly to the extant east exterior wall (this allowed for a code-compliant, pitch-to-drain waste pipe to precisely transition through the 2 x 10 floor joist cavity with no room to spare). Given the preplanning of the hallway orientation, we knew where we needed to "T" off the present floor plan. The existing exterior window at the east end second-floor corridor was reused to provide light at the top of the stair in an "art niche" harboring a large chest that had never found a satisfactory home in the original house.

A host of micromoves followed these broad strokes. The washer-drier went into the first-floor mechanical room (from our bedroom closet) to allow live-in help to do laundry without entering our bedroom. A changing table

2

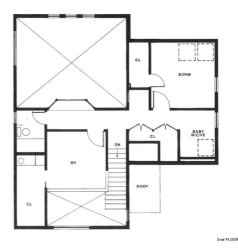

3

Figure 1 *Section. This cross section through the entry shows lowered eaves from the rest of the house, the walk-in skylight, the extended roof over the entry, and the relatively tight subdivision of internal spaces in the addition (versus the fairly open spaces present in the original home).*

Figure 2 *Floor plans. A simple "tack on" with a new entry, mud room, and bath and bedroom for a live-in au pair taking up the first floor (with the point of attachment set to the existing front door). On the second floor a nursery, child's bedroom, and storage were arrayed around the preexisting line of the second-floor corridor.*

Figure 3 *The small house expanded. An easterly expansion of a subordinate mass. To retain the dignity of the original home (left), the addition (right) perimeter has been pulled back in all directions.*

Figure 4 *The existing house. A simple box is elevated off the ground with a virtual "gangplank" of entry stairs set within the context an uninterrupted overall shape.*

Figure 5 *Easterly prospect ("the screaming-child façade"). Windows are conspired in a façade that almost no one sees. The existing home's siding, roof pitch, trim, and siding detailing are manipulated to form a visual event that would be unthinkable in the original house form.*

5

and sink replaced the laundry. We opted to use a different color palette for the addition interior: Whereas light, pale tones of yellow were used throughout the original house, light blues, violets, and pinks were used in the addition. The kitchen was brought into full family status by the transition of the former entry closet into a full-blown pantry.

Perversely enough, given the requirements of physical separation and functional accommodation for the addition, the architectural implications of adding onto the semimonolithic presence of our original little house meant that the new construction needed to be subordinate in its massing. Its roof ridge and eave line had to be lower than the original. The addition became a large-scale transitional massing element providing better connection between the ground plane and the "pod-in-the-sky" original home. This intention was symbolized by a new set of stone entry steps set in stalagmite ascendence. These steps garnered two-thirds of the height needed to enter the house and were formed between large boulders that had been removed to provide water service into the original home. The final six steps that launch visitors into the home were built as a teak bridge spanning the stone steps, which elevated the ground plane and the visually flotational home. It should be noted that this "bridge" is child-friendly with no gaps between railings or treads larger than 6 inches and with handrails set into the railings at baby, toddler, child, and adult heights, and with 3-inch-thick stringers facing the inside of the steps to allow for toy race car use.

In accommodating the aesthetic desire for a recessive addition mass, the one-and-a-half-story framing system employed was wholly different from our original home, involving balloon-framing to facilitate knee walls at the second-floor level. The low walls and roof line necessitated the use of skylights (the largest stock operable units avail-

6

7

Figure 6 *New entry A seemingly opaque box is applied, sidesaddle, to the original house form while a cascade of rocks ascends to form a new entry.*

Figure 7 *Entry steps. This new teak bridge has handrails at infant, child, adolescent, and adult height. Note that this is made of unfinished teak with each piece of wood being taken from a single piece of raw lumber.*

able on the market) set at a level to allow a 6-foot-high person to walk into the skylight well in the child's bedroom and the nursery. This was done more by necessity than design as, in order to obtain the diminished massing impact on the overall new house form, we needed to use every square inch of the cubic volume on the new second floor.

Additionally, because of the proximity of the sacred oak tree, we needed to change our foundation type to avoid any deleterious effect on its root system. The original home had the structurally minimalist design of two uninterrupted bearing walls slicing into the hillside for the entire 38 feet, 6 inch length of the house. Our rejection of a similar simple solution was derived from one of the few negative aspects of building the original home. When the original house was built, the only location available

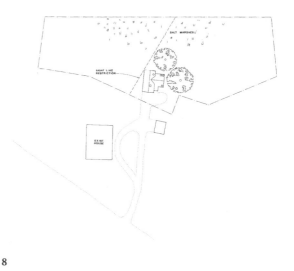

8

for our new septic system was to the west, and it had to be set at the mandatory level above the existing grade because of its proximity to the adjacent salt marsh. These requirements necessitated large amounts of clean fill to be brought in and set over the roots of a fully mature sugar maple. The tree died a slow and tragic death. To avoid more arboricide, we minimized ground disruptions by using only one bearing wall and two separate concrete piers for the addition's foundation, and we pulled the lines of the foundation from the perimeter of the addition's finished floor outline. We were thus able to avoid hitting any existing roots, and the tree healthily survived construction.

Many small moves helped escalate the cost of the addition. When we opted to limit the foundation's impact on the site, a double cantilever was employed to support the upper two occupied floors all about the addition, preempting the simple economy of the straight and consistent framing of the original building. Given the desire to internally relocate the washer and drier, provide a changing table with a new sink in the master bedroom, and provide the new "double dip" downstairs powder room/guest bathroom described earlier, the plumbing work was virtually equivalent to that of our original home. All trim material matched that in the existing home both in color (gloss white) and in profile (once again, timing forced us to purchase the trim versus milling it up ourselves). Relatively expensive, highly durable ceramic tile was used in the entryway and bled into the new bathroom. A somewhat expensive extension of the tongue-and-groove board ceiling over the kitchen was set into the new entry space as well.

Fortuitously, the potential cost of accommodating the increased heating needs was greatly reduced as we only had to add two zones to the original boiler—providing four-zone heat control within the context of an 1,800-square-foot house (the heating bills have only increased by 50 percent even though we increased the mass of the house by approximately 70 percent). Obviously, the east side foundation wall was reused, as was the interior stairway, and the electrical service also proved to be adequate although the 100-amp service panel now has every possible circuit utilized. Given the fact that neither air-conditioning nor large-scale appliances were desired or feasible, the maxing out of the available power was adequate for this house.

Similarly, the septic tank was designed for a three-bedroom house, and because there was a fortuitous (unplanned) existing linkage of the two runs of leaching fields, there was no need for any septic work to accommodate our heightened usage.

The original home relied on 2 x 4 construction with ³/₄-inch exterior polyurethane sheathing as the most economical form of insulation for the walls. With the vagaries of lumber prices versus insulation costs, this particular home achieves a similar (although slightly diminished) R value (but greater cost-effectiveness in 1989) by using 2 x 6 wall construction and 5¹/₂-inch fiberglass batt insulation. The only area where the rigid insulation was used was on the underside of the home.

Given the absolute time imperative of the imminent birth of our first child, much of the owner-driven work executed in the first home became contractor-provided in the addition, including interior painting, installation of all millwork items and bathroom appointments, and provision of most, if not all, bathroom appliances and lighting fixtures. Costs were increased, but time was saved.

Figure 8 *Site plan. The original house is built on an interior lot with the front of the house set tight to the setback, the westerly side set tight to a deed-mandated viewway, the salt marsh to the rear, and a 200-year-old white oak due east. These site plan determinates effectively located and sized the addition.*

Figure 9 *Living room. The new entryway is accommodated by an opening (left) within the context of the existing wall. The tongue-and-groove ceiling present over the original kitchen is extended into the new space (left).*

Figure 10 *Front door entry. The original front door is relocated and flanked by new sidelights. A mud room is around the corner in the background of this photograph, with a new cherry wood column set to receive the existing structural load of the original building's second floor, thus providing for the removal of a well that would have obscured the view upon entering the home. Note that the door to the right is set to the original point at which entry was achieved into the main home and now serves as a large-scale storage area set below the existing interior steps. Also note the imposition of a new tile floor in this high-traffic area.*

Figure 11 *New child's bedroom. Walk-in skylight (left) and a new window that plays off the original south- and west-facing window arrays (right) make for a lively ambience in this vaulted space. Note the low-knee wall height, appropriate for a child's room, and the highly durable quarter-sawn wood floors.*

10

Because of all the above consequences, even with accounting for inflation, the net cost of building the addition was roughly equivalent to the cost of the building of the original house—even though the addition was approximately 25 percent smaller than its parent building, and there was no septic, utilities access, or driveway work performed.

Most importantly, this project shows that a small heroic gesture can evolve and accommodate a diverse and enriched life-style. Where two people had once lived and worked, the new parents, one child, and a live-in caregiver were provided for, and in the latest microgenerational shift, two parents, two children, and a live-out caregiver are now accommodated.

As with all homes that start out as a successful fit between owner and home, fine-tuning, versus a wholesale retooling or moving to a new address, can be executed on an ongoing basis as our lives change. Ultimately, the

11

nursery alcove and the child's bedroom will be combined into one large bedroom to accommodate two children. The downstairs bedroom is now relegated to a guest room and an exercise area to help forestall the ever softening and widening bodies of approaching middle age. Despite all the new storage areas adjacent to every new space and in the extended second-floor corridor, virtually every storage area is full, but there is very little need for more storage at present. Ultimately, a storage shed will have to be built on the site. (Obviously, these storage needs are generated by the impossibility of having a full basement given the wetlands ordinances and by the decision not to have a full attic given the zoning code height limitations as well as a desire for full and open spaces.) These decisions were made with full knowledge, and the results speak for themselves.

Ultimately, this house cannot tolerate two adults and two near adults. But its life expectancy in harboring our progression from a couple through parenting preadolescents will have lasted the better part of 15 years. Typically, during this time American households have progressed from "starter home" to "20-year home," and have involved three or four moves or major additions. As of this date we've adapted our home to the ever-changing contours of our day-to-day lives without either moving an inch in distance or compromising our values.

One-Bedroom Houses

Simply Extraordinary/
Extraordinarily Simple

Amenity co-exists with economy.

S T A T S

PROJECT NAME AND LOCATION:
Employee Housing,
Sea Ranch, California

ARCHITECT:
William Turnbull Associates Architects
& Planners

COMPLETION DATE:
1989 - 1990

TOTAL HEATED SQUARE FEET:
Studio, 603; two bedroom, 703

PERCEIVED SQUARE FOOTAGE:
Studio, 743; two bedroom, 883

CIRCULATION-TO-TOTAL-AREA RATIO:
Studio, 3 percent; two bedroom,
8.3 percent

BEDROOM-SPACE-TO-TOTAL-AREA RATIO:
Studio, 18 percent; two bedroom,
44 percent

GROSS COST:
N/A - 18+/- buildings, 27 units

COST PER SQUARE FOOT:
$50

DURATION OF DESIGN PROCESS:
One year

DURATION OF CONSTRUCTION:
One year

Photos © Morley Baer.
Drawings by the architects.

THE word *housing* has many negative connotations, but there is an overarching sense of the diminishment of the individual—usually involving a desire for a higher profit margin for the housing provider. In providing housing for the employees who maintain the Sea Ranch Development in coastal California, William Turnbull Associates have created the sort of housing that has a presence and dignity which belies its low price—$50 a square foot—and its equally paltry unit sizing—603 square feet for a single-bedroom unit, and 763 square feet for a two-bedroom unit. There are some very simple rules utilized that make these homes simultaneously inexpensive and aesthetically powerful:

1. *Post-and-beam construction.* Not unlike much of the work that has gone on in Sea Ranch over the last 30 years, simple post-and-beam framing is utilized as the dominant structural system, effortlessly facilitating the differentiation of subspaces with nonbearing partitions. This system of floor and roof support is then translated to simple concrete footings, allowing the building to float over the landscape.

2. *Extruded sections forming the building shape.* Rather than using agglomerative massing, bilateral symmetry, façade-derived forms, or historicist precedent, these building forms take simple gable-ended sections and extend them linearly via the aforementioned framing bays implicit in post-and-beam construction. This system can be laterally extended via simple shed-roofed addenda—also defined by the post-and-beam framing bays employed.

3. *Cellular design.* By creating major and minor framing bays via the post-and-beam structural organization, "serving spaces" can be made inherently subordinate to the "served spaces."

4. *Consistent, natural materials.* In applying structural and insulation sheathing to the outside of the house's structural form and then applying that watertight surfacing to the outside edge, visual power and great economy are achieved throughout. The follow-through on this layered approach is that almost all materials are exposed—structure, sheathing, and siding. Natural wood can be quite cost-efficient, as it obviates the need to provide an ongoing surface treatment. The lack of a cavity wall can present certain problems in terms of mechanical systems, but in housing such as this, the economies afforded are extraordinary.

5. *Siting.* All of these buildings are sited to respect the existing tree line and present varying façades to their neighboring counterparts that

1

Figure 1 Overall view. A gentle cascade of sheds, one story (in the foreground) and two story (to the back left), utilize the stark detailing and seemingly effortless siting work to maximum advantage.

Figure 2 Unit plans. Studio, two-bedroom, and three-bedroom units are shown. These units utilize identical structural systems and framing bays and allow for manipulation to accommodate the various bedroom counts by a simple linear extension (for the two- and three-bedroom units) or for the adding of a lean-to-shed subordinate framing bay to accommodate the wet and sleeping spaces. Given the extreme costs of efficiencies that were mandated in this program, the formal and structural simplicity was essential, and large-scale covered porches were used to expand usable living areas of these units.

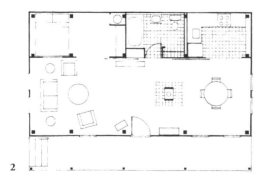

2

Figure 3 Two-story units. These double-height units vary from their single-story counterparts in the use of standard framing techniques versus the post-and-beam systems employed in the single-story counterparts, but they evidence the vertical expressionism possible when very simple plan perimeters serve as the basis for all design work.

Figure 4 Site plan. Twenty-seven housing units cascade down a gently rolling hill organized by two cul-de-sacs. Although exterior surfaces, structural designs, and strict rules of planning and site orientation are applied to all these projects, there is a marvelous sense of self-expression and kinetic interplay given the modest means of construction.

Figure 5 Living area for a two- or three-bedroom, single-story home. Simple trusses and similarly simple post-and-beam work are allowed their full visual appeal via the use of external insulation, allowing the structural sheathing to be fully expressed within the interiors of these projects. Nonbearing–nonstructural partitioning is utilized as painted sheetrock for contrast, and axial organizing is clearly seen to the left. Such a simply applied, and yet relatively large-scale, structural approach allows for a natural segregation of spaces within subordinate parts defined by it.

3

4

give all occupants a sense that they are not part of an unrelenting machine of human accommodation but rather part of an evolutionary community development realized via a common architectural vernacular.

Given the fact that these buildings are designed with no particular residents in mind and given the fact that they are intended to maximize economy, there isn't a richly textured scenario to delve into, but there are many lessons to be learned from their absolute clearheadedness—whether it be from the axial relationships of shared common spaces set to maximize a *sense* of spaciousness while affording a true minimalization of actual space or whether by the subtle use of cross-axial relationships to help define implicit duets of shared space (kitchen-dining, bedroom-living, living-porch, and so on), these homes are object lessons in how to provide maximum amenities with minimum means, both economic and spatial.

However, it should be noted that these homes do provide an absolutely minimum amount of storage space, utilize electric resistance heat (obviating the need for a mechanical room), and are without attic or basement space for long-term storage use. None of these elements are important to the actual use of these particular buildings; therefore they form a special-case scenario—one that might not be used by the majority of those reading this book. But the lessons to be learned in terms of structural clarity, formal simplicity, and spatial richness via functional interweaving are not only valuable but essential to anyone interested in maximizing the utility and aesthetic impact of a small building with the generic functional characteristics of a home.

5

Forward Retreat

Clinging to a hillside, looking out to the view, a small house answers some hard questions.

THE word *cute* is often synonomous with *small,* but small houses can transcend "cute." A small "footprint" and mass can solve some hard-nosed problems that standard-size dwellings cannot address.

So it is with a 615-square-foot, one-bedroom house in Connecticut designed by Rod Hartung. This is a second home with a twist. A couple owned a generous site with a Modernist classic already set upon it—a Hugh Newell Jacobsen home—one that would not suffer a foolish addition gladly. Given the inability to add onto an intolerant classic, the owners needed to build a "second home" within the confines of their existing lot, a place where guests could stay and also a place where a writing career could be accommodated while being quite literally close to home.

In addition, although the site was large enough to support a second home, it was hilly, rocky, and in close proximity to wetlands. This was not a rocky hill, but a hill of rock. In addition to buying the lot for its rugged, sloping hillside (and the resulting view out over wetlands), the owners also loved the pristine quality of the heavily treed landscape.

Whatever was built had to be sited to maintain the views that were present from the existing home. Given all these design criteria, there was

STATS

PROJECT NAME AND LOCATION:
Writer's Retreat, Lyme, Connecticut

ARCHITECT:
Roderic M. Hartung, Architect

COMPLETION DATE:
1992

TOTAL HEATED SQUARE FEET:
615 (includes deck)

PERCEIVED SQUARE FOOTAGE:
763

CIRCULATION-TO-TOTAL-AREA RATIO:
9 percent

BEDROOM-SPACE-TO-TOTAL-AREA RATIO:
26 percent

GROSS COST:
$132,000

COST PER SQUARE FOOT:
$173

DURATION OF DESIGN PROCESS:
Six months

DURATION OF CONSTRUCTION:
Eight months

Photos © and drawings by the architect.

only one answer: an outbuilding smaller than what you might expect given the fact that it allows for a full occupancy, involving a kitchen, a full bath, two floors, and a fireplace. This home is a viable exemplar of innovative small house use because it addresses a full range of functional desires on a site fraught with extraordinary problems.

The most pressing architectural need was to deal with the slope. This was addressed in several very specific ways:

1. *Foundation design.* The building was set on concrete piers pinned to the exposed rock with a fully open underside, involving almost no blasting and providing minimal disruption of the existing terrain.

2. *Stacked massing.* The massing became vertical, stacking the sleeping space over living spaces on the first floor. This reduced the "spread" of the house, thus minimizing the number of trees that needed to be removed and also mitigating any imposition on views from the original home.

3. *Level changes.* The interior layout of the house uses simple level changes to facilitate easy access and adaptation to the sloping terrain. The first site accommodation is a bridge that takes those entering the house above the immediately adjacent terrain, allowing the house to "float" and

Figure 1 Entry. A simple gable form gains an extraordinarily animated presence via the use of subordinate applied elements, starting with a meandering entry path/bridge set to the obscured front door located at the juncture between the ascending dormer (right) and the dominant gable roof form. The fireplace and heating plant are set to the saddlebag addendum as seen to the left, with the flues for them fully fleshed out as a vertical punctuation set before the dominant roof form. A large-scale oculus window also helps prevent a clear reading of the home's true size, while eave detailing, wood roofing, and trim provide a sense of design control and completeness.

Figure 2 Floor plans. The simple rectangular floor plan has modest projections for a heating plant, chimney, and deck on the first floor and minidormer on the second floor. Note that the entry is shown on the second-floor plan as it comes at a midlevel point and that the entry door's presence is axially received by a window set across an open two-story space. On the lower floor, the wet spaces of bathroom and kitchen are set below the loft bedroom, allowing for an open living area to be a relatively out-scaled space. The deck area to the left of the first floor has its main area covered by the house mass and effectively expands the living area, providing a highly useful perch for the extraordinary view.

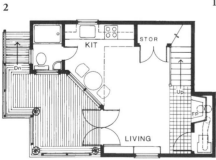

FIRST FLOOR

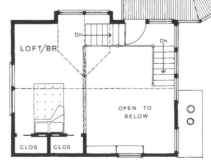

SECOND FLOOR

3

Figure 3 *Backside-downhill. The cute cottage seen from the entry is transformed at a vertically expressive mass as seen from below. A fairly heavy duty structural system can be seen underneath the recessive porch as large-scale concrete piers bear out an even larger scale concrete footing. The rustication-arboreal influence of the tree trunk columns serves to distract attention from these underpinnings.*

Figure 4 *Side view. The nature of the site is clearly evidenced in this photograph where large rock outcroppings and uninterrupted growth of first-generation forestation are interrupted by the imposition of this simple vertical mass. The positive expressionism of the lone dormer (upper left) is suitably counterpointed by the voided corner over the external porch seen at the lower right, while trim banding and expressive eaves create a cogent identity that visually hangs together amid all the natural elements that intervene.*

yet have an easy walk-in situation. The second aspect of level manipulation is the use of a half-level entry, eight quick steps down into the main living area or seven quick steps up into the bedroom.

4. *Adaptation to view.* In any small house it is always a temptation to simply let the house be overwhelmed by the view, but in this particular case Rod Hartung chose a more interesting and varied approach that belies the small scale of this house: the use of a double-height space to the *backside* of the home for the major living area. This is a space that essentially focuses upon a fireplace. There aren't too many views when the sun goes down. The double-height living room's view-directed complement is the relatively large porch that focuses upon the land-scape. Rather than cantilever out something that would extend into the landscape (thus cutting down more trees and making the house laterally expansive), Hartung chose to nestle this porch within the envelope of the house, thus providing a rainy-day outdoor retreat as well as a perfect perch for a view. By beveling one wall between the two living spaces, a natural location for a dining area was created. Set above this porch is the other spot that captures maximum view appreciation—the bedroom.

5. *Shape.* A second home retreat such as this does not want a budget that makes its presence a burden, and one of the best ways any small home can keep its own sense of self-awareness is to have a simple shape. This particular project is a model of formal simplicity, using a symmetrical gable shape with a single cantilevered dormer on the second floor that allows for headroom at the top of the stairs.

4

Figure 5 *Interior. With loft bedroom (above), living room below (left), dining area to the right and kitchen to the far right (both unseen), and covered deck beyond the glazed wall, this view is seen immediately upon entry at the midlevel between the loft and living room floors. The relatively rich appointments of this small space belie its cottagelike exterior qualities but provide evidence of the ability of small houses to be anything but predictable.*

5

In designing any small house, there are decisions that either cut corners or fully manifest the potentials involved. This house displays innovative and thought-provoking gestures that evidence the sort of rigorous interpretative work that good architects can bring to bear on the problem of designing a small house. It would be easy to focus the entry of any building on the most obvious target of opportunity, the front door, but Hartung chose to locate the entry to arouse curiosity as seen from the outside—the entry focus is set by the aforementioned bridge and the coincidence of a single subtly cantilevered dormer and main house mass. The doorway is located at the point where several competing forces collide.

By allowing the entry bridge to approach the house sidesaddle, the large-scale view is ever present alongside the home. Thus the home serves only as a partial screening device rather than a billboard that preempts the ability to glimpse the great space beyond it.

It would be easy to try to hide the small amount of mechanical equipment a little home like this needs in a crawl space or in a closet, but Hartung realized that would be a missed opportunity. As with most buildings in temperate climates, waste gases need to be accommodated from heating plants, and in this particular case, from a prefabricated firebox as well. Flues and mechanical spaces often become extraordinarily expensive and aesthetically tortuous if they are to be hidden or apologized for in one way or another. This house celebrates its mechanical aspects by harboring both the heating plant and the firebox in a saddlebag pop-out bay set below eye level at entry and by attenuating its flues as an expressive vertical gesture running up alongside the façade that dominates the entry prospect. In this way, rude mechanical elements become part of the aesthetic of interweaving trim, siding, and roof forms, allowing a very small house to have a primary hot spot of visual activity to help counterpoint and balance the aforementioned entry ensemble.

Given the site, there is direct visual access to the roofscape, and wood cedar shingles were used to great advantage. The trimwork and millwork on the interior have essentially used simple standard materials in thoughtful ways, but there is a lyric surprise in the structure that supports the bedroom loft. The extension of the support lines provided by the concrete piers is revealed by the incision of the previously mentioned deck. These could have been "tastefully done"—trimmed out columns of relatively standard issue materials. But in this one focal point—the lens through which almost everyone will see the view, a view that is both framed and filtered by the fully mature trees mentioned earlier—Hartung chose to use the naturalistic touch of full-blown tree trunks for columns, complete with limbs to create both a sense of aesthetic surprise and a visceral connection to the building's context.

Bookcases dominate many of the interior wall surfaces. Clerestory lighting, mostly from the east, allows light to flood the double-height living space.

It is also fortunate that the owners have a relatively complete palette of furnishings to complement this sweet little box shape. Additionally, closets, storage areas, and the aforementioned bookcases and cabinetry are all cleverly nestled in and about the perimeter walls to allow a fully open interior sensibility.

Small houses can often be mind-numbingly simplistic or torturously convoluted manifestations of an architect's overreaching manipulations. But in this case an experienced architect with a clear head knew that a house of this size needed to be simple—and rich. This is the opportunity of small house design, creating something that is cogent and yet delightful.

Tree House

A sculpture of structure, material, and light sits easily on a wooded site.

STATS

PROJECT NAME AND LOCATION:
Connelly Cabin, Whidbey Island, Washington State

ARCHITECT:
Arne Bystrom, Architect

COMPLETION DATE:
1993

TOTAL HEATED SQUARE FEET:
777

PERCEIVED SQUARE FOOTAGE:
1,181

CIRCULATION-TO-TOTAL-AREA RATIO:
11 percent

BEDROOM-SPACE-TO-TOTAL-AREA RATIO:
18 percent

GROSS COST:
$100,000

COST PER SQUARE FOOT:
$129

DURATION OF DESIGN PROCESS:
Six months

DURATION OF CONSTRUCTION:
One year

Photos © and drawings by the architect.

WHEN designing a retreat for creative clients, some architects gravitate toward the image of Walden, a simple bucolic respite to allow a fertile mind a chance to grow in a quiet context.

Arne Bystrom, the Seattle architect, shows a different take in this tiny one-bedroom "cabin" set upon Whidbey Island in Puget Sound.

For a vacation home compared to a home that is occupied full time, it is possible to present a clear, distilled image because of its relatively simple functional requirements, and for this home the designer has taken advantage of its relatively benign functional requirements to create an extraordinary architectural event.

Wood is an exceptionally flexible material. Its ability to be structurally effective both in compression and in tension means that it can be used for a wide variety of loading conditions. Whereas the typical stick-built American home uses plywood to absorb all the torsional-shear forces, this home uses expressed triangulated solid-wood struts, and in so doing allows some walls to be glazed infill panels, creating a large-scale connection to the outdoors that would not be possible had large planes of plywood sheathing been employed.

But beyond the structural expressionism there is an overt sense in this house that simple wood framing techniques can be made sculptural by their aesthetically aggressive use. Cantilevers, expressed end conditions, and celebrated fasteners form unapologetically ornamental structural articulation, and when continued with the semisymmetrical layout of the home's form and interior, they provide a venue for amazing interplays of light, space, and structure.

Essentially, there are two architectural systems employed: the skin (glass and red cedar shingles) and the structure (unfinished Douglas fir). The two systems confront each other as a central subordinate construction of sleeping loft penetrates a glazed ceiling to create a rather amazing cupola/trellis/crown-of-thorns that virtually explodes from the envelope. As you might expect, this vertical projection allows for an extraordinary appreciation of the views that surround the house—views that extend for a full 260 degrees of "peek-a-boo" prospects of Puget Sound.

When acknowledging their true size, small houses can have an enormous aesthetic impact if selective exaggeration can be employed in their detailing. Here, the effervescent structural expressionism is allowed full rein and projects a high level of exuberance in the context of a very simple house form. In plan organization this house utilizes a central six-bay main mass with central narrow bays flanked by larger bays. These bays align to create an axial relation-

Figure 1 *Exterior. A simple double-hipped volume has its apex explode in an effervescent wood sculpture involving multiple hierarchies of organization and sizing as well as direct structural expressionism employing triangulated members and ebulliently cantilevered extensions.*

Figure 2 *Floor plans. A simple six-bay central plan is defined by 12 columns. The column grid spawns four projections—three cantilever (the bathroom and the two decks) and one a simple gangplank, the entry. A spiral stair, wood stove, kitchen cabinets, and sleeping loft are large-scale elements within this simple context. Given the tightness of the plan (approximately 21 1/2 feet by 25 1/2 feet), virtually all functions are both embraced and described by the built-in elements: benches for the public areas, cabinetry for the kitchen area, and a fairly precise location for the dining room table. It should also be noted that the wood stove serves as the sole source of heat for this project. On the second level a sleeping loft addresses a deck that is incised into the roof, affording a look out to the extraordinary views of Puget Sound. At the point of access where the spiral stair touches the sleeping loft, a ladder is provided to a hatch that allows access to the cupola above.*

1

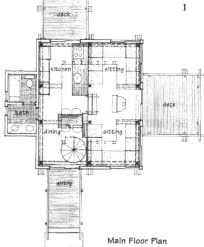

Main Floor Plan

2

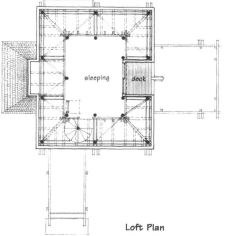

Loft Plan

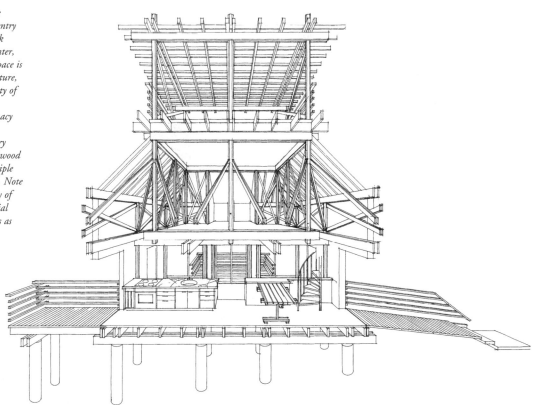

Figure 3 *Sectional perspective. The main house form spawns a canted entry bridge to the right, subordinate deck structure to the left, sleeping loft center, and celestial cupola/trellis above. Space is defined by an aggressive wood structure, and light is filtered through a variety of triangulating-stiffening structural members as well. Structural legitimacy becomes artful whimsy in the cantilevered extension of nearly every structural and ornamental piece of wood as well as the aggressive use of multiple sizings of the wood pieces employed. Note the overarching centerline symmetry of this view as well as the essential axial organization of the entry that serves as the cut line for this view.*

3

ship through the entry extending out to a deck. Held subordinate from the form are three decks (two projecting off of the axis, one forming the entry). Beyond these simple plan moves, all else is sculpture. It does not seem that Bystrom has missed any opportunity to facilitate an exuberant dialogue between stoic skin and kinetic structure, but he does utilize the basic six-bay format of his main house area to great advantage, allowing its bays to functionally segregate the house into two sitting areas, a kitchen, and a dining room, with sleeping being segregated to the floating loft above. A simple three-step level change has been employed to facilitate the view across the common areas while sitting at the dining room table or cooking.

It should be noted that the working drawings of this house were executed at twice the normal scale ¹/₂ inch= 1 foot, 0 inches) simply because the interplay between the structural elements had to be so carefully coordinated that they approached a cabinetmaker's tolerances. But it is clear that the ability to create a rather fantastic structural sculpture was gleefully embraced by the builder, abetted by the fact that Bystrom is a master at creating details that are both builder-friendly and architecturally exuberant (a combination not often found in most architect-designed homes). Cantilevers are employed to support the bathroom, the decks, and large portions of the sleeping loft. Aggressive use of all of the wood members makes a monomaterial structure visually come alive. Windows and doors are all stock items, as are lighting fixtures. There is a large amount of custom roof glazing and, as one might expect, some impressive three-dimensional mitering employed, and this did make the cost of this building go well over $100 per square foot. The complex connections were simplified by the fact that the columns employed have been octagonalized to receive all the triangulation employed.

There was an overt attempt by the architect to create a "forest within a forest" where the sleeping loft and the cupola-trellis are intended to be a symbolic re-creation of an arboreal form replete with structural "branches." These aesthetic evocations are important, but by minimizing the home's footprint via the utilization of a vertical

Figure 4 *Living room side view. The house's form is set diagonally to the tilted plane of a fern-filled hillside, amid the uninterrupted fabric of tall trees. Note the incised walk-out deck that addresses the sleeping loft and its simple coincidence with the wood stove flue (the wood stove serves as the only heating source for the project).*

4

organization, the home minimally disrupts the environment on which it sits and is allowed to become an event not unlike the break in a climax forest, where bright light cascades through an overarching forest canopy's deep shade.

This home represents the full flower of professional experience. The ability to recognize the potential for structural expression while maintaining a clear-headed understanding of what is needed to make that expression both technologically feasible and financially affordable evidences the highest level of skill that an architect can bring to bear on such a small building. Virtually every connection of this building had to be detailed as though it were being built in a shop (versus in the field). In this way, Bystrom puts a lie to the fact that small house design is the stepping-stone for inexperienced architects on the way to a glorious career of big building design. The opportunity to create a fully formed piece of art is rare, but rarer still is Bystrom's skill, which takes the opportunity and fully maximizes its impact.

Figure 5 *Sleeping loft. With unending views framed by structural stiffening and mullions, this bed faces a simple walk-out deck incised into the glass roof. The sense of a tree house is both overt and intended.*

Figure 6 *Interior. A fish-eye lens is required to capture the essential quality of a sheetrock and glass envelope enclosing an expressive array of wood components that sit within its context (the columns that dissociate themselves from the walls) or burst through its enclosure (the trellis-cupola set directly above the sleeping loft). In all cases the structural identity is unmitigated, and the aesthetic potential is thoroughly recognized.*

Figure 7 *(opposite) Structure/loft/diagonal bracing. Expressed bolt fasteners, custom-fixed skylight glazing, and lighting interweave with railings (both steel and wood) and primary structural elements of floor joists and columns to create a sense of kinetic expression, both spatially and structurally. Note the interconnectedness of inside and outside worlds as well as the various light levels that filter through the multiple levels of structure and skin.*

5

6

High (and Low) Art

Pieces and parts form a house.

It can be said that the ideal vacation home manifests the most distilled vision of what a house can be. However, this thoroughly personalized image is usually at odds with the limited funds often available for its construction. Fortunately the primary use of such buildings is inherently limited—focused on regenerative activity (or inactivity). Often this limited building program facilitates just the sort of reductionist imperative that this book focuses upon. Even though there are few "second homes" relative to their full-use counterparts, lessons learned in their design and habitation can be used in the design of any home.

This particular project has a multitude of components classically applicable to the small vacation house building type. First and foremost, the house has a singular focus: relaxation. Site selection for second homes reflects the desperate desire to "detox" from urban stress, and this project is no different —6 acres in rural Long Island. Often the house-as-sanitarium imperative is driven by two-career couples, and such was the case with Kathy Douglas and Bruce Dohrenwend, young professionals locked (for the weekdays) in the catacombs of Manhattan.

When their intense career paths led them to search the eastern horizon for a safe harbor, they discovered 6 acres that had a pool and an 825-

square-foot, 1960s prefab, two-bedroom box. As with many late twentieth century single-family construction projects on good sites, a "tear-down–rebuild" master plan was always envisioned, eliminating the original home. Maintaining their clear focus on recreation, Douglas and Dohrenwend immediately built a 600-square-foot pool house with accommodations for guests and proceeded to cast an eye toward the elimination of the 1960s box in favor of a home they could legitimately call their own.

Again, a common by-product of development of rural land by the urban elite is community resistance manifest in regulation. So it was with the best-laid plans of Douglas and Dohrenwend. When they purchased their 6 acres and built their guest house, all was right with the small world of local zoning officials. But in the interim influx of cash-engorged, exurban invaders from the West, the Amagansett zoning officials changed the rules and declared that only one structure could be set upon any one building lot. Fortunately (almost predictably when dealing with weekend exiles from New York), Kathy Douglas was a lawyer and was undaunted.

If they needed two structures to fulfill their dream and they had a lot that was more than twice the minimum acreage, then they could subdi-

---

S T A T S

PROJECT NAME AND LOCATION:
*D & D House,
Long Island, New York*

ARCHITECT:
BumpZoid

COMPLETION DATE:
1991

TOTAL HEATED SQUARE FEET:
924 (not including carport)

PERCEIVED SQUARE FOOTAGE:
1,356

CIRCULATION-TO-TOTAL-AREA RATIO:
5 percent

BEDROOM-SPACE-TO-TOTAL-AREA RATIO:
9 percent

GROSS COST:
$257,000 (including carport)

COST PER SQUARE FOOT:
$278

DURATION OF DESIGN PROCESS:
Three months

DURATION OF CONSTRUCTION:
Six months

Photos © Langdon Clay.
Drawings by the architects

1

Figure 1 Entry prospect, northwest view. The focal point of the composition, the high living room, gains height and presence by its attenuated eaves with overtly painted undersides and adjacent fascia as well as the double-canted chimney. This form's use of a voided corner window orientation stands in contrast to the background bar building where windows are essentially perforations of a continuous, uninterrupted plane.

Figure 2 Floor plan. A canted bar building collides (left) with a cubic pavilion (right) with both shapes being set in the context of an underlying deck whose shape is seemingly rendered by the imposition of the canted bar. The geometry of the plan corresponds to a functional distinction as well, and the low canted bar building houses progressively more private spaces from right to left, as kitchen and dining give way to a bedroom, and finally, after an intervening open porch, to a secluded study set to the far left of the plan. The kitchen is set to coincide with the main living space within the high cubic pavilion. Amid all these formal planning moves is a detached folly cum carport seen at the lower right. Note that the canted bar building turns its broad face to the southerly sun, providing summertime shade for the vast majority of the deck space set between the two building components.

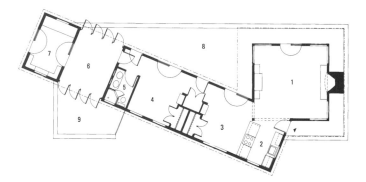

Key

1. Living Room
2. Kitchen
3. Dining Room
4. Bedroom
5. Bathroom
6. Screened Porch
7. Study
8. North Deck
9. South Deck
10. Carport

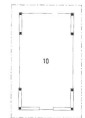

2

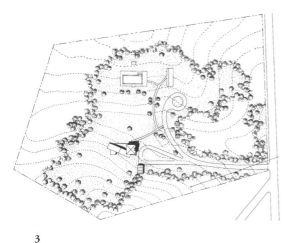

3

vide and create a paper-thin distinction between the built parts of their compound. Good idea. It worked. It took two years—and a new second well, an elongated drive, and some artful pathways to interconnect the pool, pool house, and their new house.

All of these moves had to be made prior to the ultimate move of building a personal idyll. Years of extracurricular stress were layered over the normal pressure cooker of urban life simply to "get away from it all." Ultimately, perseverance will out, and the results were definitely worth the long wait.

The BumpZoid design duet of architects Ben Benedict and Carl Pucci encountered a classically minimalist second-home design program. No need for guest bedrooms (they were in the pool house built soon after the Douglas-Dohrenwends purchased the property). Storage needs were limited—no need for an attic, a full basement, or large closets. One bath was fine since there was an outdoor shower. There was only one transcendent amenity for this and most second homes: relaxation. A "no-fuss–no-muss" aesthetic of spatial flow amid the "dense-pack" kitchen, bath, and closets is the rule.

But the similarities of this project to other second homes ends with the preceding generalities. The composition of forms and materials applied to this house were unique to this project and reflected the expressive quirkiness of BumpZoid. Since there was no view to be worshiped, the lightly rolling, tree-flecked, 6-acre site could have passively overwhelmed a 924-square-foot house unless the architects could seize the day (as BumpZoid has) and capture the site with some high-impact massing and siting moves.

To Ben Benedict and Carl Pucci, the form of this house had to reflect the character of its use. Vacation homes often seek to manifest the escapist aesthetic of picturesque massing and siting, and that runs the risk of becoming a sickly sweet parody of whatever imagery is dear to the hearts of the occupants. But BumpZoid created a home that was anything but sentimental: a two-part harmony using a bit of dissonance and some clever tertiary elements to complement the bold massing and playful use of materials.

In challenging the passive site and the sentimentality of the classic vacation house form, BumpZoid could have created the untouchable scaleless sculptures masquerading as "architect-designed homes" that dot affluent Long Island. As with all successful residential design, the ideas of the design respect the reality of living within its walls.

An attenuated gable-roofed wing locks into a pyramidically roofed tower—unpainted cedar-shingled walls abut a gray vertical tongue-and-groove shaft, and horizontally extruded windows sidle up against their vertically stacked counterparts. The "Low House" (horizontal-gable-shingle) harbors *personal activity:* cooking, eating, sleeping, bathroom. The "High House" (vertical, extended eave-painted) harbors the *social* and *contemplative:* music, reading, talking. So the contrasts employed counterpose shapes that are domestic and materials that are familiar, then aggrandize the latent properties of those shapes and take care to detail standard materials in ways that sustain interest and delight for those who look closely at the final product.

The Low House has a zooming vault of angled ceiling spanning over whited-out subordinate single-story interior construction harboring semimodularized bathroom-storage facilities. Even in an idyll, work can be a necessary evil. An office space is set to the extreme opposite end of the Low House from its intersection with the tower. Secluded from all other spaces by a screened porch but sharing the common roof and perimeter walls, this tiny island of the urban life is paradoxically held within the context of the oasis and terminates the long entry axis set at the opposite end to the primary point of collision between "High" and "Low."

The High House has a cubic-static singular space capped in plywood panels cut to the square shapes that symbolize its stolid, fixed presence. Consistencies between the two forms are also present: centers of roof peak are recognized in window placement, window specs and trim color match, and a deck "oozes" between both forms.

In the siting of the home, the High House directly addresses the attenuated driveway while the Low House is skewed off the High House ordinates. The secondary design elements act to "root" a potentially site-dissociative building. A folly cum carport is set on the ordinates of the High House and frames the "backyard" view. The aforementioned low deck is also set to parallel the tower's organizing end and has its plane symbolically voided by the

Figure 3 Site plan. A natural clearing within a grove of pine trees and a gentle slope are the context for this complex, involving a preexisting pool (upper top, center) with a new pool house and guest sleeping quarters to the right of it. In the lower center of the plan the dashed rectangular outline is the removed original home, and the new home is seen to the left of it with the carport set at the center bottom. Note the lightly arcing pathways that link the three major elements of the project to the driveway.

Figure 4 Entry prospect, northwest view. The focal point of the composition, the high living room, gains height and presence by its attenuated eaves with overtly painted undersides and adjacent fascia as well as the double-canted chimney. This form's use of a voided corner window orientation stands in contrast to the background bar building where windows are essentially perforations of a continuous, uninterrupted plane.

Figure 5 South: low building. In contrast to the extraordinary attenuation of the high building forms, the modest extension of this attenuated gable form serves to create a sense of wall—one with an oversized perforation in the form of an internal screen porch from which a deck suitable for sunning seemingly projects. Note that there is also an outdoor shower, and in the background there is a folly cum carport to the right. All the construction techniques are very simple to execute, and the materials are generic to the region.

Figure 6 Folly cum carport. Utilizing a curving roof form in contrast to the pyramidal high tower roof and the gable low bar building roofscape, this is an overtly ornamental-sculptural component set to stake out the turf that the main residential complex sits upon. Utilizing some custom-crafted steel components, this is an elegant project that manipulates semistandard building components to great advantage.

4

5

6

Figure 7 *Low bar building interior. An overarching ceiling of cedar tongue-and-groove boards relegates the interior subdivisions to a subordinate role. Note how standard light fixtures gain a sense of presence given their blank context and orientation to millwork, fenestration, or interior openings. Material contrast and overarching order create a sense of power and visual presence despite the use of simple construction techniques and generic materials.*

8

Figure 8 Living room: High House interior.
Voided corners and focal fireplace and lofted
ceiling utilizing matching book-match
veneered plywood paneling provide a sense of
both simultaneous containment and vertical
expression.

9

Figure 11 *Reflected ceiling perspective. This view looks up into the spaces created by BumpZoid and effectively reveals the strategies for the building components of the project. To the right the high building is a centered vertical presence with the bar building evidencing a rhythmatic positive-void-positive, do-si-do of open and closed spaces progressing until the most open space to the left, virtually a screen porch, and the most closed end point, an isolated study space. There is a sense that the high/living space has a singular identity whereas the bar building is a progressively evolving array of space and shapes under the bonnet of its extended gable roof.*

Figure 12 *Access. Set to the northside of the bar building, a single-loaded corridor is formed by the considered alignment of the sheetrock-shrouded storage and wet spaces to the right and the rhythmic perforation of the bar building to the left. A main entry portal is set at the end of the axis framed by the point of collision between the two building forms quietly expressed by the lone column.*

Figure 9 *Living room/joint. The voided corner at the left with its bared column is set at the coincidence between the two main building masses. The use of squared shapes for both windowscapes and millwork organization creates a sense of order via the alignment of the wall material break to window head (right) or window centerline (center). Note the change in flooring direction seen at the coincidence of the two wings as well.*

Figure 10 *Northwest elevation. Flanked by the carport (left) and the low bar building to the right, the central and pivotal high living tower is the center of attention of the complex.*

10

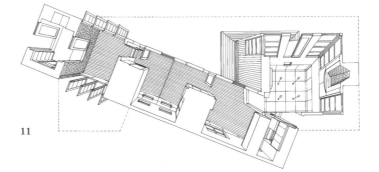

11

12

"cranked" orientation of the Low House. Wood walkways (easy on shoeless feet) are cleverly built in linear, arcing miniboardwalks, hovering over the sandy soil and providing a light, sinuous interconnecting system between the main house, pool house, and guest house (despite the code-complying site subdivision).

Stock materials are used throughout: veneered plywood, clear-finished cedar tongue-and-groove boards, strip-oak flooring (it's easy to guess which "house" has the winning floor orientation when they meet), plastic laminate cabinets, painted flat stock trim. Color (the least expensive expressionist gesture) is used on the exterior to great effect at the extended "tower" eave, providing a relatively massive green "cap" to the High House, violated only by the lightly beveled chimney mass (formed by standard brick set to a subtly expressive, three-sided cant).

In small houses the expressive and the expected go hand in hand to create a rich environment in tight confines. If a small house merely replicates extant clichés, it voids any house design's obligation to fit the occupants' functional idiosyncracies and manifest their exquisitely personal vision. Often in striving for innovation and/or personal expression, architect-designed small houses also leave out these client-oriented design criteria. Walking the high ground between the banal and the esoteric, BumpZoid has shown that the paradigm of "vacation home" can handle the edginess of innovation without losing the domestic touch.

Artfully Done

An artist and architect create a simple shape and wonderful spaces.

Bernard Wharton (along with Allan Shope, whose work appears later in this book) is one of the two partners in the firm Shope Reno Wharton in Greenwich, Connecticut. This firm has risen from designing three garage additions in its first year of operation in 1980 to designing some of the highest profile residential projects in the United States in the 1990s. The homes designed in their office often go beyond 10,000 square feet in size (and occasionally multiples of that dimension), so it is extraordinary to see what Bernard Wharton has helped midwife for his own house. When architects design their own homes, they often view them as opportunities to distill their aesthetic outlook. Often these homes can be seen as petri dishes for the enhanced growth of nascent ideas.

In the first house Wharton built for himself, he had a potent design focus—his wife, Elaine Anthony. It was not simply love that made Elaine's input powerful; it was the fact that she, like her husband, had become prominent in her own field, fine art. She has been a painter all her life, and much of what goes on inside this home has to do with her aesthetic vision. But more importantly, the design had to accommodate her needs as an artist since this home was where Elaine Anthony would "go" to work every day as a painter.

Surprising to all but the architects who read this book, very few architects, even those who have achieved Bernard Wharton's success, are wealthy. The same is true for painters. Thus several methods were employed to rein in the budget. The cost per square foot was relatively high (almost $200 a square foot for finished heated space), but the shapes employed and materials used would have given this house a far higher price tag had not some very rigorous cost containment strategies been employed. The total cost remained feasible because of its tight plan layout, only 1,100 square feet.

The first budgetary hurdle for any house is the cost of the site. This site is in Weston, Connecticut—a place of almost bucolic ambience despite its proximity to the hubbub of nearby Greenwich, where Bernard Wharton's office was located. What set this lot apart from more generic (and thus more costly) lots was that it had ledgy subsoil conditions where bare rock often came out of the ground. Even in the one area where there was some percolation for a septic system, "hard pan" was found—a subsoil that simply sheds water rather than receive it. The expense of bringing fill to the site and digging out a full basement would have frightened—not inspired—most buyers. But Wharton knew that designing a home with a full basement was foolhardy since this home was to

Figure 1 *Entry prospect. A proud prow of conical studio roof greets those who enter the site with a secondary beckoning gesture in the wake of this nautical mass in the form of the lone dormer that in turn locates the entry. Note the large quantity of bared bedrock which forms an inorganic sea on which this little ship sets sail.*

Figure 2 *Floor plan. A simple four-part harmony, a common kitchen-living-dining area is formed by a squared room (right), with its counterpart, Elaine Anthony's studio, a fully circular presence at the opposite of the plan (left). Connecting these dominant end points is a perspectively skewed corridor (center, top), and the bedroom and bathroom are nestled between these three public areas. Note the rhythmic imposition of a large-scaled south-facing double doors and the inherent cross-axiality of the entry with the most easterly set of these openings. Built-in storage is insinuated at most interstitial areas of the plan, and the fireplace's dominant masonry mass is set to receive the inherent center axis of the kitchen cabinets.*

Figure 3 *Entry. Centered on the backside gable, this entryway in turn centers upon the south-facing double doors set across the living-dining space it accesses. In the one overtly antihistoric gesture, Wharton created a steel prow roof at the entry point, utilizing bolt patterns, material contrast, and an undeniable edginess to contrast the home's semi-shingle-style detailing.*

1

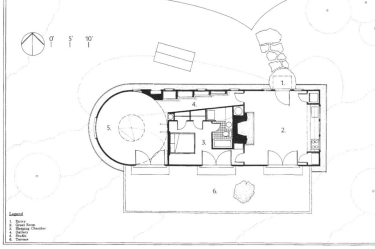

Legend

1. Entry
2. Great Room
3. Sleeping Chamber
4. Gallery
5. Studio
6. Terrace

2

3

Figure 4 *Entry north. The out-scaled banding of clerestory windows and trim serves to aggrandize the animated roofscape and obscure the true size of this house, fostering a sense of ambiguity which is further heightened by the oddball outbuilding to the left (a construction that hides the oil tank for the heating plant). Note the dark trim work set in contrast to the inexpensive asphalt roof shingles.*

Figure 5 *Bedroom. Bold colors and art allow a built-in bed (center) to be nestled amid a seemingly out-scaled space. Note that over the bed the projected wall plane allows the exposed joists to run uninterrupted and again focuses upon the local center of the room—not unlike the fireplace in the living room.*

be built upon solid rock, and with no full-time children present or planned for, a "standard-size" home with three or four bedrooms was not needed. Because of its geological baggage, this lot was affordable.

Beyond the literal "in-house" quality of the architect employed, Wharton and Anthony were their own general contractors, and they performed much of the finish work themselves. Their focus and commitment were evident when they were married on the job site after the foundation slab had been poured.

The next basic economy can be seen in the home's simple outline: a 20-foot-wide rectangle culminating in a hemicycular end. The floor plan is but a four-part harmony, with a circular studio to one end and a square kitchen-living-dining space at the other, interconnected by an ever-widening hallway cum gallery. Amid these three semipublic spaces was the serving area of the home: the bedroom, bathroom-laundry, hot water heater, central hearth, and storage. The delightfully continuous and unbroken perimeter holds together these four distinct elements with unexpected ease.

To compensate for the lack of a basement, Wharton created very large loft-attic spaces with twin dormers to allow emergency sleeping accommodations. This attic also houses the heating plant and serves as storage space. Because of its ongoing use, this area has a fairly ceremonial access in the form of a custom-designed ladder-stair set to the studio space.

5

Because of the cost-saving measures of careful site selection, owner design and general contracting, and the inherently simple plan perimeter and layout, the owners did not need to scrimp on the quality of the detailing and materials. In fact, the choices they made make their project a prime example of sound budget prioritization, that is, the determination of what should blow the budget and what can be safely backpedaled.

Determining budgetary priorities is critical to making any home affordable and cost-effective. Among those items determined to be high priority in this house (and thus relatively unencumbered by budgetary restraint) was the employment of the studio's fully curved walls and conical roof and skylight. Wharton opted to use 4-foot-wide, 8-foot-high custom doors of the highest quality available. The finish trim work is extensive and large scale. A fully realized masonry fireplace is central to the house. Lofty 9-foot-plus ceilings were provided for most of the house, as was the fully realized conical ceiling in the studio.

To afford these amenities the house contours to the budget and the priorities of Wharton and Anthony via a list of carefully reasoned compromises. Asphalt roof shingles were used

Figure 6 *Living room/connecting axis. Set within the context of the high ceilings, a semi-stonehengesque firebox surround of split granite fully realizes the potential latent in a simple room. Beckoning to the right is the ever-deepening set of book shelves that utilize the rich qualities of built-in trim at its corners plus top lighting to create a sense that there is something quite interesting to be seen beyond this very sedate and centered living area. Note the arcing cornice of a projecting wall plan centered on the fireplace that allows the ceiling framing pattern to be uninterrupted and at the same time reinforces the central organizing axis of the entire house (it also provides a nice pocket for built-in speakers).*

Figure 7 *Kitchen-dining area. A simple strip of countertop affords cleanup (left) and cooking (right with the refrigerator set behind the closet door to the right. The complete absence of upper cabinets wonderfully eschews any sense of "kitchen" and in its place leaves an uninterrupted sense of casual dining. Note the arcing presence of the steel structure set above the context of this space; centered upon the windows and reminiscent of the entry overhang, it has its geometric counterpart in several other spaces within the room, resonating with the projecting plane of the fireplace wall opposite. Note that the windows look like double-hung units but in fact are out-scaled casement units that provide maximum ventilation and ease of operation when reached across the countertop.*

(versus wood). Wharton designed a delightfully diminutive kitchen (which effectively hides the refrigerator within a closet!). A stackable washer and dryer was set within the only bathroom in the house—a model of functional efficiency. Additionally, a custom-designed bed allows for the full utilization of its underside for storage, thus eliminating the need to provide space for bureaus and drawers within the confines of the master bedroom. Other measures included the aforementioned lack of a basement and the lessened quantity of windows (compensated for by some large-scale openings).

But the greatest savings derived simply from reducing the home's size to fit the occupants. Thirty years ago a 1,100-square-foot, one-bedroom house would have been viewed as impractical, but that is not true today. Wharton and Anthony are in love with their refuge, and it is the physical focal point of their relationship. The house has been designed for future bedroom expansion: a bedroom/entry tower has been designed to be set directly to the north of the home and the septic field has been designed to accommodate one additional bedroom.

Despite its small footprint, the exterior of the house has a scale-ambiguous presence. It's hard to discern a real "size" given its eave height, which is seemingly somewhere between one and two stories, steeply pitched roofs (all well over 12-in-12 pitch), the aforementioned conical exclamation point proudly poised to be the focus upon site entry, and the aggrandized chimney mass. When these manipulations are combined with out-scaled doors and tiny windows all held to a brilliantly dark green trim and an eave datum that wraps around the entire length of the house, a vague nautical sensibility is developed and helps create a "tightly wrapped" form. The one window set in the curve is a truly curved window—not cheap, but again this is one place where money should be allocated, as it benefits the home's most prominent aspect, an aspect fully realized in the conical skylight.

Beyond these broad-stroke moves, Wharton has evidenced his extraordinary skill at detailing to mitigate some domestic eyesores. In rural ledgy sites it is almost impossible to bury oil tanks, and Wharton has opted to house his in a garden pavilion, canted to dissociate its mass from alignment to the "mother ship." The pavilion detailing directly harkens back to the home, and the miniclerestory windows allow an enigmatic visual perforation. As this demitasse object sidles up to it, the 1,100-square-foot home again seems a bit larger than its true size.

Electric meters have to be set at a certain height and at a certain location and are as visually appealing as a microwave oven lag-bolted to the side of your home. But in this house Wharton has turned this potential eyesore into a lightly beckoning gesture and has presented the one true voidal aspect of the home by taking advantage of the ability of wood shingles to contour and bend, making folds and bows to create an enigmatic slot within the context of the long, unbroken north-facing entry facade.

Additionally, in creating a home with a tight unbroken perimeter such as this, it is often a good idea to figure out a way to shelter those who are about to enter your home. This could have been easily accommodated by a iconic roof form (typical in New England architecture). But Wharton has chosen to transform this functional necessity into a prominent aesthetic feature—virtually a cantilevered steel sculpture—as unexpected as the aforementioned meter-accommodating void. It is the only antireferential, overtly unprecedented element in the entire façade.

For a small house, the windows and doors show extraordinary variety, from the very small (facing north and entry) to very large (facing the south light). This southern exposure helps defray heating costs and also serves to provide natural illumination for some of the large-scale wall spaces that are provided for Elaine Anthony's artwork.

In harboring two fully mature artists, evidencing the work of one and providing for the work of the other, this home has a unique interrelationship between its genesis and use, right down to trim details that incorporate the letter forms W and A. This home symbolizes the efforts of two people dedicated to their craft and to each other.

Figure 8 (opposite) Studio. The heavy articulation of the bared structure and ornate trim work of the main body of the house are contrasted by this semitrimless, scaleless space. The studio is a place without corners, and most of its light cascades down from a central oculus. Anthony's artwork is the essential focus of this space, and a central axial relationship derives from the custom ladder (left) and the curvilinear window set opposite it. Industrial lighting follows this centerline as well, providing a metering influence for a potentially abstract space.

Axis and Cross Axis

Passive solar intentions and symmetry infused with a Japanese sensibility.

A married couple (two doctors) wished to find a retreat from busy careers in Berkeley, California. In their mind's eye, Japanese architecture had a timeless simplicity and honest materiality that evoked a sense of peace and perspective for them.

Traditional Japanese homes are definitely small by western standards. They also have a series of spiritually interpretative and culturally derived functional constraints that render them problematic for habitation by typical American occupants save those devoted to Japanese culture. So when the couple hired Alex Riley to build their home in rural California on a 3-acre lot, it was clear that this conceptual overlay would be more a motif than a studied academic re-creation of Japanese architecture.

In hiring Alex Riley, they chose an architect who is clearly masterful in the expressive use of natural materials and in the use of the sun to provide heat. The desire for a Japanese ambience reinforced Riley's latent desire for material expression. However, the site chosen by the clients for their vacation home definitely stood in the way of creating a home in which the use of artificial heating would be minimal.

Many vacation homes are sited to appreciate views, to provide psychological relief from the effects of a dense-packed urban work-a-day world. In this case, the site did present an extraordinary view out over the hills of rural California. The only problem was that these views face due north on a hillside that is diametrically opposed to the best place for meaningful solar gain—unless an innovative architect can re-invent the "rules" of the game. Given the implications of the marriage of architect, client, and site, the house that results evidences an intricate architectural interplay set in the context of an 1,174-square-foot, one-bedroom home.

This book openly advocates the use of axial and cross-axial relationships as well as the use of three-dimensional space to defeat the sense of spatial constriction present in most small homes. No project better evidences the liberating sense of spaciousness afforded by these axial and spatial manipulations than the one depicted here. The house has a single roof ridge oriented in a north-south direction, a spine that is the essential generator for all the home's massing. Essentially, the roofscape and subsequent massing follow a telescoping formal progression, with mass ever widening from the upside south to the downside north. Riley used the interplay between the constant ridge line and the descending ground plane to create spaces that are both loftier and larger as the floor planes of the house descend and rooms widen progressively to address the view.

1

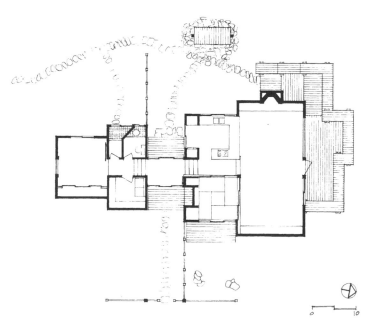

2

Figure 1 Entry. A traditional Oriental archway serves to signal the point of entry for those encountering the house. The entry sequence is complete with custom-built exterior lighting indicating the preferred pathway into the building.

Figure 2 Floor plan. Five bays of construction are cross-axially linked at their common centerpoint. For most private (bedroom) to most public (living room), a left-to-right progression is breached amidships via a recessed entry slot. This voidal entry serves as a cross-axial linkage/perforation which connects the home to the immediate landscape. Ascending (to the left) from this entry slot is the master bedroom suite with sleeping space at the end point, bathroom to the top, and closet-laundry to the bottom of this self-contained, tripartite ensemble. To the right and down is the duet of kitchen and dining area. Note that the dining area is formed by a 4.5 tatami mat module. The end point for this axial orientation is the large-scale living room, which accepts views from both the kitchen and dining areas. A meandering deck transitions around two sides of this living area. A pavilion is set opposite to the kitchen sink and serves to extend the building's vernacular into the landscape. Note the use of wing walls to similarly attenuate the cross-axial influence of the entry.

Functionally, the house has a progressive quality as well. The 50-foot central axis is the physical link between five bays of space all bisected by the line of the roof ridge. From the narrowest and most private (bedroom) to the widest and most public (living room), the home evolves functionally as well as formally. The dominant ridge/corridor axis is counterpointed amidships by the cross axis of site access and house entry. This cross-axial bay uses tempered glass roofing set in the same plane as the rest of the roof and supported by the same expressed structure used throughout the home. The use of wall-to-wall sliding glass doors in this "slot" gives the house a completely clear and pure opaque skin.

An unrelentingly logical organization can be stultifying, but Riley uses the underpinnings of a rational mind-set to facilitate the use of some animated detailing based on the Japanese motifs mentioned earlier. Although this home eschews a traditional Japanese entry, soaking tub, veranda, and other elements in favor of western planning and functional accommodation, the overt sense of integration (right down to a 4.5 tatami mat–sized square dining area) helps to suffuse the house with a sense of abstraction that belies the specificity of its aesthetic underpinnings. The interplay between linear organization, lyric craftsmanship, and structural expressionism creates a quietly dynamic ambience. The structure uses post-and-beam technology, cross-referencing white walls with clear-finished wood structure, cabinetry, and railings. The design is extended into the landscape via an extended asymmetrical deck and a conscientiously noncentered Japanese-style "folly"—an outdoor covered work table rendered as a gateway-altar.

Such a thorough coordination of circulation, space, structure, roof form, and landscape might be enough for most architects, but for Alex Riley there is an abiding imperative to utilize solar heat to warm the interior of the house and thus root the entire ambience of the house to nature. Riley chose to link the dominant formal and functional axis with the sun. The method of this linkage is a continuous ridge skylight running the length of the house that allows light to cascade into the ever-increasing volumes of space, transcending all the functional layering mentioned earlier.

This passive solar intent would have been an empty gesture had there not been something present for the sun to warm. In a typical late twentieth-century American home, white wall surfaces are presumed to be gypsum wall-

3

Figure 3 Roofscape. *Evidencing the dominant organizing principle of this project, the tiled roof has its spine celebrated with skylights and wood trim and has its planes extended (down and to the left) and incised (at the point of entry). A garden pavilion (left) serves as the classical function of folly distilling the base identity of this roofscape into a bite-sized reality.*

Figure 4 Central axis: living room view. *With the entry perforation fully evident to the left, the ascendent skylight-lined roof ridge marches unrelentingly toward the view (center). Note the double bay support forming either side of this axis and the multiple utilization of trim and structural elements to reinforce the latent arts and crafts aspects of this design, including the built-in ladders that facilitate access to modest lofts (to the right) and above the kitchen area to the left. It should be noted that all surfaces set close to the skylights are stucco, designed to help provide a modest amount of radiant heating during cooler periods.*

Figure 5 Axis to entry and beyond. *Large-scale timber construction serves as an out-sized presence amid the interweaving trim and wall work. Note the tatami mat organizing influence in the dining area (left) as well as the recessed niche this room centers upon. The open kitchen-cooking area (right) shares space with the living room as well as visual access to the intermediate entry slot (far right). The stepped floor plan is in evidence as steps separate the entry slot (center) from the formal part of the house (foreground) and the bedroom suite (set center right). Two lofts are also evident (upper left and upper right). Note the complete customization of virtually every element of this construction including lighting.*

4

5

board, compounded and painted. Wallboard is a material of relatively low density and thus has a low ability to accept, store, and radiate heat derived from the sun. Riley opted to use a full coating of stucco for all the walls adjacent to this skylight and thus provide a large square footage of relatively high density material to accept the sun's warmth (despite its reflectance) and store it for the mitigation of the radiant cooling caused by the large-scale glazing which accommodates the northerly views mentioned earlier.

Symbolic of his intention to express materiality and to integrate his design environmentally, this ridge skylight draws attention to itself via ornament as its divisions are graced with extended wood trim. Set upon a sea of cement tiles, this spine becomes a visual focal point upon entry and serves as a highly visible common denominator to the progressive and expressive extensions of the roof form.

The large-scale planning, massing, and material gestures are complemented by a large array of details, both structural and aesthetic, involving the expressive use of the wood. These articulations—some overtly symbolic (the use of a anomalous cantilevered support) and whimsical (the subtly expressive ladders to access the aforementioned loft spaces)—create a sense of controlled animation in contrast to the ever-present linear axis that controls and orders virtually every aspect of the house. There is a sense that every aspect of the home has been designed under the aegis of a single controlling influence: Light fixtures, handrails, custom windows, and cabinetry are all completely coordinated with a sense of customization that is rare, which is reflected in the budget with a cost approaching $200 per square foot in 1987.

If any one of the competing architectural influences had subordinated or trivialized another, a dysfunctional hybrid would have emerged. Japanese motifs are interpreted with California Arts and Crafts techniques and detailing under the transcendent influence of the view. Amid all these influences, the sure and steady hand of Alex Riley is seen throughout this small house, which is an expressive and controlled product of an experienced and careful designer.

Basilical Shed

Art and technology interweave, bathed in light.

HOUSES usually reflect two mind-sets: that of the designer and that of the occupant. Few projects could more clearly reveal its architects' essential attitude and occupant's life-style than this one-bedroom home. The context is a community of tight, interwoven rectilinear lots in La Conchita, California. Built as a summer studio for an artist, this 1,300-square-foot home is a classic example of the tail wagging the dog. In most homes, the home office represents between 5 and 10 percent of the overall square footage, leaving the 90 to 95 percent of the main body of the house for eating, sleeping, bathroom activities, and leisure. In this particular house there is an inversion of that ratio with about 15 percent of the total area of the house given over to day-to-day living and the vast remaining bulk of space dedicated to the occupant's work space—a place to create art.

The artist-occupant spends his fair-weather months in Chicago, also the home of the architects, Stanley Tigerman and Margaret McCurry. The Tigerman-McCurry office has a remarkable diversity of projects involving a wide variety of design programs. Amid the diversity of their project list Tigerman-McCurry have evidenced a fascination with the stepping three-bay section of the early Christian era basilica—a double-story, gable-roofed form with two

---

STATS

PROJECT NAME AND LOCATION:
Private residence, La Conchita, California

ARCHITECT:
Tigerman McCurry Architects

COMPLETION DATE:
1992

TOTAL HEATED SQUARE FEET:
1,300

PERCEIVED SQUARE FOOTAGE:
1,859

CIRCULATION-TO-TOTAL-AREA RATIO:
8 percent

BEDROOM-SPACE-TO-TOTAL-AREA RATIO:
4 percent

GROSS COST:
NA

COST PER SQUARE FOOT:
NA

DURATION OF DESIGN PROCESS:
One year

DURATION OF CONSTRUCTION:
One year

Photos © Tim Street-Porter.
Drawings by the architects.

---

flanking single-story lean-to sheds. In this incarnation of their sectional predilection, the architects have found an almost perfect marriage of form, function, and site.

The site in question is a 60- by 75-foot lot set amid houses all registering to a small grid of roads that interconnect the entire community. The basilical form obviously has "ends" and "sides"—in this particular case the lot geometry dictated that the one "end" of this extruded section would front on the street. This perfected form stands in stoic distinction from its higgledy-piggledy neighbors. But the measure of the basilical form's true applicability to this particular site is its use of the upper portion of the basilical shape (above the flanking lean-to sheds) as a massive monitor roof, providing enormous quantities of indirect light while successfully avoiding the visual intrusion of the adjacent homes into the studio space.

Additionally, the basilical form has the opportunity for structural expressionism via the interweaving of the two roof forms (gable and shed). It can also facilitate spatial subdivision either by imposing a column grid or by simply using the latent spatial properties defined by the building's shape. Here a single span roof superstructure embraces the ever-changing needs of an active artist.

With plenty of light and space to harbor the occupant's creative efforts,

1

Figure 1 Front. A dominant basilical form is flanked by two offspring. In mass and scale not unlike its counterparts (left), its shape and architecturally conspired clarity are relatively unprecedented to the area. Note the use of standard cladding materials (stucco siding and sheet-metal roofing) and the careful sizing of fenestration. Note that the porte cochere to the right serves as the major entry portal despite the fact that large-scale doors directly address the street itself.

Figure 2 Floor plan. A three-part complex with each component having a three-bay longitudinal organization of redundant transverse bays (five for subordinate flanking components, six for the central dominant home). At the top is an enclosed garage, and at the bottom is an open porte cochere/carport that serves as the main entry for the entire building. Dominated by axial symmetry, this plan presents an inversion of the typical plan layout with the most intimate spaces (bedroom and study) occupying the first bay orienting to the street (left) and the most public areas orienting to the open-ended backyard (right). Central to this private-public spatial organization are the points of entry set between the main house and its subordinate garage and porte cochere, and its bathroom-kitchen-laundry wet core occupying one of the six bays. Note the two curb cuts providing vehicular access to both sides of the site, allowing for loading and off-loading of the artist's materials. Note also the screen of palm trees that is set as a buffer across the front of the building.

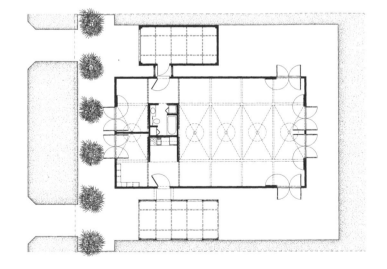

2

Figure 3 Studio space facing the backyard. Art, architecture, and technology fuse in a play of light, space, structure, and scale affording a stoically simple centered ambiance counterpointed by inflections of color and dancing light and shadow play.

Figure 4 Site. An isolated grid of high-density construction set between the mountains to the left and the seaside to the right. Note that the main highway and railroad are set between this grid and the sea. The site in question is set to the upper right (the darkened-in building plan). Note that the backside of this particular site leads to the largely undeveloped open and relatively flat landscape, providing a private orientation to the large-scale art studio that inhabits more than half the total area of the home.

Figure 5 Living room facing the street (front). The wet core of kitchen and bath-laundry is behind a finish trimmed wall set to clear the overarching presence of the expressive roof trusses that allow for a full-span roof structure above the entire ceiling. Note the polished concrete floor, the bypassing lighting and mechanical systems, and the overtly expressionistic utilization of bared structural elements affording a semifactoryesque presence amid the overtly "hip" furnishings.

Figure 6 Porte cochere. A demitasse structural distillation of its parent building, this porte cochere has an interesting dynamic between a stolid semisymbolic roof construction and a completely open and voided (one might say naked) lower construction that utilizes bared structural supports heavily cross-braced with post tensioned steel rod; these supports echo their structural counterparts in the roof of the main building.

Figure 7 Site situation. As one of many elongated buildings set along a tight street grid in the otherwise low-density lowlands, this project is sympathetic in scale but distinctive in geometry and abstraction to its neighbors.

3

Tigerman and McCurry designed the human component of the home, using the kitchen, bath, bedroom, and dining spaces as a buffer between the outsized studio space and the street. Thus the dominant activity, art, is held away from the hubbub of street activity by two of the six bays that form the house.

Similarly, automobiles need to be accommodated in any urban situation, and this project uses car storage to buffer the studio space from its neighbors via an enclosed garage and an open carport set to flank the house. Two entries are set between these outbuildings and the central house form, neither of which in any way visually keyed to the street. The design of this house enhances the mystery of artistic expression, whereby a beckoning form has

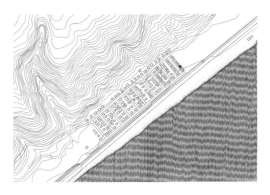

no obvious visible means for human access. This attitude is lightly reinforced by the use of a palm tree screen carefully set in front of the home—six evenly spaced trees whose gaps accommodate cars and which simultaneously screen openings that address the street.

Given the lot's size, it's not surprising that site development is quite simple. Ninety percent of the available site is paved with the carport serving as a porte cochere, allowing unencumbered passage of vehicles straight through to large doors at the back of the studio for easy loading and off-loading of artist's materials and finished art. In this case, the site development reinforced the essential character of the architectural elements that celebrate the industrial over the visceral—to a point.

Areas of whimsy and delight can be found in the secondary elements of detailing that are gleefully present once the stark impact of unapologetic

4

forms is fully digested. The first indication that this is not a simple warehouse conversion is the use of flanking outbuildings as toylike pavilions, chicks set close to the flanks of the mother hen. The unabashedly honest structural systems of the main house become semisymbolic as applied to these service buildings. They become large-

5

6

7

scale ornaments, and have carefully rendered distinctions from each other.

Similarly, on the interior of the main building, although the triangulated steel stays of the truss roof structure are the dominant visual focus of the interior, the subordinate interior wall system that houses the "wet" core of kitchen and bath is carefully trimmed to become out-scaled furniture in the context of this overarching space.

In addition, the aesthetic manipulations of the structural work play with scale as well. A simple truss spans from wall to wall and has a miniaturized offspring sitting atop its peak to form the vertical "push" of the central gable roof, thus creating multiple replications of the geometries employed.

Although this is not a "bare bones" industrial shed, relative economies are employed by using off-the-rack materials indigenous to the region. Acrylic stucco and corrugated steel roofing are set over rigid insulation throughout, with wall surfaces utilizing an in-fill system of wood-framed and sheetrock-covered cavity walls. In such a consistent palette there has been careful development of window types, colors, and final finishing of all the subtextural surfaces.

It's easy to attain visual impact when a dynamic referential form such as this is employed, but it is harder to sustain interest via the careful use of scale changes, detailing, and material selection. Tigerman and McCurry have done all these things and provided a home that uniquely embraces the art and soul of its occupant—a home that not only has plenty of elbow room but the sort of visually active and yet functionally passive space which presents an overarching embrace of the act of artistic expression. Small houses do big things well when they have a sense of their own true size.

Two-Bedroom Houses

"Do Not Use Residential-Style Elements"

Taken from the specs for a poolside lesson in economy and delight.

I F a building does not live up to its potential, it's easy for architects to use the canard of a bare-bones budget to plea-bargain their culpability for dereliction of aesthetic duty. On the other hand, someone wishing to build a small house is terrified that an architect will take his or her hopes and dreams and simply squash them with budget-blind, egomaniacal, artistic zealotry that creates a design so expensive that it is virtually unbuildable.

This little project puts the lie to both of these scenarios. Walter Chatham, a New York City–based architect, endeavored to fulfill both the present and future hopes of his niece, Louise Chatham. There was a paucity of funds (all of $35,000) and a plethora of hope (this is virtually a beachhead for a future "real" house).

In trying to be both innovative and thoughtful, Chatham realized that if anything was to be built, there had to be one simple rule: The project must contour to the funds available to build it. One of the central premises of ensuring buildability is that the size of the house and budget correspond to each other—the smaller one is, the smaller the other can become.

Beyond this rather obvious syllogism, Walter Chatham happened upon two equally obvious, but far less commonly employed, vehicles for economy that architects are loath to embrace. These design imperatives

---

S T A T S

PROJECT NAME AND LOCATION:
*Pool House, State Road,
North Carolina*

ARCHITECT:
Walter F. Chatham, Architect

COMPLETION DATE:
1992

TOTAL HEATED SQUARE FEET:
280

PERCEIVED SQUARE FOOTAGE:
600

CIRCULATION-TO-TOTAL-AREA RATIO:
0 (no dedicated circulation space)

BEDROOM-SPACE-TO-TOTAL-AREA RATIO:
35%

GROSS COST:
$35,000

COST PER SQUARE FOOT:
$70

DURATION OF DESIGN PROCESS:
Three weeks

DURATION OF CONSTRUCTION:
Four months

Photos © Walter F. Chatham.
Drawings by the architect.

---

can be applied with a breadth and scope that ensures their applicability to any project. The mind-set of these premises had to form the base line of whatever was to be built for Ms. Chatham.

The first axiom implicit in this project is an old saw, "Keep it simple, stupid." In this particular case, *simple* might equate to the word *redundant.* Two barely two story buildings are set kitty-corner to each other with a diagonally arrayed single-story screen porch set between them. Beyond the simple planning, the "buildings" themselves are almost identical in all aspects save minor changes in window positioning and in the interior sleeping lofts that inhabit each form. Architects will appreciate the fact that these buildings are so similar that the long elevation depicting this project is identical when seen from both sides. Another symptom of simplicity is that this entire project was drafted on one 2- by 3-foot format sheet with but two framing details. What makes this distillation almost poetic is the fact that the project was computer-drafted, thus lending a quality of an industrial catalog illustration to the project's rendering.

The quality of the graphics employed depicts the second axiomatic approach which was that all the materials used to build this project would be available from a single source—the local Hog Farmer's

Figure 1 *Poolside. Composed of materials derived from a single catalog, this innocent and expressive construction utilizes two identical dominant buildings, forms that sit kitty-corner to each other with an in-fill porch. Unabashed material contrasts are employed (corrugated steel siding and roofing, Plexiglas barn doors, prototypic rotary ventilators, and so on).*

Figure 2 *Working drawing. Computer-generated, this single drawing served as the entire set of working drawings for the house. Note that the lone longitudinal elevation is presented only once (upper left) simply because its opposite counterpart is identical to the vantage depicted. Two identical two-story buildings are joined by a single-story open porch, with the entire ensemble centering upon a 20- by 40-foot swimming pool. Local centerlines are continually reinforced via simple orientations of openings and minor manipulations in the interior development of the two towers. The entire complex is levitated off the ground plane by piers.*

1

2

Cooperative Store. Despite its use of factory-made materials, this minicomplex evidences the best lessons of home construction that were in force prior to the advent of the Industrial Age. In primitive cultures, simple dwellings were typically constructed from materials that could be harvested or quarried directly from the land the home sat upon. As transportation of materials became commonplace, "better" materials could be obtained to make the home more durable, functional, or aesthetically exotic. In late twentieth century America, the economy of building materials has less to do with the distance of transportation between a product's source and its ultimate market than with the kind of customization that building materials are subjected to once the house is built. Many architects pay lip service to the idea of "industrial" materials. Early twentieth century Modernists would often use plate glass and steel in ways that symbolically rendered an "industrial" building that was, in fact, as hand-hewn as any "traditional" chateau or mansion. Given the fact that very few groundbreaking Modernist homes had any meaningful precedent for their factory-grade detailing meant that there was an inherent hypocrisy in their final built form.

Unlike their predecessors, the house Walter Chatham designed virtually uses a single catalog for its component specifications, and the harmony implicit in this approach is readily evident in the playful richness of its built form. Needless to say, all doors, windows, screening, light fixtures, and so on, are off the rack.

In eschewing customization, Chatham could have simply "rolled over and played dead" and allowed a simple shed to sit beside a pool, declaring it a triumph of the mundane. But rather than be cowed by the potential banality of these materials, Chatham was inspired to use them in ways that evidence his resourceful and rigorous approach to design.

The buildings themselves are of minimal dimension (10 feet wide by 18 feet long, each) with the screen porch being determined by the same 10-foot-wide bay but continuing that bay for two more 10-foot modules, creating, in effect,

3

4

Figure 3 *Inglenook. Simple painted-wood flooring and galvanized-steel wainscoting stand in contrast to the naturally finished plywood walls and white-painted ceiling of the loft.*

Figure 4 *Backside entry. Essentially providing access into the home away from the poolside of the project, the starkness of this prospect stands in contrast to the more open and urban of the poolside ambiance.*

two 10- by 20-foot rectangular shapes "lean-to'd" together to create a central 10-foot-wide gable connector between the two two-story buildings. However, to maintain the appropriate scale for this project, the architect has taken complete control over the dimensioning of all heights employed, keying the vertical dimension of the first-floor height to the simple module of a 6-foot, 8-inch-high door with 6 inches of trim above it, thereby creating a 7-foot, 4-inch space below the two sleeping lofts that are set within each "building." The spring point for the pitched roofs in these projects is taken from a 6-foot point above the loft floor with all but the very tall able to stand in the lofts. It must be said that these tight height constrictions might not be appropriate for a full-time residence, but given that this is an outpost of civilization, homesteading for a future "real" residence, these ingenious moves are wholly palatable. There is also a sense of miniaturization that allows these extraordinarily tight buildings a sense of scale and dignity that belies their true size.

In forming spaces, Chatham uses a similarly no-nonsense approach that simultaneously facilitates a paradoxical sense of control and spatial lyricism. The 6-foot ceiling heights of the loft space and the 7-foot, 4-inch-high bath and inglenook spaces set below these loft areas are counterpointed by the 14-foot-high ceilings in the main body of each building. Similarly, the insulated flat ceilings of the two two-story spaces are counterpointed by the cathe-

5

dralized porch roof framing that "glues" together the two building forms. These competing forces of horizontal and vertical spatial expansion serve to enliven the entire experience of the project and tend to animate the very "normal" building materials employed to the point where these are not rude sheds but spaces and shapes acting in a conscientious choreography to create a singular image.

The detailing employed enlivens the project as well. Classic galvanized-metal rotary caps are used both for the stove flue and the kitchen fan exhaust and are (of course) carefully centered on each gable and located to the "inside" of both ridge lines to create a central, vertical focus above all the construction. Eaves are extended beyond walls a full foot in both directions, and the whole complex centers on the pool by using a platform cum plinth that fairly oozes around both buildings and screen porch to create a singular presence. A corrugated fiberglass panel is used as a large-scale shutter to protect the main double doors that access both buildings, and standard galvanized steel is used exclusively throughout for the roofing, siding, ceiling material, and loft access ladders; the steel is complemented wonderfully by the expressive use of paint and raw Douglas fir plywood. Corrugated steel is also used to create a semienigmatic pyramid at each end of the pool to house pool equipment.

It is now virtually trite to say "less is more," but it is never a cliché to say that any imagination limited by money is not very imaginative. Like many projects in this book, this one proves the point that it is not enough to build small. Building small has to be complemented by building well—and that usually means utilization of a thoughtful, imaginative, and, in this case, gifted architect.

Figure 5 *Pool: landscape view. Flanked by enigmatic, corrugated-steel pyramids housing the necessary appliances and appurtances of pool maintenance, this proud little construction basks in the sun.*

Figure 6 *Bathroom-kitchen interior. A bedroom loft is set above the project's lone bathroom, which accommodates a standard refrigerator to one side. Note the use of galvanized-steel wainscoting and galvanized siding material for the ceiling of the project, fully highlighting the bare-bulb lighting fixtures. Steel wire and galvanized pipe as well as a stock aluminum ladder are employed, and when combined with a brightly colored doorway into the bath and natural wood furniture, a wonderfully playful palette of contrasting materials enlivens the potentially blank box of space.*

6

Invisible Order

Symmetry and cellular design are masked by a natural context.

THE second-home design program is a natural vehicle for innovation in small-house design. Whereas homes built to harbor full-time occupancy need to accommodate secondary and tertiary activities (homework, bill paying, storage of off-season clothing and equipment, and so on), second homes are merely repositories for the mind and body—not necessarily for the activities that make distant relaxation a necessity rather than a luxury. Secondarily, these homes usually are held to a fairly stringent reality check when it comes to their building budget. Typically vacation homes are the product of dream fulfillment evidencing years of planning by their owners to facilitate the creation of something which has a use that is, by definition, limited. Second homes are often set in the context of extreme topographical or geographical idiosyncrasy. All of these specialized design criteria apply to the Kempton Cabin designed by Seattle architect Arne Bystrom.

Given that it is set on an island in the Puget Sound, this 1,025-square-foot home is relatively inexpensive (less than $100 a square foot) and successfully deals with a ledgy subsoil condition, extraordinary views, and the desire to minimize the disruption of the existing trees that were on the site. The added twist to this project is that it employs some classic design

STATS

PROJECT NAME AND LOCATION:
Kempton Cabin, Obstruction Island, Washington State

ARCHITECT:
Arne Bystrom, Architect

COMPLETION DATE:
1992

TOTAL HEATED SQUARE FEET:
932

PERCEIVED SQUARE FOOTAGE:
1,418

CIRCULATION-TO-TOTAL-AREA RATIO:
5 percent

BEDROOM-SPACE-TO-TOTAL-AREA RATIO:
55 percent

GROSS COST:
$100,000

COST PER SQUARE FOOT:
$93

DURATION OF DESIGN PROCESS:
Four to six months

DURATION OF CONSTRUCTION:
Four months

Photos © and drawings by the architect.

principles to facilitate a greatly enhanced sense of space while at the same time facilitating affordability. Without looking at the plan layout, these two central organizing features of this project are essentially invisible when the building is seen from any vantage point.

The first abstract architectural strategy employed was cellular design. Essentially, three separate "cells" were designed to have consistent massing, construction, and materials. The second organizing principle was symmetry, whereby the flanking cells are centered around an aggrandized and recessed central cell.

These methods of organization are not abstract constructs but methods by which significant economies can be achieved via redundancy (the nearly identical cells) and structural efficiencies (the symmetrical alignment of these three cells allows for the structural "double-dipping" of the footings employed). Symmetry and modular construction also facilitate axial organization, helping to interconnect the three cells via two aligned "bridges," thus greatly enhancing the interior perceived space.

If this project were set on a barren hillside (as in a classic villa or farmhouse), these organizing features would be obvious—perhaps even problematically so. But set amid the wild growth of this wind-swept island, these two organizing princi-

1

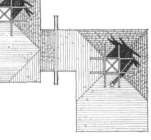
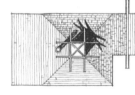

ROOF PLAN

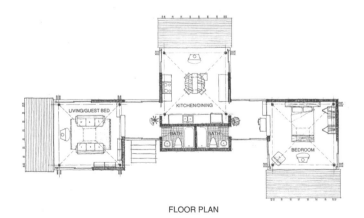

FLOOR PLAN

2

Figure 1 *Northwest orientation. Semi-identical pods, or cells, turn their "visors" at different orientations with their expressive cantilever enhanced by the full-width glazing set to wrap around the corners from which the roof cantilevers. Note that all glazing is accomplished with stock sliding glass doors.*

Figure 2 *Roof plan/floor plan. Three replicative "cells" are axially linked in an implicitly symmetrical order. The central cell harbors the wet core of bathroom and kitchen spaces as well as the dining area, with the flanking pods harboring a permanent bedroom occupancy on one side and a living room with a guest bedroom capacity on the other. Entered at the joint between the guest bedroom/living room and the kitchen-dining area, the living area is set two steps down and the bedroom area set two steps up. Projecting from each of the three cells— each in a different orientation—are three heavily cantilevered decks, each completely covered by an equally aggressively cantilevered roof. The roofscapes essentially meld three pyramidal, cupola-capped roof forms complemented with a wood stove flue pipe. Roof planes are extended to form the joints between the three cells or attenuated to provide the cantilevered roof overhangs over the decks mentioned earlier. Note that the post-and-beam construction is distinctively held away from the wall enclosure system and from any adjacent millwork elements, and that all structure is allowed to have its cantilevered end points fully expressed. Note also the use of seamless sliding glass doors to form all of the glazing.*

3

Figure 3 *Entry, south elevation. A central pod, or cell, has its backside shape manipulated into a double-sawtooth form that recognizes the double bathroom set underneath its roofscape.*

Figure 4 *Site plan. Possessing an entire peninsula projecting out into Puget Sound, this remarkable site affords incredible views and some fairly rough weather. The site plan reveals that the formal concavity formed by the symmetrical arrayed building elements provides an entry courtyard that addresses this site's lone point of access—a dock.*

Figure 5 *East: typical visor-lantern-deck. Simple rectilinear and pyramidal shapes are manipulated to create large-scale forms reminiscent of the rough-hewn character of the site.*

Figure 6 *North and south elevations. The north elevation, primarily oriented toward the view, displays the extraordinary simplicity of three pyramidal roofs gently stepping down a hillside, each spawning a glazed cupola-lantern-light well. The south elevation is slightly more complex, allowing for entry (center left) and providing a slight formal sawtooth indication of the double bathroom seen at the center. The absolute consistency between the building systems, geometries, and materials reinforces the semimechanistic quality of this playfully evolving construction.*

SITE PLAN

4

ples are simply not apparent. The potential for predictability amid the redundancy is mitigated by the developments of each individual cell as well. Each cell has simple cantilevered decks set to address three separate views, and all have attenuations of the existing 45-degree roof slope over each deck area, creating an exuberantly cantilevered "visor." The large-scale voids under each visor and simple massing of the cells are intended to be replicative of the "in-and-out" quality of the dense but inconsistent tree patterning that envelopes this house. Each cell also possesses a wood stove set at a different orientation. Additionally, each cell is set at a different level, cascading down the gentle hillside.

Another development that preempts predictibilty is the use of some fairly expressive, even latently ornamental, features—all derived from the unabashed love affair this house has with wood. In a gesture of structural annunciation, the heavy double-timber framing system is allowed to cantilever beyond the perimeter of the house as are the ends of the deck framing. Similarly, and more dramatically, cupolas projecting out through the top of the

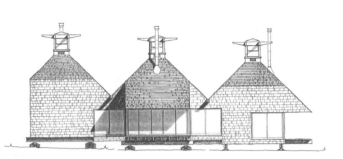

NORTH ELEVATION

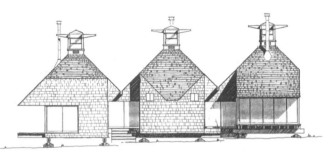

SOUTH ELEVATION

6

5

pyramidal roofs serve as lanterns for natural light to cascade down to the interiors of each cell and provide venting for the roof cavities for each of the roofscapes as well. These architectural exclamation points are zestily enhanced by cantilevered "horns"—mute gargoylesque attenuations of the perimeter framing at the top of each cupola—and by the proximate location of the flue pipes of the aforementioned wood stoves. In a similar gesture of aggrandized detailing, the point at which the three dominant roofscapes join over the connecting bridges has attenuated scuppers extending far out beyond the eave line.

Low-tech cleverness is used in the heating and ventilation system. Unabashedly using a loophole in the state energy code (which has since been closed), this project relies on individual wood stoves instead of a central heating system. This provides a significant economy and a practical application of rudimentary technology to a situation in which heat is a very sometime thing (especially considering that this is a site accessible only by small boats!). Additionally, the need for any air-conditioning is mitigated by the extreme overhangs that provide shading wherever there is massive glazing as well as by the surrounding trees and by the use of the lanterns as vertical flues to naturally ventilate each cell.

In short, this is a house of extreme contrasts—three stoic cubes with symmetrical roofs being activated by the cantilevered extensions of roof and floor planes, counterpointed by the absence of roof overhang in all other areas. Its symmetry order is counterpointed by progressive level changes and idiosyncratic articulations of form and stove location. Easily recognizable standard materials have their normative presence distorted by large-scale manipulations to create visual interest. In short, this house evidences what architects can offer in the design of a small house:

Figure 7 *Interior corner. Simple post-and-beam framing is allowed to express itself with those timbers carrying the heavily cantilevered roof that provides a miniloft space. Note the integration of lighting and the attenuation of the main carrying timbers set to stiffen the perimeter walls. Note also the use of contrasting sheetrock set disocciatively from the heavy timber construction.*

Figure 8 *Ceilingscape. Expressly attenuated wood stove flues are centered upon the penultimate skylight-cupola. Out-scaled geometries mesh with structural fine-tuning to provide a sense of scaler variety and vertical expression given the small-scale spaces employed.*

7

8

Figure 9 *Axial view. As seen from the entry "gasket," a long axial relationship exists between all three cells. Note the expressively cantilevered end pieces of the large-scale timber construction and the orientation of the column grid to be set off from the wall enclosure system. This is truly an out-scaled space given its true dimensions.*

the perspective to provide for overarching economies of order and material selection combined with the inspired aesthetic expression.

This house benefits from the functional distillation that a vacation house affords—each cell has but one simple use: one for sleeping, one for kitchen and dining, and the third for a living room and guest bedroom function. Despite its modest intentions, the house does have some amenities beyond those of a bare-bones cabin: two full baths, the expressive cupolas, and the extensive use of wood surfaces throughout all the ceilings of the house. There is a healthy sense of innovation as well, such as the use of inexpensive wood decking as an interior floor surface. By dissociating the essential frame construction from the sheetrock walls and combining lighting with the exposed structure, the level of contrast is heightened, and the potential for "cheap thrills" is enhanced. Additionally, large-scale, wall-to-wall use of the cheapest glazing available on the marketplace (the sliding glass door) allows their presence to become abstracted, to become the now-classic "glass wall."

Clearheaded abstraction can make the prosaic poignant. It is too easy to throw money at the problem of making a good home, and it is simply irresponsible when a home is downsized specifically to facilitate economy. It is not enough to make a home smaller unless its impact and presence are vibrantly distilled. Perspective and vision are the province of good architects, and Arne Bystrom has formed an uncompromised construction.

9

Contained Quartet

Four building blocks set within a squared plinth.

ARCHITECTS are often described as "form givers." Walter Chatham can be described as a "forms giver." This project was built over a decade ago and evidences the seminal design notion that houses can be composed of a subtext of rooms that are in and of themselves formally rendered as "houses." Chatham likes to create kitty-corner symmetries and do-si-do ensembles of space and mass, creating a sense of a miniaturized village crafted to house a family.

In this home, Chatham used a pre-existing foundation as the ordinate for his role as "forms giver"—in fact, there is a significant amount of archeology present on this site on the island of Nevis, West Indies. A pre-existing foundation is left untouched adjacent to this nineteenth-century stone plinth. As you might expect, this home's environmental outlook has more to do with eschewing the sun and heat than any other project in this book; therefore a design approach that fosters shade and direct access of sea breezes between, in, around, over, and through all parts of this minicomplex makes great good sense out of something that could be perceived to be an academic exercise intended to undo the implicitly monolithic image of a typical American home.

In this case, the act of breaking up the components of a typical home

STATS

PROJECT NAME AND LOCATION:
Adams House, Nevis Island, West Indies

ARCHITECT:
Walter F. Chatham, Architect

COMPLETION DATE:
1985

TOTAL HEATED SQUARE FEET:
1,500

PERCEIVED SQUARE FOOTAGE:
1,867

CIRCULATION-TO-TOTAL-AREA RATIO:
0 percent (all exterior)

BEDROOM-SPACE-TO-TOTAL-AREA RATIO:
22 percent

GROSS COST:
$90,000

COST PER SQUARE FOOT:
$55

DURATION OF DESIGN PROCESS:
Nine months

DURATION OF CONSTRUCTION:
Eleven months

Photos © and drawings by the architect.

into fully expressed constituent parts of living, dining, kitchen, and bedroom has only one modest overlap—the master bedroom is set above the kitchen, obtaining the best breezes and views available and providing nocturnal separation from the single-story guest bedroom building. In the context of this formal and functional separation, the unifying perimeter of preexisting stone foundation served as the point of departure for the detailing of all the materials used as well. There is an overt sense of trying to replicate traditional Caribbean detailing via twentieth-century stock materials.

Unlike other projects in this book, this particular work uses the classic Caribbean technique of steel-reinforced, small-scale concrete frame construction with concrete block infill. But rather than embrace this construction technique with an industrial aesthetic, Chatham preferred to foster a direct interplay of several building systems, all playing off of the stone skirt that defines the extent of the project's perimeter.

Concrete block is set as an exterior skin for most of the pavilions and allows a secondary system of painted-wood construction to be revealed in the clerestory/second-story aspect of the pavilions. Unabashedly interweaving with these two approaches are expressed concrete beams, columns, and lintels. Corrugated-

Figure 1 Water-facing view. Living area to the right and open dining pavilion to the left sit above the rough-hewn, preexisting plinth. The large living area uses deep-set cantilevering shutters below and clerestory louvers set in a square-within-square motif above. The fractured formal manipulations present in this house provide for the distinctive elaborations of material and shape. Note the lamination of concrete block to the right which attempts to mimic the antique stone structural system in tone and pattern, held shy of full enclosure and enhancing the sense of a construction that evolves and opens up to the water.

Figure 2 Floor plans. Set upon an existing plinth, four distinctive "houselets" semipinwheel within its rectilinear context. Major entry is achieved between the guest bedroom block and major living area (right) with dining being set as an outdoor pavilion (lower left) and kitchen, mechanical, and master bedroom spaces set to the upper left. The subordinate components of dining and guest bedroom are kept at a single height status with an elevated roof of the living area and a double-height master bedroom providing a formal ascension that provides for further animation.

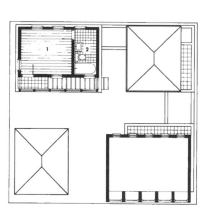

Second floor plan

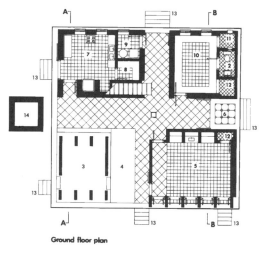

Ground floor plan

1 Master bedroom
2 Bath
3 Outdoor dining pavilion
4 Planting
5 Living room
6 Existing marble pavers
7 Kitchen
8 Pantry
9 Laundry
10 Guest bedroom
11 Outdoor shower
12 Closet
13 Existing stone steps
14 Cistern

2

3

Figure 3 Model. Perhaps the best overall view of this project given its relative formal complexity is in this artificial bird's-eye view where the subordinate elements of open dining pavilion (bottom center) and guest bedroom (top center) allow the intermediate-height living room (right) and its kitty-corner counterpart master bedroom set above the concrete block plinth of dining and mechanical spaces to provide a sense of complexity and coordination that belies this home's true size.

Figure 4 Entry. This photograph clearly shows the preexisting plinth of cut stone (at the bottom edge). The new perimeter wall construction facing landward (of concrete block), with the unabashed use of precast concrete structural elements (the lintels, top), has a sense of abstract composition evidenced by the secondary lintel that serves as the hinging point for the double entry doors seen flanking this entryway. Note the precast concrete wall cap at the top and the incorporation of the preexisting stone cistern as the focal point for this threshold (center background). Plantings and multiple eave heights lend a sense of a "microvillage."

4

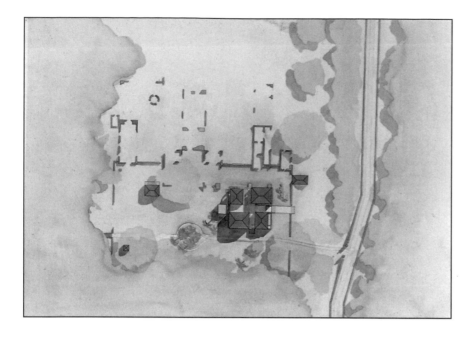

Figure 5 Site plan. Set within the remains of a large mansion, this quartet of spaces literally reinhabits a far grander outpost of civilization.

Figure 6 Living room interior. Imaginative treatments of openings allow for shading and air movement. Clerestory louvers are set to the outside and face of a pier support system while inside louvers both cantilever out as a sunscreen and open as traditional doors below to further allow for shade while facilitating airflow.

5

6

7

Figure 7 Dining pavilion. *This open-air dining pavilion acts as the symbolic structural manifestation of the water-side buildings where piers allow for an effective sunscreen and provide ample visual support for the fairly stout pyramidal roofs employed. This photograph also evidences the extraordinary appeal of a Caribbean site situation.*

steel roofing is used in lieu of costly terracotta tiles. In shape, texture, and orientation the concrete block, corrugated roofing, and simple wood siding give a first-blush appearance of traditional island construction, but on a closer look there is a crisp, clean, and decidedly intellectualized application of their detailing and construction techniques. Similarly, the colors employed are also allusive, yet expressive. Although the project is far from stark, it does have a lean quality, seasoned with the rigorous and ever-present rhythmic annunciation of structure and fenestration. A preexisting cistern locates entry steps that are set beyond the edge of the perimeter wall. This access point is respected in the organization of the project on a major axis and minor cross axis that orders the different massings employed.

With all the organizing aspects of rhythmic fenestration, choreographed roofscapes, a constricting architectural plinth, and the implicit subtext of structural organization, there is a significant dose of expressive and energized detailing employed on a variety of levels throughout the complex. Chatham sets each of the double-hipped roofs at a slightly different height and makes each plan perimeter slightly different. Various shading devices are used, both integral (in the recesses, in piers as a brise-soleil, and in the micromanagement of solar intrusion via the extensive of use of the classic louvered shutters). Dining and living spaces are given the greatest possession of the winds and views, with the elevated master bedroom uniquely orienting to the views as well.

There is always a danger implicit in creating demiarchitectural forms such as these. If human scale and structural efficacy are abandoned in favor of imagery, the final product is inherently dishonest, eschewing utility in the cause of architectural symbolism. Here the assiduous abstraction is combined with expressive materials in concert with evocative massing to create a building that overlays the sense of ensemble with the emotional roofs of "house."

In designing small houses, a rigorous respect for utility needs to be applied to the desire for expression, but without a sense of invigorated massing and detail, a small house simply becomes a warehouse for its occupants. This particular house maximizes intrigue without forgetting its true size and function. Cleverly conspired architectural distinctions allow any small house a sense of depth often expected of larger homes. Using its antique plinth as its reality check, this home, like a family, has singular identity born of diverse parts.

"Sacred Centerline"

A "shotgun shack" vacation home is invigorated.

S T A T S

PROJECT NAME AND LOCATION:
Knight Home, Front Royal, Virginia

ARCHITECT:
McInturff Architects

COMPLETION DATE:
1989

TOTAL HEATED SQUARE FEET:
1,321

PERCEIVED SQUARE FOOTAGE:
1,960

CIRCULATION-TO-TOTAL-AREA RATIO:
18 percent

BEDROOM-SPACE-TO-TOTAL-AREA RATIO:
20 percent

GROSS COST:
$125,000

COST PER SQUARE FOOT:
$95

DURATION OF DESIGN PROCESS:
Nine months

DURATION OF CONSTRUCTION:
Eight months

Photos in Figs. 1, 4, and 5 © Walter Smalling and in Figs. 6 and 7 © Julia Heine. Drawings by the architects.

all successful homes, opportunities are celebrated, and the restrictions are invisible in the final built product.

As one might expect, the two bedrooms harbored within the house shy away from the view and are sized to be mere repositories for sleeping occupants. Even more recessive are the two bathrooms that are set deep within this simple form. The kitchen, also centralized, looks out over the relatively large-scale living and dining area through a set of windows on to the seemingly infinite view beyond.

Counterpoising this run-on sentence of a building is the cross-axial relationship of the entry—an in/out space cantilevering beyond the building's perimeter into the central wet core of bath and kitchen mentioned earlier. Flanking the sacred centerline are linear axes on the perimeter of the building, affording indirect access to the trailing bedrooms and instant access to the living and dining area. In the context of a sacred ordinate, there are a host of minor variations that energize the sensibility of the house.

The first of these enlivening elaborations is the use of the site's slope to provide a progressive descent into the living and dining area—two double steps down open up the space as the living-dining area is entered and allow its cathedral ceiling height to be even more impressive. This downward movement to the living-dining

1

Figure 1 *View, side. A simple form stands proudly in a meadow, overlooking a terrific view.*

Figure 2 *Floor plan and elevations. Essentially an extruded gable form with two bays of circulation flanking its longitudinal axis: outside (below) and inside (above). A central entry/wet core with entry opposite to two bathrooms and a central kitchen are centered upon the open vaulted living area (right). Two bedrooms (left) are set away from the view, and two minor level changes segregate the private left side of the plan from the public right end. Note that the nonview bedroom end employs a false window formed by trim.*

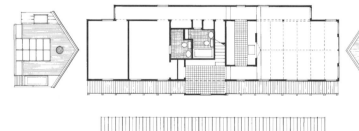

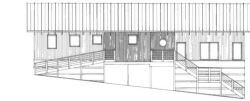

2

Figure 3 Skeleton/skin. An extraordinarily simple framing design (right) has industrial-grade cladding layered upon it (left). Formal moves are greatly emphasized by the variety of textures, colors, and material used. Note the sublimely simple foundation: two rows of footings with the flanking circulation zone simply cantilevered off their central location.

Figure 4 Longitudinal prospect. A dominant single-ridge gable form has secondary constructions layered upon it, permutational windows dancing along it, and a variety of colors and textures applied to it.

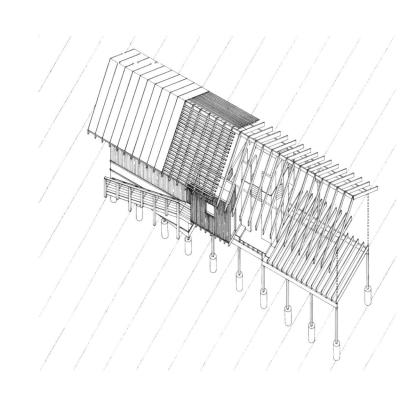

3

area is contrasted by a minor stairway going up to a loft that overlooks this large area, thus fleshing out the active up-down/in-out spatial entry interplay.

Rather than completely harken back to a the shotgun shack tradition of cheap materials from local sources, McInturff has conspired to use relatively expensive clear-finished top-grade wood trim to contrast with the dominant painted-sheetrock surfaces. McInturff has also picked his spots in other areas, combining bright colors, linear trim used as connective tissue, and painted-metal collar ties. This lively approach to materials and color is complemented by the occasional oddity—an expressive clear-finished column set below aggrandized knee braces, the aforementioned stair to the loft that becomes more ornamental millwork than rude physical accommodation, and the occasional presence of semi-high-tech elaboration on the porch and access stairs.

Additionally, absolute code and ergonomic minimums are used for the necessary evils of corridors, bathrooms, kitchen, and closets. The net space of the wall cavity that is available to the inside of closet doors is used to allow full hanging space. Corridor width is 1 inch greater than the code minimum. The dimension between counters in the kitchen is 3 feet. Occasionally, walls between closets utilize standard 2 by 4 framing set on the flat, thus creating a 2½-inch-thick wall and saving a precious 2 inches from the norm. Doors going into bathrooms are the absolute minimum: 2 feet operable width. While these minimums might become constrictive with a full-time occupancy for most people, in a vacation house they are a tolerable efficiency that experientially herds you into the relatively unrestricted living-dining area.

Structurally this house evidences the oxymoron of commonsense ingenuity. By utilizing a small basement (20 feet by 14 feet, 7 inches) to accommodate the forced air heating and cooling system, the vast majority of structural support is provided by simple wood columns bearing on concrete piers. By double cantilevering the floor off either side of this foundation, only two bearing lines defining a 14-foot central framing bay are used to support the entire mass of the house. The latent savings derived from these moves are functionally and visually invisible and easily accommodate the aforementioned level changes.

The bold strokes of axial massing and linear planning are complemented by the lyric and sometimes technologically symbolic gestures of the substructures employed. The loft has a noble prow of clear-finished wood project-

ing into the living space; the track lighting has an enthusiastic marriage with steel collar ties; skylights and roof fan housings mesh; and round seminautical windows mesh with metal siding. The corrugated-steel entry contrasts with the deep-green painted board and batten siding, indicating a functional intervention amidships (resonant with the wet-core spaces within). Additionally, a calculated use of horizontal and vertical lines of trim, siding, roofing, window, and door alignments create an intermeshing sense of conspired design that allows a very simple structure to have a richness beyond its size and budget.

The most prosaic elements imaginable—dimensional lumber stairs, exposed rafter tails, trimless windows, and semi-industrial grade siding—provide a sense of presence and power by zesty interrelationships. For example, the seaming of the roof panels aligns with the exposed rafter tails. The dimensional lumber entry stair uses stainless steel wire as its code-compliant barrier. The alignment of windows is enhanced by the use of radically different trim dimensions between top and side, and these trim choices stand in contrast to the absolutely trimless windows set within the board and batten siding. There is an unabashed exaggeration of eave overhangs as well—not only to help preempt unwanted solar gain and the wear and tear of rain but also to ennoble the roof form and give it a sense of overarching presence under which all the various material and fenestrational activities can occur. Similarly, the view-addressing windows become an out-scaled wall of glass, where non-view-addressing windows become apertures set within largely uninterrupted planes of siding.

In short, Mark McInturff left no stone unturned in trying to create an extraordinary house with a minimum budget. As an architect, his working drawings evidence extraordinary ingenuity as well, using $^{1}/_{8}$ inch=1 foot scale sections to indicate the basic structural intent set in the context of the more traditional $^{1}/_{4}$ inch=1 foot scale working drawings. Additionally, soft-line sketch perspectives were used as part of the working drawings to indicate the techniques involved as well as the intent of the design.

The forced-air heating system was thoroughly laid out and integrated into the context of the structure—not often the case in custom home design where subcontractors are left to quietly curse the architect's lack of integration. Given the high impact and spatial needs of forced-air systems, this layout can be critical to the viability of a small-house design. The resourcefulness employed in these drawings contrasts with the norms of the architectural profession, norms that often hold abstract graphic consistency over utility and clarity.

This dense-packed little house is as clear and utilitarian as the drawings that describe it. Its gleeful use of generic materials and commonsense detailing toward a decidedly unpredictable end reflects McInturff's abiding obsession for innovation regardless of budgetary limitation. Following his own sacred centerline, Mark McInturff shows remarkable architectural control over an unabashedly playful shotgun shack.

4

Figure 5 *Entry and entry axes. This is the view as seen upon entry with the direct corresponding axis alongside the building set to address the landscape. A secondary axis to the left addresses both the kitchen and the living room beyond and a tertiary axis as indicated via the steps (left) facilitates access to a top-lit loft above. Again, materials, color, and light are used to contrast and beckon.*

Figure 6 *Entry. Windows reduce in a perspectively enhancing movement as an entry walkway is neither stair nor ramp but something in between. The stoic gable face (left) does not have a window but merely the image of a window, thus ensuring the privacy of the bedroom that sits behind it.*

Figure 7 *(opposite) Living-loft-kitchen. A simple exterior shape encloses a whimsically subdivided interior form where tensile steel aspects are highlighted via color and material and an isolated stoic column is rendered in relatively clear Douglas fir (right). In an almost ceremonial sense of centering, a balcony's canted prow rests above the centerline of the kitchen sink. Contrasting colors, modest level changes, and wall plane shifts reinforce the cross-referencing regulating lines, all helping to create a construction within a construction. Note the entry access to the left and the private circulation path to the right.*

Gridded Cube

*Unapologetic materials are used in an expressive interplay
of space and structure.*

SMALL houses are often used by architects to test their intuitive inclinations or intellectual presumptions. In this particular house, the architect Richard Tremaglio designed a vacation retreat on Martha's Vineyard for a naturalist and artist couple with grown children. Like many of the houses in this book, this project has rooted Tremaglio's aesthetic explorations in the real world of affordability.

The owners had their own set of design criteria as well, centering on images of Tuscan towers and Japanese houses. Such eclectic ideas, when viewed through the eyes of a thoughtful architect, can transform a predictable home into one with a fresh perspective.

Aesthetic expression can become creative innovation when a tight budget is applied to a small house, as it did in this project which contoured to a relatively tight budget for building on Martha's Vineyard—under $90 a foot—and focused Tremaglio on cost-effective materials and techniques. The massing of the house takes on a cubic volume that is voided at one corner. A three-dimensional structural grid of columns and framing bays are allowed to be completely expressed within and without. The ultimate flavor is almost diagrammatic, with interweaving layers of intersecting planes highlighted by the lines of trim and structure.

S T A T S

PROJECT NAME AND LOCATION:
*Private Residence,
Martha's Vineyard, Massachusetts*

ARCHITECT:
Richard C. Tremaglio, Architect

COMPLETION DATE:
1987

TOTAL HEATED SQUARE FEET:
1,560

PERCEIVED SQUARE FOOTAGE:
1,870

CIRCULATION-TO-TOTAL-AREA RATIO:
14 percent

BEDROOM-SPACE-TO-TOTAL-AREA RATIO:
18 percent

GROSS COST:
$137,500

COST PER SQUARE FOOT:
$88

DURATION OF DESIGN PROCESS:
Six months

DURATION OF CONSTRUCTION:
Nine months

Photos © Herb Engelsberg.
Drawings by the architect.

Beyond the basic economy of making the house smaller and structurally simpler than many of its counterparts, the architect endeavored to use recycled blackboards of a demolished school as large-scale slate siding panels, and he attempted to use a similarly "honest" standing-seam aluminum roof. These conceptually appealing symbols of fiscal restraint did not prove out when the house was bid. However, the eschewing of standard finish surfaces—the secondary layers of sheetrock, trim, paint, floor finishes, and so on—in favor of a barebones interior did save money. In rejecting these secondary layers of surface treatment, Tremaglio has celebrated the fasteners (thousands of exposed screw heads) and the reveal (an expressed gap between materials) as seen in virtually all the joinery between major panels of construction. In this case, birch plywood was used for almost all the wall surfaces, and solid yellow pine subflooring was used as a "monomaterial" combination finish floor, subfloor, and finish ceiling surface. All the joists, rafters, and columns are similarly unashamed in their unadorned presence. Beyond clear finishing almost all the wood elements employed, the aesthetic predilection toward honest materials can be seen in the incidental use of slate (*not* from blackboards) and exposed stainless-steel fittings and fasteners.

Figure 1 *View-oriented façade. Windows are both perforations of a flat plane and the voids left in the wake of a dominant grid. Extraordinarily consistent use of inside and outside materials allows for a full-dimensional read of this home as a singular construction with wholly integral interior and exterior articulations. The consistency of the linear elements employed is complemented by the use of occasional oddball materials (the glass block, lower left, the attenuated balconies with ribbonlike steel rails, and the single canted window form, upper left).*

Figure 2 *Floor plans. A square plan is subdivided by exposed structure and functional segregation with the right side of the plan given over to wet and circulation spaces. The constant utilization of cross-referencing window and trim rhythms tie this consistently cubic volume together. Push-in/push-out elements of entry, wood stove flues, and stairs provide a secondary level of interfloor consistency. Note the extensive use of center-pivot doors for larger-than-normal openings and the use of large-scale sliding panels for area subdivision in the studio-level floor, and the use of freestanding sinks on the second floor. The Modernist graphic quality of these floor plans is derived from trimless door opening conditions and quasi-ornamental wall attenuations and dovetails with the overt graphic quality of the exterior elevations, providing an abstract sense of order amid the expressly "real" aspects of materiality of the built construction.*

1

2

Figure 3 Entry/side. Overt laying of the three floor plans is complemented by the vertical alignment of window forms and trim. The remnant clapboard wall surfaces become almost abstract in their distinction from the trim elements employed. "Honest materiality" is present in the steel handrails and bare concrete retaining wall (right). Attenuated aspects include entry overhang (right), flues (top), and modest slate appointments (set at the corners and peak of the gable roofs) as well as slight attenuations. Cutbacks of planes and lines (note the pullback of the gable roof, center right, and the slight extension of the ends of the beams at the deck extensions) animate a potentially mechanistic construction. Shadow play is enhanced by the extensive use of drip edges and a variety of trim thicknesses as well as the extension of eave planes and the unabashed utilization of unadorned rafter tails set to the vertical lines of the trim (naturally).

Figure 4 Trim, window, structure. This photograph graphically displays the intention to organize this building simultaneously in three dimensions. Beams align with mullions, and window divisions conspire to align across a variety of sill heights. Flooring (below) and floor sheathing (above) are the same material but are laid transversely to each other. Lighting fixtures conspire to misalign with most linear elements employed. Honesty of materials can lead to interesting trim abutments with one seen above the upper-right-hand window of the quartet as seen at center left.

3

4

5

Figure 5 *Living room. Materials are gleefully expressed in this photograph. The visual activity of a pine floor is set in distinction to the monolithic qualities of a slate insert to accommodate the wood stove as well as slate paneling that surrounds the kitchen. Plywood is set not only to distinguish its own inherent panelization but in the figuring of the veneers reinforces the latent qualities of each piece used. Framing is equally unaplogetic in its bypassing qualities and blindly interacts with the wood stove flues that perforate each floor. Note the unrelenting use of extended linear organization of window trim, bearing lines, and material distinctions, all received by and extending a web of dados. Furniture selection enhances this animated and playful interplay as does the use of distinctive lighting and fan equipment.*

A major cost-saving factor in this home is that it is heated by three wood stoves versus a central heating system. This is wholly appropriate for a summer residence as a nonautomated heating approach can be tolerated (even ritualistically fulfilling) when the house is seldom, if ever, used in the dead of winter.

In envisioning such a complete three-dimensional construction, there is the opportunity (gleefully grabbed by Tremaglio) to expose the kinetically bypassing systems usually covered by the very layers of materials eschewed in this home. Flues race between and around framing, lighting is semi-high-tech, fans are flecked about, and finishes tend to bump up against each other in a coordinated but innocent dance. Windows often align to floors, and range from the extraordinarily small to the unabashedly huge.

With a similarly open mind, the functional layering of the house is the inversion of what might normally be expected. Artist's studio and guest bedroom are located on the first floor, master bedroom and study on the second floor, and living, dining, and kitchen areas are on the topmost floor.

A secondary organizational feature can be seen in the consistent vertical stacking of each floor's function. One side of the entire house is given over to wet spaces (kitchen, baths, and so on) and circulation (the stair and hallways). The remaining half of the three-floor construction is left open and oriented to accept the primary view facilitated by the hillside site.

Small custom home design can benefit when a very specific geometric limitation is embraced and structure is similarly clarified and simplified. Given this home's simple cubic mass capped with a predictable gable roof, all hell can break loose in the secondary and tertiary elements of lighting, heating, windowscaping, and material selection without having the overall effect sink into chaos. A secondary benefit to the simple form/exposed subsystems approach is economy. Simple shapes formed by basic structural systems are inherently easy to build. Without having to register to any precise preconceived layout, mechanical systems and finish work are easier to execute.

A secondary note that would interest those readers of this book who practice architecture is that this relatively intricate and interwoven construction was described in barely three 2- by 3-foot drawings and utilized framing plans at a $1/8$ inch equals 1 foot scale (versus the normal $1/4$ inch equals 1 foot). It is clearly evident that there was direct dovetailing of the necessity for economy in construction with the ability to describe this project in so few drawings.

A loose construction schedule also helped contain costs. Including a few breaks, the house took nine months to build, providing verification of the old builder's saw that it is easy to build with less money if you don't have a killer deadline and can plan to maximize efficiency.

There is a simple lesson to be learned from the design of this house: Great benefits can be achieved by simply rethinking the presumptions of any house's organization. The automatic use of the first floor for living space with bedrooms above can often preempt the best view for the parts of the house that are most often used. A secondary benefit is that top-floor living spaces have use of the space afforded underneath the bonnet of a gable roof. The second lesson to be learned is that it's usually cheaper to use standard, readily available materials, and these materials can gain presence when they are unapologetically used *au natural*. Similarly, mechanical systems can gain visual impact if they are allowed to express themselves rather than being insinuated, hidden, or indirectly installed. The corollary to these simple concepts is the expressive sizing and organization of windows and trim. A very large stock window does not cost a great deal more than a normal-size stock window. Similarly, conspiring trim to align and highlight areas of a house (versus frame openings) is not inherently costly.

In this house, the standard becomes delightfully customized. A simple box becomes fresh not only by its interior organization but by the expression of the materials employed.

Figure 6 (opposite) Bathroom. *The overt honesty of the materials used can be seen in this image where bare-faced, unplugged screws carefully dot each plywood panel and distinctive bolt heads are applied to the patch of slate used as a back splash. Note the nonconcentric alignment of the light fixture to the relative centerline. Right down to the attachment of the bare-bulb keyless porcelain light fixture there are no unexpressed attachments and no unarticulated joints in this construction.*

Gridded Wedge

A high-tech, user-friendly house in the woods.

ARCHITECTS are often chastised for using symbolism to the point where a building is no longer recognizable as a building. This mind-set is particularly problematic when the building being designed is the beloved American home. The project depicted here is a house of exquisitely distilled components, one whose overall form and constituent parts evidence the sort of stripped pungency that usually conveys a sense of an architect preemptively responsive to his or her vision, ignoring client needs and cultural values. In this case, nothing could be further from the truth.

Natalie O. Miller wanted a second home in Maine. Her children had grown up and moved away, and she had a site with a spectacular view of Acadia Park on Mount Desert Island. Mrs. Miller also had enormously restrictive design criteria. Not only should her home respond to environmental, structural, and aesthetic concerns but it had to make her body as "at home" as hopefully her soul would be. Mrs. Miller suffers from a hypersensitivity to a wide variety of materials commonly found in buildings, a problem for a growing number of people.

She chose Peter Forbes as her architect, a man with a national reputation who has offices in Maine and Boston. His work often uses stark forms and expressive structural artic-

STATS

PROJECT NAME AND LOCATION:
Private Residence, Mt. Desert Island, Maine

ARCHITECT:
Peter Forbes and Associates, Inc.

COMPLETION DATE:
1993

TOTAL HEATED SQUARE FEET:
1,800

PERCEIVED SQUARE FOOTAGE:
2,590

CIRCULATION-TO-TOTAL-AREA RATIO:
6 percent

BEDROOM-SPACE-TO-TOTAL-AREA RATIO:
30 percent

GROSS COST:
NA

COST PER SQUARE FOOT:
NA

DURATION OF DESIGN PROCESS:
Five minutes

DURATION OF CONSTRUCTION:
One year

Photos © Paul Ferrino.
Drawings by the architects.

ulation to create highly dynamic and visionary buildings. In this particular case his natural predilections dovetailed perfectly with Natalie Miller's baseline concerns.

Secondarily, for all of their cost-saving and aesthetic benefits, small houses provide the sort of limited contained air mass that is easy to micromanage. This feature will become more important as more people realize that semiairtight house construction, although beneficial in mitigating heat loss and preventing ongoing maintenance problems, creates the sort of interior climate that can cause some occupants enormous discomfort, and even illness, if the materials within the home are toxic or cause an allergic reaction from the occupant.

With this essential design criterion firmly in mind, Forbes went about designing a thoroughly dynamic and expressive form, one whose constituent parts are almost diagrammatic. Central to this home's conception is a three-dimensional structural grid utilizing stock steel tubing, set to define cubic volumes of space. This steel cage has floors set upon parts of it, glass adhered to it, and roofs laid upon it. Steel is the obvious choice for a structural system in nontoxic home design as any organically based product would emit gases or sustain bacterial or fungal growth, which can render a house useless to a sensitive occupant.

Figure 1 *Exterior. A simple saltbox, sawtooth form has orthogonal projects lower right and upper center, with a gridded glazing applied to it. Note the unabashedly expressed steel framing set to float the form above the terrain.*

Figure 2 *Floor plans. A four-level construction with each level being regulated by the superimposed structural-enclosure grid. The basement (left) occupies the central slot of the three long bays, the first floor-plan fully realizes the entire grid's presence, the second-floor plan is limited to a circulation area (left) and a loft-bedroom (right), and the fourth level, a dormer, echoes the second-floor plan's layout but with a greatly diminished bedroom space. Note, however, that this bedroom has direct, centered visual connection via the roof to the fireplace beyond. In general, this is an open plan with a dense-packed service core at the entry side (lower area) of the plan. Bathrooms occupy the central slot of the second and third floors with basement stair, half-bath, and pantry being oriented to this area on the first floor. The kitchen is essentially a floating island (right side of first-floor plan) with stairs being lyrically canted and dissociated from the overall structure and enclosure systems. The firebox, at the downside central aspect of the project, reinforces the interior central organizing axis that is manifest formally in the uppermost floor of the house. This fireplace is flanked on one side by a screen porch and on the other by an entry vestibule.*

1

2

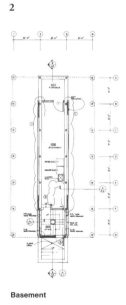

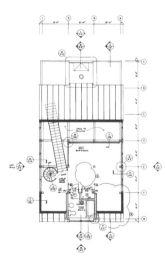

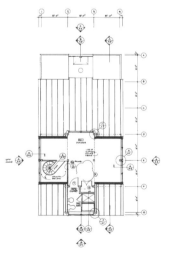

Basement

First Floor

Second Floor

Third Floor

Figure 3 *Night-time view. A grand double-height stairway takes full advantage of its dissonant angularity set in contrast to the overarching structural grid. The consistency of interior materials and semiabstracted glazing pattern underscores the dynamic interplay of material, form, shape, and line of this building.*

3

Forbes then gave this dominant grid some lightly competitive elements. One cubic bay accommodates a semi-symbolic stone and concrete fireplace, wood storage, and the heat plant flue, and, interestingly enough, it functions as a large-scale scupper-downspout addressing the dominant roof plane. Other subordinate elements within the context of this cage are artfully cast about, distinguished by their disorientation with the structural grid and by the use of colors contrasting the white superstructure. Wood elements are used throughout the project for a large array of built-ins, flooring, and ceiling material, all of which are finished in a nontoxic water-based clear finish. A canted and rakish stair leads up a full two stories to the upper-level bedrooms, and has its spiral complement (also rendered in steel) going from the stair landing to the loftiest bedroom perch. A tiny elevator is set to be blissfully ignorant of the overarching structural grid and is painted a bright red in contrast to the wood-tone floors and the white-painted steel structure. Other subordinate elements in-fill the grid and respect its patterning. Quarter-sawn oak cabinetry is detailed to be visually inert, lightly contrasting the wide-board maple floors. The ceiling lightly touches the structural cage and uses expressively figured, clear-finished cedar. Opaque gray-stained tongue-and-groove siding is used to create in-filled walls at the backside of the house.

Beyond these lyric and subordinate contrasting elements, Forbes has manipulated this superstructural grid to facilitate interior circulation, voiding one corner of the first floor of this grid to accommodate the two-story stair run, and the cage stagger-steps up to allow an unbroken rakish roof pitch. The three-dimensional grid asserts itself vertically by perforating the rakish roof pitch to form the uppermost bedroom and laterally extrudes to accommodate the fireplace and flanking areas of vestibule and backside entry portal.

Out-scaled structural designs such as this can have enormous power in the context of a small home. In this particular case the grid has an 8-foot on-center module in all directions meshing with the 16-inch module used in stan-

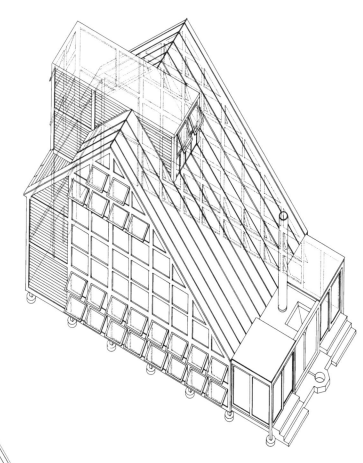

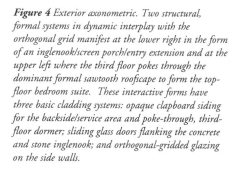

Figure 4 *Exterior axonometric. Two structural, formal systems in dynamic interplay with the orthogonal grid manifest at the lower right in the form of an inglenook/screen porch/entry extension and at the upper left where the third floor pokes through the dominant formal sawtooth roofscape to form the top-floor bedroom suite. These interactive forms have three basic cladding systems: opaque clapboard siding for the backside/service area and poke-through, third-floor dormer; sliding glass doors flanking the concrete and stone inglenook; and orthogonal-gridded glazing on the side walls.*

4

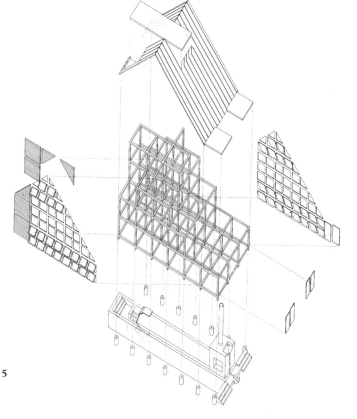

5

Figure 5 *Structure/skin. A central three-dimensional orthogonal grid serves as the armature for a series of skin treatments all set upon a semidiagrammatic concrete plinth that expresses itself as a firebox on the first floor. Standing seam metal roof covers the majority of the interior with flat membrane roofing for the inglenook and dormer projections. Note operable glazing occurs at the top and bottom of the saltbox profile, providing maximally efficient airflow (and responding to those areas of the glazing that are ergonomically available for easy operation).*

6

Figure 6 Stair. *Set amid the thoroughly conspired orthogonal grid, window screen, flooring pattern, and background surface, this lone "odd-ball" element is playfully mechanistic right down to its point of attachment to the floor: two small-scale wheels. Wire supports weight-saving round punch-outs, and the antiskid tread surface treatment invokes an image of out-scaled gangplank dynamically positioned to enhance the distilled quality of the structure. Note that a single horizontal member of the orthogonal grid has been simply voided to accommodate the uninterrupted path of this two-story stair. Note also that bare-bulb light fixtures and wire hangers follow the cant of the stair rather than the overarching order of the structural system. Set beyond all this activity is the almost symbolic spiraling of the upper-level staircase. Almost an iconic reference, this is the final beckoning gesture to the promised land of the lone, unseen space from the large-scale living room. Note in the background that there are several grilles that facilitate the movement of treated air within this semisealed airspace. Note also the coy placement of the one-person elevator to the left rear. The hyperorganic chair is the solitary focal point of this flanking bay.*

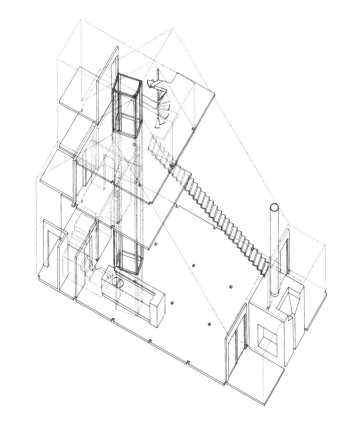

Figure 7 *Interior diagram. Vertical linkages of elevator and stair provide vertical consistency amid the rakish spaces defined by the sawtooth roof form. Upper floors are defined by the three-dimensional grid system with the intermediate floor formed as a loft and the top floor having a sense of spatial isolation as a projecting dormer set above the angled roof. Set in contrast to this spatial openness is the stoic and solid fireplace.*

7

dard light frame construction, but this spacing is far tighter than necessary in solely structural terms. Items that register to its dimensions include a cranking stair going down to the basement, bathrooms, and the fireplace-wood storage-roof scupper block.

This is a home of formal and structural dialogue where the three-dimensional poetry of the cubic module serves as the unabashedly dominant influence on all elements save the roof. Its 12-in-12 pitch is in concert with the diagonals of an equilaterally orthogonal cage, but its form limits the superstructural ascent and spread except for the vertical and horizontal projections mentioned earlier. The large-scale glazing is subdivided into 4- by 4-foot modules organized by the grid.

The building is visually floated over the landscape, hovering via the extension of the grid's vertical lines 2 feet over two-thirds of the terrain. An unseen central slot of full-height basement space is set to align with the central bay of columns. This space harbors all mechanical equipment including laundry, furnace room, and stairway access.

The "stripped" program of a second home is well accommodated by such architectural abstraction. The means and methods are in full agreement with the homeowner's central desires. Beyond the aesthetic imagery, this home is enveloped by and focuses upon the natural world. The home's tight footprint and vertical massing minimally impose on the woods. The extraordinary sweep and scale of its main space and glazed walls provide a sense of complete envelopment within the trees.

It should be noted that every aspect of this home's construction is custom crafted, often utilizing steel. Given this level of design and craftsmanship and the conscientious rejection of standard building materials, this is not an inexpensive form. Fortunately, the level of drama and dynamism of the built product has an impact that corresponds to a higher-than-normal price tag.

Aesthetic vision does not preclude utility. The conflicting aspects of aesthetics and functional viability are easier to resolve if the home is small. Rather than limiting the opportunity for success, the scale of a small house can provide the conceptual datum that leverages the sort of creativity that Peter Forbes masterfully evidences in this expressive construction.

Figure 8 *Living-dining room interior. A virtual forest of steel structure has a natural-wood sky and floor. Note that the flooring pattern reinforces the orthogonal grid and that the simple built-ins set about the space are organized by the lines of the superstructure and out-scaled glazing patterns. Also note in the background the large-scale firebox whose semisymbolic stone lintel is held by an overtly artificial set of concrete piers.*

Figure 9 *(opposite) Lofted bedrooms. A second-floor bedroom level utilizes built-ins as a visual barrier to the living areas below, while a spiral stair–accessed lofted bedroom creates the lone intimately scaled space within the entire project. Note the materially expressed elements of ceiling, stair, floor, elevator, railing, structural grid, lighting, and so on. The relative flexibility of the steel structure can be seen in the incidental wire attachments used to support the two-story gangplank (stair) as well as the simple angled perforation of the floor planes of the self-supporting steel-caged elevator.*

8

A Simple Triumph

A tough site is conquered by a straightforward house.

I F you want to build a new home within the context of suburban America, there are fewer and fewer simple options left. During the housing feeding frenzies of the 1920s, 1950s through 1960s, and 1980s, the vast majority of "easy" sites were gobbled up. Left in the aftermath of these orgies of building are the problematic sites that were previously deemed much too difficult to deal with. Such a site confronted Paul Zeisler and Elizabeth Devermond. They had found a steeply sloped site at the intersection of three curvilinear suburban streets. The site had an odd semitriangular shape further complicated by town regulations involving typical setbacks and a limitation that buildings could not be built on grades greater than 25 percent. Consequently, there was precious little buildable area left on their wooded suburban lot. Enter Nagle, Hartray, architects from Chicago. They realized that not only was the building site limited but the budget was tight for this area as well (just over $100 a square foot). These pressures helped spawn a 2,000-square-foot, three-bedroom home of considerable innovation and presence.

This home conquers a very tough site with a minimum of means and, as such, evidences the greatest gift architects can give their clients: an overarching perspective that allows a clear vision of their house amid a sea of uncertainty and limitation.

Economy dovetailed with necessity as the tightly restricted buildable lot area facilitated a simple extended rectangular plan perimeter of 21 by 78 feet. This simple shape allows for a clear span between the long foundation walls via the use of prefabricated 2 by 4 trusses for both floor and roof construction. Since the economical span is in the short direction, the home is capped by an attenuated gable roof with rafters set upon the ascending walls.

The use of engineered wood products is a trend that will become more and more evident as the material used for simple framing lumber becomes more and more expensive. In this particular case, the cost-effectiveness of these engineered products had even greater utility given the fact that the clear net span of over 19 feet could not be easily accommodated by anything other than a product that was as much manmade as naturally derived. The open web of this prefab truss allows for great mechanical flexibility as it accommodates the interweaving of systems across the direction of joists and rafters. There was one structural consequence to the relative thinness and height of this building form. Plywood-sheathed sheer walls were needed to stiffen the overall structure. These were easily inserted given the internal wall locations.

STATS

PROJECT NAME AND LOCATION:
Zeisler/Deyermond Cottage, Michiana, Michigan

ARCHITECT:
Nagle, Hartray & Associates, Ltd.

COMPLETION DATE:
1991

TOTAL HEATED SQUARE FEET:
2,000

PERCEIVED SQUARE FOOTAGE:
3,243

CIRCULATION-TO-TOTAL-AREA RATIO:
7 percent

BEDROOM-SPACE-TO-TOTAL-AREA RATIO:
34 percent

GROSS COST:
$235,000

COST PER SQUARE FOOT:
$118

DURATION OF DESIGN PROCESS:
Eight months

DURATION OF CONSTRUCTION:
Eleven months

Photos © Hedrich Blessing.
Drawings by the architects.

1

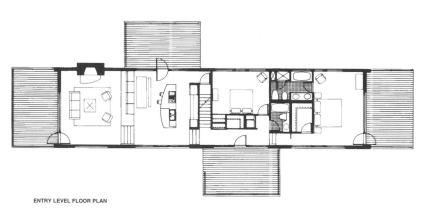

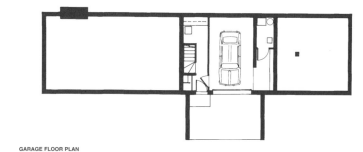

SECOND FLOOR PLAN

ENTRY LEVEL FLOOR PLAN

2   **GARAGE FLOOR PLAN**

Figure 1 Exterior. Screened by dense overgrowth and obscured by the ragged terrain, this simple plan perimeter becomes an ascending form when seen from below. The dynamic quality of the steel-stayed, cantilevered decks launching out into space is highlighted by contrasting color from the monolithic house form. Similarly, an outside stucco flue shroud (upper left) counterpoints the rakish form.

Figure 2 Floor plans. The entry-level plan graphically displays the simple duality of a central bar building with pirouetting decks, one set to each side of the bar. Center right is the point of access for both the building itself and the upper floor loft area, with wet cores and dense-pack storage (right) separating the two bedrooms from each other and from the entry hall. The kitchen space dominates one deck-defined area's space and the common living area staking out one end of the house (left). Its complement, the master bedroom, is set to the far right. The house cascades from uppermost master bedroom to the right to lowermost living room to the left. It should be noted that even in such a small house a full walk-in closet and fully operational master bath are provided. On the second-floor plan, a loft area complete with built-in desk is fully open to the floor level below (to the left). Storage area is provided to the right of this plan as is a full bath for the occasional guest who uses the fold-out sofa. Note that the windows on this level are set to align with the roof ridge line of the building form. On the garage floor plan, the terrain provided for a single slot of garage space, but the deck above this space provides shelter for a second car. Given the terrain and cost limits, a full foundation barely occupies one-third of the overall building footprint and provides simple storage space, a mechanical area, and access to the upper floor.

The home's interior has four levels entered at a relative midpoint. The master bedroom is set on the upside of the entry and the kitchen-dining space at an intermediate level cascading down into the living area. All of these individual "trays" of space are accessed via single-loaded circulation that serves to form a house-long axial coordination of all spaces, both functionally and experientially. Set opposite the entry level is a guest bedroom and above that another guest den/sleeping space ascends into the space available as the roofline climbs to its apex. Each one of the sleeping spaces (including the den) has a full bath directly adjacent to it, and there is relatively commodious closet storage throughout as well as a large quantity of built-in storage to mitigate the need for furniture that would clutter the bold sweep of space facilitated by the home's simple shape (and to compensate for a lack of a full basement).

Four cantilevered decks pirouette from the four sides of this "slab"; two are directly extended from the downside ends of the roof and are literally suspended by steel stays to the main mass of the house. The remaining two flanking deck forms project out from the long walls of the house with the front-facing deck centered upon entry. The other transverse deck extends the kitchen-dining space out into the landscape. Each deck is set to its relative floor level, and they all provide a viable sense of connection with the surrounding wild and wooly terrain.

Suburban decks are often treated as rude manifestations of a rough carpenter's wood butchery. In this particular home, the expressive steel suspension and complementary semi-industrial railings create constructivist art springing forth in lively contrast to the relatively stoic house form. All four decks share a common vernacular of detail, material, and color and serve as light inflections upon the relatively unrelenting formal progression (either ascendent to roof peak or descendent down the slope of the hill itself).

As noted, costs were mitigated by limiting the full-height basement space to only a small portion of the building's overall footprint. In most suburban homes the garage is the first large-scale focal point seen upon entry. This sloping site forced a garage location upon the design, and it is both celebrated and transformed by some clever orientations and façade treatments. To provide vehicular access, the surrounding terrain had to be greatly manipulated, and this is an obvious focal point of attention, but rather than attempt to obscure the unavoidable, Nagle, Hartray and Associates celebrated its location by using it as the baseline culmination of a vertical façade axis centered on the penultimate apex of the gable roof form. An array of architectural elements from tripartite window to suspended trellis to dramatically extended deck rail to the deck itself, on down to retaining walls and garage door, form an ensemble that is anything but a predictable suburban icon.

The interior of the home has a unified spatial sensibility resulting from its out-scaled form. All walls are painted white, millwork is relatively simple (site built to facilitate affordability), and space is thoroughly celebrated with wood tongue-and-groove ceiling material complementing the use of wood flooring throughout the first floor. A large, lightly curvilinear central cooking island is the focal point for three-quarters of all the spaces in the home, reflecting the evolution of the American kitchen into the dominant altar of sociability. While set at different levels, these spaces bask in the common denominator of a transcendent spatial flow facilitated by a large-scale simple building form.

Despite the crisp coordination of the built product, its original conception was greatly altered to contour to the budget. The owners originally perceived this to be a true high-tech log house, utilizing rustic horizontal lines in direct contrast to the unrelenting tree trunks set about it. Additionally, they had hoped for a wood-shingled roof to follow through on the aesthetics of simply hewn natural materials. Unfortunately, the building budget dictated that the horizontal lines of logs give way to the simpler and more affordable lines of horizontal clapboards and red cedar shingles give way to asphalt. In a final derustication, a hoped-for masonry fireplace was supplanted by a prefab metal fireplace, in this case cleverly encased in a consistently tapering interior-exterior monolithic stuccoed form. When combined with the use of site-built millwork, instead of millwork custom-fabricated in an off-site shop, the house became affordable and maintained the vast majority of its inherent appeal.

It is tempting to view small houses as being cute manifestations of an architect's whimsy, reflecting the nonthreatening idiosyncracy of optimistic occupants. But in this case a small house solved a multitude of problems that are common to all those seeking to build their own home, whether big or small, and ultimately evidences the tangible benefits of designing to a tighter-than-normal standard.

Figure 3 *Site. The irregular peninsula shape of this site is flecked with a dense canopy of trees (providing a visual separation to the three streets that encounter it) and has extraordinarily steep slopes—most of which so steep as to prevent the building's occupying of many parts of the site area. Note that a central access point is used for cars as well as pedestrian access, and this "slot" that is cut into the hillside is centered by (or locates) the penultimate ridge line of the overarching roof form.*

Figure 4 *Section. A simple gable form covers several levels—entry, kitchen-dining, living area, bedroom space, and one celestial loft area—while the overarching roof form spawns a lightly canted attenuation (left) centered upon the fireplace and covering the living area of the house. Note the strategically located band of skylights set at the interface between the loft and the open area below. Note also the sawtooth ceiling form of the master bedroom (far right) as well as the modest utilization of a full basement area (center). In addition, note the utilization of steel ties to tether the cantilevered deck forms off the main mass of the house (right and left) and the hidden large-scale gutters that are set to preempt the cascade of water from falling upon the decks' unprotected planes.*

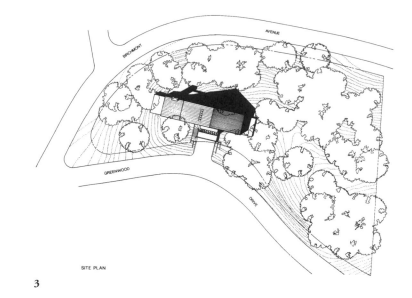

SITE PLAN

3

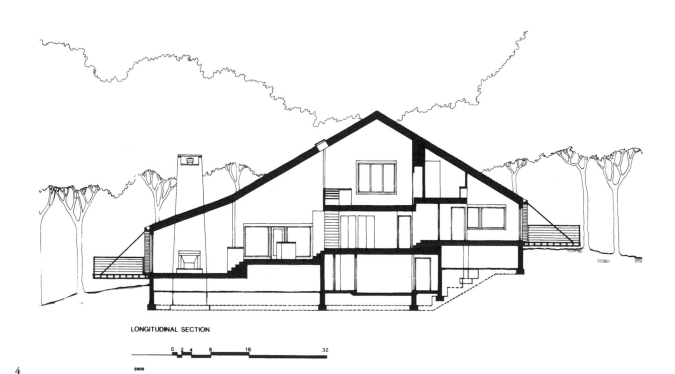

LONGITUDINAL SECTION

0 2 4   8   16   32

8909

4

Figure 5 Entry. The rugged terrain is manipulated at the point where cars and people must gain access to the building. Normally a suburban embarrassment, the garage location in this particular case reinforces the celebrational peak of the overarching roof form with steel rod–stayed trellis being set above a deck-terrace, which in turns serves as a demicarport, allowing a second automobile to be covered (almost a necessity given that there is only room for one car to be set within the minimized basement space). With the conspired coordination of peak, window, trellis, deck, and garage, the presence of a front door is unmistakably keyed to those entering the site.

Figure 6 (opposite) Interior. An ascending ceiling form of bleached wood provides a dynamic linearly reinforced spatial progression to a celestial loft that is top lit by an array of skylights. Level changes provide for an animated sense of spatial interplay as well. Note the use of field-built simple oak-veneered cabinetry that separates the dining area from the living room space and the use of the deer antler chandelier as the lone remnant of the client's original desire for a log house, set in the sea of sheetrock and steel railings that is their home's final manifestation.

5

Finish with a Bang

Formal fine-tuning culminated by structural exuberance.

small house cannot be all things to all occupants. The inherent constriction of maintaining a tighter-than-average volume of space dictates that a measure of versatility be replaced by a dose of custom tailoring. Similarly, the reduced size implicit in a small-house form limits the capacity for elaborate massing manipulations. When small houses overreach themselves in an attempt to miniaturize the eccentricities of their larger counterparts, they become caricatures rather than buildings that convey their true size. To maintain formal integrity, a small house must "pick its spots" and limit its major articulations to those that play off a clearly dominant shape or organizing feature.

These observations are elegantly accommodated by Bohlin Cywinski Jackson in a 2,400-square-foot, three-bedroom house set in the Pennsylvania woodlands. The home is sited to appreciate the intersection between a fern-filled deciduous forest and secluded lowland woods that are filled with meandering streams. In addressing a sloping site, the architects opted for a semiconfrontational orientation where the long axis of the house rests perpendicular to the slope of the hillside. Although this orientation had cost implications due to a relatively complicated foundation that steps down the hill (versus paral-

S T A T S

PROJECT NAME AND LOCATION:
*Barth House,
Bear Creek, Pennsylvania*

ARCHITECT:
Bohlin Cywinski Jackson

COMPLETION DATE:
1987

TOTAL HEATED SQUARE FEET:
2,400

PERCEIVED SQUARE FOOTAGE:
3,610

CIRCULATION-TO-TOTAL-AREA RATIO:
9 percent

BEDROOM-SPACE-TO-TOTAL-AREA RATIO:
15 percent

GROSS COST:
$315,000

COST PER SQUARE FOOT:
$131

DURATION OF DESIGN PROCESS:
One year

DURATION OF CONSTRUCTION:
One year

Photos in Figs. 3 and 7 © Wayne Fuji
and in Figs. 4 and 6 © Scott Dorrance.
Drawings by the architects.

lel to its line), the resulting house form presented a marvelous opportunity to foster a sense of experiential evolution. The diminutive massing encountered at first blush becomes an elongated form set in contrast to the hillside as those approaching draw near. There is a single dominant roof form with an unbroken ridge traversing the length of the home, and as the hillside descends below it, the massing of the home seems to proudly launch itself out of the hillside.

It is at this final culmination of massing that the formal elaborations take hold, allowing for the extension of the roof ridge to create a clerestory dormer as the roof double-hips itself around its end where it simultaneously extends its eave line, seemingly pushing the building's perimeter out from walls that had consistently aligned. Additionally, the roof line at the entrance is bent to form an eyebrow, allowing a singular focal curvilinear manipulation of the dominant roof form to focus the attention of those descending the hill to obtain entry.

There is an interesting connection between the home's formal evolution and its proposed functional planning. Although the owners, Bruce Barth and Joanna Douglas, had grown children and this was a home meant to reflect a new empty-nester life-style, there is a further functional evolution planned into its floor plan. It is not

1

2

3

Figure 1 *First-floor entry plan. The first-floor entry reveals two large volumes of space at the end points of an elongated plan. The garage (top) is sized to accommodate the future use as a shipping-receiving area for an in-home business. The entry is set as a platform within the context of a double-height living room (bottom). Between these two out-scaled spaces are a series of rooms, oriented and subdivided for future use in an in-home business. To the left will be offices that presently function as a den, and to the right is a guest bedroom and bath that can also be used as ancillary office space. Note the curvilinear aspects of the inserted entryway and stair and the diagonals springing forth from its ebullient form that are located by the corners of the living area. Whereas the garage is an opaque utilitarian form and the intermediate connective tissue of subdivided rooms has windows set as perforations, the wall of the living room has a screen of glazing set to allow for the full appreciation of views. Note that the connective subdivided rooms create subordinate axial relationships that provide background order for the spatial energy of the living room and that the centerline of the garage and launching pad for the celebrational structure stair is ceremonially recognized by the linking corridor and ultimately received by the pattern of the glazing in the living room (bottom).*

Figure 2 *Ground-floor plan. The public spaces and the master bedroom suite control this lower area of the plan. The master bedroom suite (upper left) is set to appreciate the lateral hillside views and is held distinct from the living room by the hot tub/sitting room that is a semienclosed space which acts as a buffer and has the hot tub itself covered by slip-in floor panels. Set to the upper-right-hand corner is storage space, a laundry, and a half-bath with a J-shaped kitchen cabinet array nestled underneath the lofty point of entry. Note the axial orientation of the walk-out deck at the bottom of the plan, which is directly linked to the balcony above, which is in turn centered upon the axis point to the master bedroom. The skewed stair and kitchen peninsula serve as intermediate massing elements in the context of the out-scaled space with the secondary axis of this large-scale space being defined as the orientation of the centered doors to the paved terrace (left) orienting to the main prep space of the kitchen (right).*

Figure 3 *Entry aspect. This skewed vantage is seen upon the encounter with the home with the "tail end" of the house not visible in this photograph. The bowed roof, custom door, abstracted entry seat, and skylight serve to collect visual interest in the context of the unrelenting, attenuated, roof peak line, and the simple siding employed.*

surprising that living areas are set to enjoy the view of the interweaving foliage types mentioned earlier, forming the "head" of the attenuated massing. At the "tail" of the home is a large garage set at a level above the view addressing the living floor. The garage end of the house addresses a large motor court—the internal rear entrance off this garage reveals a central corridor flanked by a suite of interconnected rooms on one side and a bathroom and bedroom suite on the other. These spaces were designed with soundproofing and utilities to facilitate the future accommodation of offices for the owners' package design business. Additionally, it is envisioned that children and grandchildren might also be occupying these spaces at some point, so the second floor effectively "stakes out turf" for a variety of uses. These simple spaces are experientially bypassed by the central corridor, which acts as an axial "launching pad" leading up to the ultimate encounter with the expressive Great Room. Set below the relatively prosaic spaces on the upper level is the master bedroom suite, which also opens onto the Great Room. The home's formal entry is also set to address the Great Room, serving to focus almost all activity on the final act of a dramatic little house.

It is a simplistic truth that small homes benefit from big spaces. Tight planning can mitigate the impact of the serving spaces (kitchen, baths, closets, and utility areas) while allowing the served areas (living, bedroom, dining area) the luxury of an open spatial sensibility often involving double-height spaces or at the very least cathedral ceilings. In this particular case, all of those axioms hold true, but this particular project evidences the sort of the structural and spatial pyrotechnics that allow a large space to be a delightful one.

After several design iterations, Bohlin Cywinski Jackson conspired to provide a significant measure of drama for this final event of the home's progressive massing by the imposition of an explicit structural sculpture in the form of large-scale truss-column-hip rafter braces oriented to the upstairs axial entry and front door. This constructivist ensemble implicitly and explicitly subdivides kitchen, dining, and living spaces below. By integrating stair, custom cabinetry, and ceiling-scape, the entire ambience is one of unexpected and explosive architectural expressionism. The scale of the space is reflected in the use of a large glazed wall looking out at the untainted natural world. The detailing of the ornamental and structural elements, as well as the lighting and secondary openings, suggests a building's exterior rather than an enclosed, finished space. All of these moves contribute to the sense of surprise and delight that overcomes any possible sense that this is a "limited" or simply small home.

Although the rest of the house does its job of paying the functional dues for this exciting space, there is no abiding sense of compromise in the orientation or detailing. Below the office-guest bedroom upper level, the master bedroom suite has an unrestricted view out the side of the house while centering its long axis to the Great Room. Set as a gasket between the Great Room and the sleeping space of the master suite is a large-scale hot tub room— a room that is anything but limited in function as the architects had the good sense to allow it to be turned into a fully functional sitting room. The tub is set below the level of the surrounding floor plane, and more often than not, floor panel inserts are set in place over it. Large pocket doors allow for discrete separation between this room and the sleeping space. Large-scale cabinetry is used to dense-pack storage to compensate for the fact that this home does not have a true basement.

Because of these functional accommodations, this home has the capacity to be a study in axial and cross-axial relationships. A semisculptural balcony serves as a final recognition of the central unifying ordinate. It is a relatively pristine perch into the natural world with its railing broken to respect the ultimate power of this dominant axis. Cross-axially, the long direction of the family room is organized by the relationship between the kitchen's main cooking area and an outdoor terrace that presents the only "civilized" outdoor area present in a relatively pristine site. Additionally, the aforementioned formal entry is set as a secondary cross axis on the upper level, utilizing skylight orientations and the space provided between the aggrandized column-truss structure and the backside wall of the main wing of the home. Additionally, the two bays of bedroom-offices upstairs have their openings cross-axially centered on these same skylights and one opening is in turn the centering influence for the opening to the hot tub room mentioned earlier.

This home is also a study in the way architects can compress and release building mass, interior space, façade openings, and circulation to obviate the sense of compromise in small-house design. In evidencing a mastery of architectural control, Bohlin Cywinski Jackson proves that designing homes that are smaller than average does not limit creative opportunity. It is harder to do better with less, but a reduced scale also can help create more pungent and exhilarating buildings when in the hands of capable architects.

4

Figure 4 Master bedroom axis. As seen across the hot tub room (with the tub fully covered in flooring panels), this coordinating axial vista links sleeping area with the marshland (to the right are windows that address the more heavily forested hillside). The rakish presence of the steel stairs serves as a beckoning promissory note of the outsize structural theatrics in the living room. Note the variety of light levels present. These are crisply defined by the simple pocket door openings.

Figure 5 *Site. Given the heavily treed and contoured aspects of this site, the formal massing of the home is best seen abstractly in this site plan. A tendril-like driveway splays to accommodate day-to-day traffic and has the splayed parking spaces addressed by meandering walkways that descend the hillside to the home's entry. To the right of this coincidence is an outsized parking lot set to the home's garage; this area might be given over to a future office use.*

The central spine of roof peak is extended to form a small dormer that in turn indicates the center of the interior axis and the structurally expressive interior of the living room. Note that the roofscape telescopes out as the starting point centered garage expands to accommodate potential office space and then ultimately living area, and that these lateral extensions project the house form down corresponding to the hillside upon which it reposes. The home is set at the juncture between heavily treed highlands and lower-level wetlands—a lightly forested marshland subdivided by a meandering creeks.

Figure 6 *Entrance. Simple stone steps ascend to a centered doorway beckoning to a skylight-lit entry platform with the promise of some zesty architectural events teasingly evident from this prospect. The brightly colored, custom-built, abstracted, and playfully formed entry seat (left) serves as a promise that something interesting just might happen.*

6

5

Figure 7 *(opposite) Living room interior. Two column-buttresses crease a zesty angular event within the context of a double-hipped roof. A skylight set over the entry and the axially oriented clerestory dormer serve to top- and back-light this interior construction, the elements of which transform from millwork below to outsized buttress, shaft, custom steel connector, and stock framing lumber struts explicitly set to buttress the underside of the diagonal folds of the ceiling. A rakish steel stair is set in distinction to the wood and painted elements and serves to fully flesh out this interior architectural sculpture. Note the similarly canted and rakish kitchen cabinets set behind the stair and the dining table set between. The lightly curvilinear aspect of the entry porch and its lower, supportive cabinetry in coordination with the lightly bowed light fixture create an extraordinary visual treat amid the context of simple sheetrock and flat stock trim.*

Highest and Best Use page 118

Power and Poignancy on a Budget *page 126*

The First House *page 164*

Temple to a Great View *page 144*

Temple to a Great View *page 144*

"Sacred Centerline" page 72

"Sacred Centerline" page 72

Artfully Done page 38

Tree House page 24

"The Vertical Dimension" *page 178*

"Make No Small Plans" page 132

Gridded Wedge page 84

Modest Intentions, Vigorously Expressed page 218

Setting Sail page 152

Multiple Personalities with a Single Focus *page 226*

A Sweet Sunlit Box *page 112*

Three-Bedroom Houses

Grounded Aspiration

A vertical imperative and aesthetics rooted in tradition.

YOUNG architects who design houses for themselves have unique obstacles to overcome. The first of those is inexperience. The lack of a professional track record can create gaps between desire and do-ability. The second hardship is not limited to architects—the chances are the younger you are, the less your financial resources. So, when architect Dennis Wedlick and Curtis DeVito decided to build a second home in the country to escape the confines of New York City, it was only youthful enthusiasm that left them undaunted at the prospect of showcasing Wedlick's talents and at the same time designing something that could get built.

There is, however, an inherent advantage to being young. The young often do that which they "shouldn't." Conventional wisdom kept most people away from the lot that Wedlick and DeVito decided to purchase, a parcel with apparently no focal point or view to be worshipped. However, there was in the eye of the architect the ability to create the *illusion* of something special. If the house could act as its own focal point and the contours of the earth could be changed to create surprise once the house was entered, then the simple act of construction could reinvent the essential character of the site that was to be built upon.

S T A T S

PROJECT NAME AND LOCATION:
*DeVito-Wedlick House,
Kinderhook, New York*

ARCHITECT:
Dennis Wedlick

COMPLETION DATE:
1988

TOTAL HEATED SQUARE FEET:
1,000

PERCEIVED SQUARE FOOTAGE:
1,211.5

CIRCULATION-TO-TOTAL-AREA RATIO:
14 percent

BEDROOM-SPACE-TO-TOTAL-AREA RATIO:
42 percent

GROSS COST:
$135,000

COST PER SQUARE FOOT:
$135

DURATION OF DESIGN PROCESS:
Six months

DURATION OF CONSTRUCTION:
Nine months

Photos in Figs. 1, 5, 6, and 7 © Dennis Wedlick
and in Fig. 4 © Michael Fredericks.
Drawings by the architect.

The central and simple vehicle for this reinvention was the use of an extraordinarily attenuated massing. It is as though a standard farmhouse with a stout 12-in-12 pitch had been plasticized and stretched to a point where its roof became giddily and irreverently aspirational. Rather than a 12-in-12 pitch (a 45-degree angle relative to the ground plane), this house-'s roof has almost a 24-in-12 pitch—virtually a 60-degree angle to the ground. This one simple geometric move is reinforced by virtually all the other moves present in the house's design, both inside and out. The net effect of such an exaggerated roof form would be lost if this roofscape rested upon a multistory box, but Wedlick wisely kept the entry wall of his house only one story high and in fact, further focused attention on this extraordinary roof form by placing a recessive porch below its eave.

An exaggerated shape such as this can get old fast without a complementary aesthetic subtext, and Wedlick enhances his vertical imperative by the use of carefully crafted and intricately scaled elements that set upon, respond to, or perforate this dominant roof form. The first of these seen upon entering the site is the demidormer set directly above the entry door. More dramatically, Wedlick creates a tower form on the backside of the house capped by the

Figure 1 *Entry, northwest prospect. A tiny footprint gains grandeur via a hyperbolically attenuated roof form. Visual interest is sustained by the multiple layers of trim and consistently interweaving motifs of shape and material. The dormer centered over the entry (right) is the offspring of the larger gable at the end of the house (left). Corner windows (lower left) use out-scaled trim to become an acknowledged large-scale component of the façade, and a prow bay has its spikiness set within the context of one of the bays defined by the porch columns. Note that the porch in this case is little more than a symbolic form as it has a greatly reduced width (approximately 4 feet). Note the careful eschewing of corner board trim on the first floor set in contrast to the horizontal banding that wraps the major eave and sets off the various elements of the gable form, a shape that has its latent graphic identities enhanced by the use of a secondary surface treatment of staggered wood shingles. The north-facing window array seen on the second floor uses off-the-rack columns to create a semi symbolic entablature.*

Figure 2 *First- and second-floor plans. The house is organized by three bays: two major and one minor central bay that is utilized for circulation. On the first floor the southerly flanking bay is used for wet spaces and the chimney flue, while the north-side bay utilizes corner glazing to define a living area and a prow bay to define the dining area. Note that there is but one bath in these floor plans and it is not on the bedroom level—a conscious choice to provide maximum sleeping space for a weekend home. The porch columns announce this organization to the outside, and this central slot of circulation is received by the spiral stair that leads to the through floor corridor on the upper level. Not shown is a full basement with bath that is accessed by a trapdoor in the living room and a loft space accessed via a stock library ladder from the second-floor hallway. Note the cross axis on the second floor set between bedrooms and the double doors (French and pocket).*

2   1

a. Entry Porch
b. Dining Area
c. Living Area
d. Kitchen
e. Bath

First Floor Plan

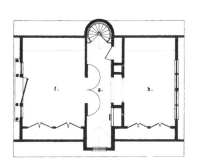

f. Bedroom
g. Hall
h. Bedroom (loft above)

Second Floor Plan

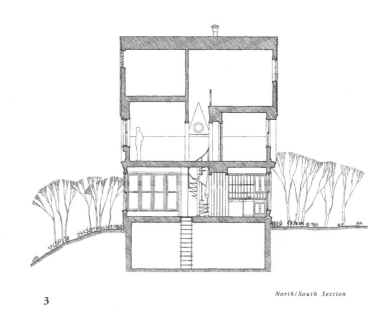

Figure 3 *Section. A full basement accessed via a trapdoor compensates for some of the possible storage problems; and given the fact that the basement is a full walk-out amidships (not shown in the section), the house effectively has four levels of occupancy. This section faces into the kitchen (first floor right) and living room (first floor left) and shows the varying ceilings of the second floor with a ceiling set higher (left). On the opposite side of the central corridor (right) a more compact bedroom utilizes its reduced ceiling height to accommodate an open sleeping loft set above it (upper right). Localized reductions in ceiling height can be seen between the corridor and the smaller bedroom and between the living room and kitchen that help create thresholds and provide spatial variety within the context of a very small home.*

3

North/South Section

same gable roof form that he used on the front dormer. The flanking gable elevations articulate the attenuated roof form as a strong, singular triangular shape. On one side a columnated window array and on the other aspect a hypervertically oriented attic window provide focus for a strangely proportioned pediment. These considered differentiations make a strong form palatable beyond the first blush. Beyond the roof work, the aforementioned voidal porch has a prow-shaped bay projecting into its shape, and windows span from water table trim to one attenuated eave trim that bands the building.

All these exterior architectural moves have three clear scalar categories, set in a clear hierarchical order. Obviously all is subordinate to the roof and its base—a simple, unforgettable shape. This radical shape is given scale and visual "sustain" via complementary formal moves: the voided porch, the violative tower, highlighting dormer. Lastly, linear trim and windowscaping all interconnect and coordinate the first two levels of scale and have enough inherent complexity and richness to prolong visual interest.

Beyond all these architectural moves there is a simple site manipulation that allows a potentially abstract form to mesh cogently with its site. In digging a full foundation, a relatively large amount of earth is moved, and in this case the earth was further manipulated to allow for a walkout basement. Wedlick used this leftover fill to form a raised and bermed front entryway. This allowed the front entry to be "squeezed" (the one-story entry facade) and the rear entry to launch the aforementioned tower form.

Make no mistake about it, this is a tiny house, and all of these large and small manipulations have a strong underpinning of highly articulated exterior materials and trim. All elements employed are from a traditional palette, but they are used with a sense of coordination and animation that only a clearheaded architect can employ. Trim is not used simply as picture framing but as linear "glue." The sash lines of windows are extended to mesh their shapes with eave conditions. Wood shingles, clapboards, crowns, columns, and tongue-and-groove material are used to reinforce all of the latent geometric properties of the building parts. For example, curve-accommo-dating cedar shingles are used on the tower, and windows are set in it with a trimless joint, cutting through the shingled skin like a knife through butter.

The interior layout involves three bays clearly defined by the spacing of the columns of the recessive front porch. The central bay contains circulation—front door, central hall, and spiral staircase (it should be noted that in most municipalities a spiral stair cannot be used as a primary means of egress). Wedlick has utilized a traditional method for functional overlap by allowing a stair accessing the walkout basement to rest below an out-scaled hatch set within the living room floor. Given the fact that the basement is a walkout, the problematic qualities of opening this 7-foot, 6-inch-long by 3-foot-wide hatchway are greatly mitigated. Complementing this middle bay is a fire-place set central to the floor plan addressing the large-scale living and dining area. The second bay, the living area,

Figure 4 *Living area. This space is subtly defined by a lightly projecting corner window bay. Note the use of Shakeresque trim elements and yellow pine flooring. Resting just below the right-side rocker of the rocking chair closest in this view is a handle for the large-scale hatch that affords access to the basement.*

4

orients to the north side, reflecting the idea that the living space in a summer home is best kept cool. The remaining bay is the service/wet core of the home, involving a kitchen and bathroom on the first floor and a bathroom in the basement. On the upper floor the central hallway/stair bay is flanked by two bedrooms with one bedroom having a separate sleeping loft set into the apex of the ascendent roof. Opposite this sleeping loft is an attic used for storage and for the passive venting of unwanted summer heat.

Although the outside of this project can be seen as a modified Queen Anne–early Victorian mélange of trim and siding lines and textures, the interior overtly attempts a Shaker-style attitude, but in a way that eschews the ascetic qualities of the Shaker aesthetic. There is a celebration of windows and openness. The spiral stair set within tubular tower and complementarily bulging prefab fireplace shroud offer considered animation that takes this traditional motif into a new light.

As you might guess, a second home for two young adults need not have the vast kitchen or storage area of a full-time residence housing children; nevertheless, the full basement and aforementioned attic plus the presence of two full baths lend a functional legitimacy to this house. It should be mentioned that there is no bathroom on the bedroom level, obviously reflecting the value judgment that social engagements and sleeping capacity have more functional "weight" than the immediate hygenic accommodation of those who sleep in. Electric resistance heat was employed as well, its high cost per Btu forgiven for its low installation cost—a reasonable compromise given the limited use of this house during cold weather. Although its primary means of budgetary accommodation was in its downsized scale, the architect specifically used off-the-shelf standard materials to make the vast majority of the detail work affordable. This stock mind-set makes the obvious effervescent ambience of this house even more remarkable.

The constant aspect of all of these large-, middle-, and small-scale manipulations is the abiding sense that this is a compact home in which the basic occupiable house interior is seldom more than 16 feet wide and never longer than 26 feet. These dimensions relate to *one* bay of a typical center-hall Colonial residence. There is a heroic sense of triumph in this little house that is a mirror for the open mind of an innovative architect.

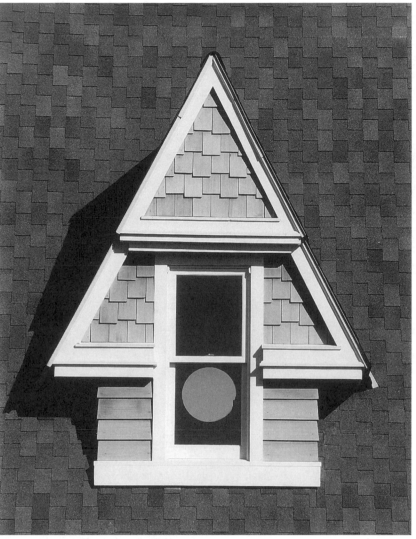

5

6

Figure 5 *Entry dormer. Careful use of standard materials can allow a great deal of visual activity and enrichment. Mitered corner clapboards create shadowlines that stand in stark contrast to the flat stock-trimmed linearity that surrounds the staggered shingles seen in the triangular in-fill of the gable roof itself. The lowest eave line has trim applied to align with the horizontal sash of the double-hung window. Multiple layerings of simple flat stock trim create a dance of line and shape. Note the use of staggered asphalt roof shingles to create a sense of an interweaving fabric rather than a surface of layers.*

Figure 6 *Northeast prospect. As the terrain falls away at the backside of the home, the turret cum stair tower perforates the attenuated roof's eave line and provides an overt focal point subordinate to the home's semiradical massing.*

Figure 7 *(opposite) Stairwell/fireplace. Shaker trim and crisp walls are animated to form a lightly curvilinear focal point within the context of the dining room-living room.*

A Sweet Sunlit Box

A home built in the early eighties has some meaningful messages for the next century.

Why would a book written and published in 1995 present a house that was designed and built over a decade ago? It is simply because its organizing principles are at once timeless in their simplicity and extraordinarily relevant to the coming generations of home design and construction.

All of the houses in this book are implicitly more energy efficient than standard homes of similar functional capacity because they are smaller than the norm both in square footage and in cubic volume. In particular, this home evidences the sort of spatial parsimony and prosaic structural detailing that inevitably lead to an efficiently functional building regardless of its specific approach to energy efficiency.

Fossil fuel energy is cheap in the 1990s, but by definition this is a limited resource and one that will inevitably become more expensive to obtain and use. However, free-market economics being what they are, the historically inexpensive energy of the last decade has been translated to a diminishment of concern for energy efficiency, as there is simply no evident payback given the costs involved when technologies are employed to mitigate heat loss or generate passive solar heat gain.

Therefore, throughout the northern latitudes of the United States, the last decade has seen a wholesale lack

---

S T A T S

PROJECT NAME AND LOCATION:
*Eck House,
Newton, Massachusetts*

ARCHITECT:
Jeremiah Eck Architects, Inc.

COMPLETION DATE:
1982

TOTAL HEATED SQUARE FEET:
1,150

PERCEIVED SQUARE FOOTAGE:
1,517

CIRCULATION-TO-TOTAL-AREA RATIO:
14 percent

BEDROOM-SPACE-TO-TOTAL-AREA RATIO:
29 percent

GROSS COST:
$70,000

COST PER SQUARE FOOT:
$61

DURATION OF DESIGN PROCESS:
One year

DURATION OF CONSTRUCTION:
Five months

Photos © Paul Ferrino
Drawings by the architects.

---

of consumer interest in passive solar design as a generating force in the physical planning of homes. Consumers are very willing to spend a few extra dollars on more insulation, better windows, and proper venting. But there is a fearful sense that double-height convection spaces, high-density thermal masses, or active solar collectors will not have any real net cost benefit in the average home's life cycle. Therefore, it is left to those with high sense of environmental ethics to make symbolic gestures of environmentally correct design. It's homes like the one Jeremiah Eck designed for himself in Newton, Massachusetts, that evidence the inherent wisdom involved in commonsense orientation, planning, and detailing that has very little to do with high-tech or heroics.

This is the simplest form of house, a "squished Cape" as it were, simply an extruded-gable form with a slightly oblique roof pitch (14:12 versus the more normal 12:12). Its 21- by 34-foot perimeter is absolutely typical of thousands of Cape homes that dot the American landscape from coast to coast, especially in New England.

The segregation of common spaces down and bedrooms up, the use of shed dormers to mitigate the roof pitch's imposition in the floor plan, and a centralized core of hearth and wet spaces have direct precedent in

Figure 1 Southerly prospect. Out-scaled glazing addressing the living room and solar attic presents a surprising perforation of a simple gable form. A gentle shed dormer allows headroom for part of the major bedroom space as well as the bathroom.

Figure 2 Floor plans. On the first floor (left), three distinct spaces are interwoven: entry and stair (right) kitchen and dining room (left), and living area (top). Out-scaled glazing in the living room addresses south-southwest, providing late-afternoon heat gain while a bay window in the dining area (bottom) captures due east sunlight for a toasty breakfast. The wood stove, pantry and coat storage, and wall oven and refrigerator create a central deep wall element surrounded by circulation. On the second floor (right), the original layout can be seen where three bedrooms stake out corners and a high-tech "solar attic" was intended to provide supercharged solar-heated air via water-filled tubes with the heated air collected and recirculated through the house. This experiment in active solar heat gain has been jettisoned in favor of a legitimately sized bedroom-studio space. Note that the circulation about the stair is held to an absolute minimum and that closets are relatively diminutive. Note also the expanded storage capacity of the elongated bath vanity.

1

2

3

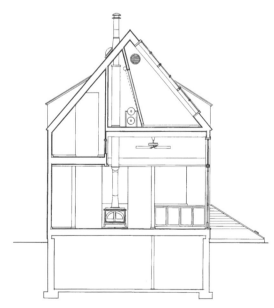

Figure 3 *North, entry. A semiwindowless form is a study in parsimonious perforation. Note the beckoning void in this stoic Cape shape at the left, with the sole ornamental aspect (the column) and its corollary bypassing out-scaled rail. Window placement is overtly nonaligning and random, but the carefully layered elements of the façade have extraordinary coordination. Note the diminished corner boards and the out-scaled water table trim. Note also the use of a venting skylight to the side of the shed and the venting fan set adjacent to the wood stove flue. Both are set high—the fan to evacuate unwanted heat in the summer and the flue with the vast majority of its heat-generating presence subsumed within the house mass to allow as much heat transfer as possible prior to the evacuation of waste gases.*

Figure 4 *Section. Set through the high-ceilinged living room space and solar attic, the out-scaled south wall glazing and attic skylights can be seen as well as the wood stove's uninterrupted flue, which in turn has its heat given over to the aforementioned solar attic. The attic's space had the potential to have its heat-generating portion sealed with roll-down insulation at night and have the heat generated from the sun and woodstove flue collected via the round vents seen at the top of the drawing. The rather oblique sawtooth space of the extraordinarily diminutive third bedroom can be seen at the left—a space that has had its fairly problematic shape mitigated by its integration with the attic space now that its active solar heat function has been jettisoned.*

4

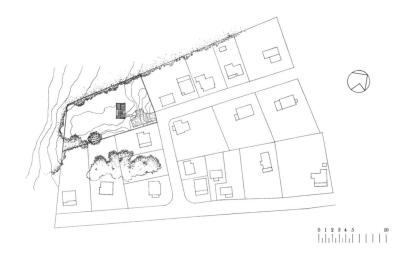

Figure 5 Site plan. Set at the corner of a street, this lot afforded topography that fell away as it addressed the south and provided an open area set before the out-scaled living room glazing. These are important site amenities when southerly glazing is set to accept the sun's heat.

5

0 1 2 3 4 5 10

traditional New England home construction. However, this house design by architect Eck (who also served as the general contractor on the project) displays the inherent wisdom in questioning tradition and tweaking it to effect both fresh aesthetics and a better environmental fit.

It is interesting to note that within this 1,100-square-foot, two-and-one-half-bedroom house (one space is so small that it really has to be used more as an emergency bedroom or nursery than a full-use sleeping space) is evidence of some obvious compromises. There is but one bath located on the second floor, the bedrooms and their closets are quite small, and the dining area is equally "wee." However, there are compensations. First, there is a full basement accessed by a full-width straight-run stair and by exterior access doors, and large-scale windows grace an 11-foot-high living space. Additionally, master planning was part of the home's construction and site location, allowing for additions to the west and the north.

Symbolic of the last decade's "reality check," the one high-tech element employed in the original design was a south-facing "solar attic," which has been decommissioned in terms of its active solar use and reconfigured as a working studio and true guest bedroom. This solar attic had the full complement of passive solar collection technology using Trombe wall water-filled cylinders and high R value glazing. Fortunately, this noble attempt at energy production was born of "normal" building technology rather than the "tack-on" technologies that scream out their aesthetic presence whether they work or not.

This modest technological experiment is gone, but its first-story counterpart—a simple Great Room facing south with an elevated ceiling to allow full solar penetration to the backside of the home—has remained and is in active use. The floor registers that allow air to convect from the wood stove and solar-heated first floor up to the bedroom level are also in active use. In fact, this tight box will likely never have the energy consumption of the average home of similar occupancy, which is more than twice its size.

With all of these technological intentions and evolutions, this home represents a model of functional efficiency. It is one thing to diminish the size of rooms used, but it is a happy circumstance when the relatively light occupancy elements such as circulation space and single-function rooms are kept to a minimum. In this particular case there is very little space given over to what could be deemed hallway. Also, the functions of kitchen and dining and formal and informal living all completely overlap each other on a relatively open first floor.

On the home's exterior, it is in the detailing of the façade that a clear-headed and ingenious architect's hand can be most overtly seen. Eck delights in tweaking the scale and character of details such as an attenuated deck rail whose height is set to align with the central sash rail of an oversized double-hung window, the aggrandizement of trim at the lower water table level, or the marriage of basement access doors to a large window. These out-scaled elements are complemented with the diminishment of trim at all corner boards or the absence of detail for the whole second-story façade and gable face. These details are arranged in façades that use a balanced, but largely asymmetrical, location of windows. Eck's aggressive manipulation of building elements can be seen in the extreme

Figure 6 *Kitchen. An open prep cooking space (left) stands in contrast to a dense-pack oven-pantry-refrigerator space (right). A careful incision (left center) allows full appreciation of the living room's southerly wall. Cabinetry employed is almost Shaker-like in its simplicity.*

Figure 7 *Living room. A completely outsized doorway sets the tone of the one grandly sized space in the house. The mullion patterns integrate with the relatively heavy-duty superstructure (left) while the minimized mullion and muntin patterned window wall stands in contrast to the boldly sized (and ruggedly checked) timbering of the ceiling joists. Note the formal manipulation of the wall that separates the kitchen (left) from living (right) area and the simple void that allows a coy connection between the kitchen space and the living area.*

6

out-scaled sizing of the south-facing glazed wall and doorway and skylight array. Contrast is also employed when a solid color (green) is set against the aforementioned neutral white trim and in turn contrasts with the natural-cedar clapboards. All these elements are held suspended in the context of this simple gable form that is absolutely typical of traditional New England architecture.

Homes designed and built by architects for themselves are often experiments. Hopefully, the heavy-duty solar gain of the south-facing living space is mitigated by shading during the summer months. The "deteching" of the solar attic evidences that this home is an open-ended ongoing experiment. However, the baseline truths of simple form, diminished size, and commonsense site orientation are timeless and have latent benefits that no amount of cheap energy can cause us to ignore.

As with other elements in our culture, the key to our housing future lies in our past and, in this case, our recent past. Without some sense that there will be an ever-changing capability for us to heat our homes in ways we have grown accustomed to, architects beg the question of long-term utility, let alone adequately address the ethical quandaries when finite resources are wasted via careless design. The trendy advocacy of a "green" consciousness when designing homes utilizing materials that are recycled, renewable, or at the very least nonhostile to fragile environments has a conceptual lure. If "earth friendly" materials are set in a context of inefficient, bloated, or simply poorly designed buildings, their positive characteristics are merely wallpaper set upon a corrupt construction of rationalizations. Without focusing on making homes more efficient (and thus smaller) to dovetail with an occupant's idiosyncrasies, no building can claim to be truly environmentally friendly in the largest sense.

Our forefathers knew this when they designed shapes like the Cape or saltbox, orienting their homes to gain heat in the winter and allow for natural ventilation in the summer. No amount of trendy technologies, politically correct materials, or symbolic gestures toward energy efficiency can compare to the basic benefits of spatial thrift so ably evidenced in these homes.

7

Highest and Best Use

Invention within the urban fabric.

THE problems of New Haven, Connecticut, are the problems of urban America. The twin economic engines of manufacturing and the middle class that made urban America a vital and evolving center for community development and architectural expression have fled almost all the urban centers of America, forming a suburban halo that surrounds virtually every major metropolitan area in the United States. Not surprisingly, this evacuation has left large-scale craters of underdevelopment and blight in its wake.

Within the statistically richest state in the union, New Haven is one of the poorer cities in the country. Crime has rushed in to fill the void left by a deteriorated job base. Family structures are devolving to the point where meaningful demographic analysis becomes almost impossible. In this seemingly hopeless situation, New Haven's most famous institution, Yale University, has offered up some of its best and brightest to help reverse the tide of degeneration in both a symbolic and absolutely tangible way.

The Yale Building Project was formed almost three decades ago by Charles Moore and Kent Bloomer to take advantage of massive federal funding of innovative constructions—often housing—and to give the rarified ivory tower of the Yale

---

S T A T S

PROJECT NAME AND LOCATION:
*1993, Yale Building Project,
New Haven, Connecticut*

ARCHITECT:
*Michael Levy, Russell Katz,
Jae-Yun-Cha*

COMPLETION DATE:
1993

TOTAL HEATED SQUARE FEET:
1,190

PERCEIVED SQUARE FOOTAGE:
1,830

CIRCULATION-TO-TOTAL-AREA RATIO:
21 percent

BEDROOM-SPACE-TO-TOTAL-AREA RATIO:
29 percent

GROSS COST:
$56,000

COST PER SQUARE FOOT:
$47

DURATION OF DESIGN PROCESS:
Seven weeks

DURATION OF CONSTRUCTION:
Twelve weeks

Photos © Yale University.
Drawings by the architects.

Architectural School some down-to-earth experience in how materials are used to build buildings. These exercises had drifted into the construction of architectural follies, a band shell here, a park pavilion there—buildings that were more often than not structural sculptures set to evidence the cleverness of young student designers in a way that had more to do with art than "the real world."

Things changed in 1990 when the Yale Building Project started to collaborate with the local branch of Habitat for Humanity, an organization that is explicitly geared to provide housing for those who are often cast adrift in this changing social environment and that often uses those to be housed to help build their own homes. The results over the first three years of this collaboration were true gifts to the community—carefully crafted constructions of thoughtful massing and referential detail. But the project of the 1993 collaboration has some extraordinary and innovative aspects to it, and thus belongs in a book that strives to deal with the practical applications of the art of small-house design.

From the mouths of babes have come some controversial truths. Those who have not had their heads filled with preconceptions can often see through problems with a clarity that older minds envy. So it appears to be with this 1993 effort. The

Figure 1 *Front view. A proud presence held distinct from the street, this project has lightly referential material and shapes, but is overtly reinterpretive of its context while it eschews the more normal enfrontment presented by its neighbors, left and right. Behind the two-story "tower," note the double-height wall which in fact serves as the entry portal from the street side of the project—a minimalist perforation of plywood and batten construction.*

Figure 2 *Floor plan. The first-floor plan evidences the "backward," or at least "sideway," approach to the typical urban lot. Rather than enter the home on the short-street end (left), the home is entered amidships (bottom). The porch to the left is made overtly inaccessible to the street and addresses a multi-purpose room that could serve as an office, additional bedroom, or even secondary living area. This room has its counterpart on the second floor, a bedroom. This semidetached, semitowerlike, street-facing element facilitates a great deal of functional diversity while at the same time creates a barrier to the street. The middle section of the plan is given over to circulation, entry, and a courtyard-lightwell, providing the sort of finished and secure space on a scale that is unprecedented in this neighborhood. This courtyard is partially enclosed with a gentle egress to the backyard to the upper right. The third element of the construction is a rectangular building (right) that harbors the kitchen and living-family room on the first floor, as well as a main staircase, which (not surprisingly) turns its back on the street to provide second-floor access directly to the backyard. Wet spaces are kept to one side of this linear plan, and window sizes and orientations help reinforce the qualities of the exterior forms and elevations. Cross-axial relationships abound, circulation is celebrated, and exterior spaces are overtly possessed and controlled. Although untraditional in nature, this home is not without its own internal logic and formal and spatial rationale.*

1

2

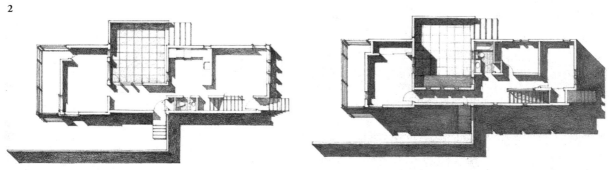

design team of first-year Yale graduate architecture students indicated in the "stats" box executed this project with Paul Brouard as their advisor, and the entire first-year architecture graduate school class had a part in its construction.

The site that this young group encountered was both generic and special. Centrally set in an urban block of single homes, this lot was indiscernible from its neighbors. However, at the backside it widened to a double-lot width, providing a very unusual amenity. Almost all of the surrounding dwellings occupied barely one-half of their lot's full depth—not surprising as these homes are set tight to the street to provide the maximum amount of "backyard" space for safe play and socializing. The expanded backside portion of this particular lot is set behind the typical rear lot lines of most of its neighbors.

Additionally, this particular lot had a secondary street directly facing its frontage. This small urban site was pressurized at its front and relieved at its back, and the scheme that was employed recognizes both of these aspects in a way that is quite unusual in the context of the surrounding community.

The design shown here was the winner among four schemes presented to the faculty, students, Habitat for Humanity representatives, and the family that was to be housed. If this project had been chosen by Ivory Tower academics or even by those who did not know or live in the neighborhood, this project would have been quite controversial. But the jury (or juries) were unanimous in their judgment that this site and this neighborhood could be challenged by its unprecedented sensibility.

Rather than follow the rhythmatic streetscape by rote, the Yale design team pushed the building back to allow the "soft underbelly" of the building's shape to accept light and air from the open void across its adjacent neighbors' backyards. Given the sideyard setbacks, the resulting form is still centered in the short direction of the lot.

The home's front form abstractly respects the gable-faced fronts of the surrounding buildings. But the largest part of the home is set to open up to the aforementioned expanded backyard. The three-bedroom, two-bath home so often seen in this context as a singular form becomes a three-part harmony, with forward-facing front block, a transitional linkage that spawns a large-scale terrace, and finally its largest building piece, a rectangular form capped with a single-pitched roof ascending to fully embrace the expanded backyard.

Materials are used reinforce the various identities of the building components. The front block utilizes horizontal vinyl clapboards to lightly mesh with its surrounding buildings. The central soft spot/connector terrace has siding formed by plywood gridded with battens all painted white, presenting a unified, light-reflecting presence at the center of the composition. The backyard-facing block is covered in vinyl clapboard where it's visually accessible to its neighbors while maintaining the plywood and batten siding addressing the central soft spot.

The site gestures that are the genesis of this house's form are reflected in the large-scale features applied to these forms as well, involving not only the aforementioned terrace amidships but an almost symbolic front porch and the various roofscapes mentioned earlier. The smaller moves also lightly reinforce and articulate the abstracted aspects of the constituent parts of the construction: Roofs are held distinct from walls via recesses in the façade, virtually painted-out "gaskets." Windows are ganged together to form a larger-scale element that is set to project from the façade, a gesture that almost makes them a kinetic presence.

No doubt these exterior moves are unprecedented and provide a sort of standoffish quality from the neighborhood. However, in breaking with the traditional site orientation and massing, this building intends to give a beacon of hope rather than a message of despair. By taking a generic site, finding its hidden virtues, exploiting them functionally, and underscoring them aesthetically, this project provides hopeful vision for the community.

The functional distinctions of the interior act in concert with the site-determined form and have a similarly reinventive attitude as well. The road-facing vertical block is revealed to be a semidetached, ground-level, multipurpose room and porch with a bedroom set above. One should note that this porch is accessible only from the interior—it is not an entry porch—and in fact the "soft spot" amidships is the main point of entry. This entry is set at right angles to the long dimension of the lot line and is part of the connector. The kitchen, family room, half-bath, and stairway are located in the rear-facing block. Above this backyard-facing block are two bedrooms and a full bath. In dissociating the street-facing block of bedroom/family room, a variety of tenancies can be accommodated. The first-floor room can be utilized as a secondary bedroom or even an office, and the entire street-facing block can house an in-law style subordinate occupancy.

Figure 3 *Site plan. The site context encountered by the design team served as a genesis for the entire project approach. Eschewing the normal enfrontment of houses typically present to the streets of this urban neighborhood, this house takes a different approach. Utilizing an extraordinarily large backyard, the home's footprint slides back to facilitate a situation that none of the other homes in this community have—significant light and air in the middle of the house form—while allowing the rear of the home direct access to an isolated backyard. The net result of these moves, which responded to the peculiarities of the site, is that a very large frontyard is obtained, an amenity that is overtly standoffish from the context of the streetscape but responds to the imposition of a secondary thoroughfare T-ing in across the street. Note that the entry is set to the middle of the long wall to the right, addressing the alleyway to the right of the project, while a terrace-courtyard as set to the left has one-story walls preventing unwanted physical and visual intrusion while at the same time allowing the sunlight access from the open space between the neighboring building and its garage to the rear.*

Figure 4 *Section. Street-side tower (right). The soft center of entry-courtyard and circulation (middle) and the true "house" (left) have their identities reinforced by roof line, material, and spatial properties. While the street-facing tower (right) presents a gable face to the street and provides optimal spatial expression on the second floor, the "house" to the left has its roof ascending to a large backyard with a correlative attenuation of the ceiling-scapes within the rooms that progress down its length. The living room/kitchen of the "house" is rendered as a single space lightly subdivided by kitchen cabinets. Note that the stairway involved directly addresses the backyard (left) rather than the street while the front porch (right) is an outlook rather than a extended stoop as it is rendered as an item that is completely inaccessible from street level.*

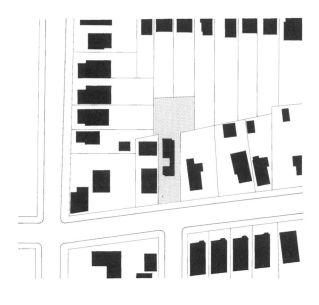

3

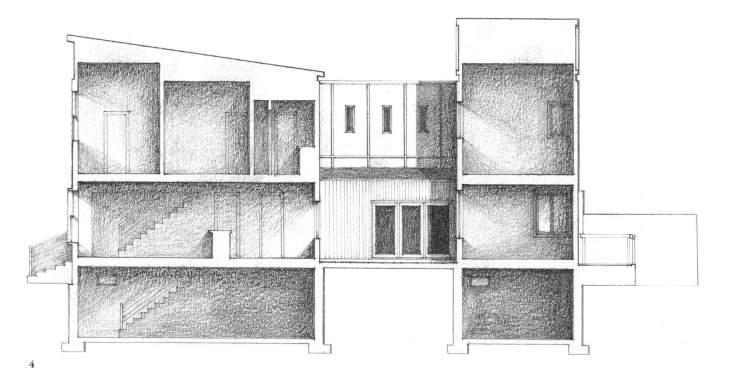

4

5

Figure 5 *Courtyard, sky. The formal distillation of the próject is mirrored by the graphic qualities of the plywood and batten siding used for the project's "soft underbelly." The street-facing tower (right) opens up windows to this central area as does the entry foyer (lower left)—a glazed space that serves as an interior light well to the entire house. On the second level a recessed hallway has visual access obscured by slit windows. The presence of the backyard-facing dominant rectilinear component can be seen at the upper left.*

6

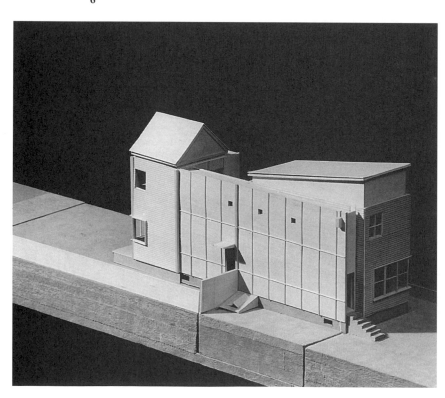

7

Figures 6, 7 *Presentation models. The semiabstracted formal genesis of the project can be seen in these models, models that were dropped into the neighborhood context for the final presentation to the students and faculty at Yale as well as to the sponsoring agency, Habitat for Humanity, and the family that would live in the house. Despite its architectural expressionism and antireferential qualities, this project was a clear winner among its competitors and represents the sort of original take that challenges the conventional wisdom of contextualist theory while at the same time recognizing the legitimate conditions that exist for this particular site. Note that the roofs are rendered as semidetached elements, both kinetic and symbolic, and surface treatments are rendered to enhance either the underbelly aspect of the courtyard or the superscaled wall sensibility of the entry. Note that the entry itself is but a perforation in this wall with a modest overhang (yet to be built) while the backyard access is available at two locations, both generous and focused. These elements effectively render linkage to the street as a necessary evil and, in one sense, recognize the latent properties of what many of our urban neighborhoods have become. Note that windows are flecked about in ignorance of whatever centerlines may be present, superscaled to be a wall of glass (addressing the courtyard), or manipulated to wrap around corners.*

The Yale Building Program's original intent—giving students practical construction experience—is evidenced by the simplicity of the detailing of the interior, but there are some exciting gestures as well, mostly in the custom-crafted steel handrails, both inside and out, that have overt structuralist-sculptural intentions successfully realized. Wood floors are used in most common areas, and the panelized plywood system that is used for the soft under-belly siding is also used to create the central terrace's enclosure. It should be noted that there are full-perimeter walls for this enclosure, and they do not allow easy access nor views into this central part of the house but take full advantage of the lack of adjacent building mass to provide the vast majority of light and air into the center of the house. This is distinct from most row houses where most light and air comes from the end points of the construction.

Functional innovation, interweaving the site's characteristics with the building's form, aesthetic concepts of solid and void, transparent interrelationships, axial organization, the creation of semisymbolic elements—all of these are abstract concepts often learned in school by architects. To see them exploited to create an affordable building with a high degree of utility for a desperate population is indeed the highest and best use of what the architectural profession and architectural education has to offer. It is in this way that seemingly out-of-touch institutions such as Yale can evidence the fact that we are all residents together, whether it is in the confines of New Haven or anywhere else in the United States.

Figure 8 *Courtyard. The plywood and batten siding of the home makes a direct transition into a freestanding wall. The existing grade is controlled and raised to provide open and easy access to the large-scale backyard that this home's unique site provides. While the wall prevents unwanted visual intrusion at eye level from immediate neighbors (right), it sill provides full accessibility to light and air to the center portion of the house—an amenity that its neighboring counterparts simply cannot have.*

Figure 9 *(opposite) Interior. Spaces within the house are relatively stark given the tight budget and the nature of the workers available for construction, but there is some legitimate craft and artistry evidenced in both the handrails and the windowscaping.*

8

Power and Poignancy on a Budget

A small house has extraordinary presence despite its diminutive price tag.

STATS

PROJECT NAME AND LOCATION:
*Stone/Mahn House,
Eden Creek, Washington*

ARCHITECT:
The Miller-Hull Partnership

COMPLETION DATE:
1989

TOTAL HEATED SQUARE FEET:
1,300

PERCEIVED SQUARE FOOTAGE:
1,739

CIRCULATION-TO-TOTAL-AREA RATIO:
11 percent

BEDROOM-SPACE-TO-TOTAL-AREA RATIO:
37 percent

GROSS COST:
$103,000

COST PER SQUARE FOOT:
$79

DURATION OF DESIGN PROCESS:
Eight months

DURATION OF CONSTRUCTION:
Five months

In the minds of most people, architect-designed, custom-built homes are out of their reach—both in terms of their financial ability to pay for the added amenity and in their conceptual ability to deal with an architect's crazed conceptual meanderings. This home undercuts both those presumptions. This is a three-bedroom, 1,477-square-foot home, professionally designed by The Miller-Hull Partnership (Bob Hull and Philip Christofides in charge) and general-contracted.

The total price tag when built in 1989 in Eden Creek, Washington, was $103,000, not including land. As with any low-budget, high-art building, there are a few compromises, but unlike many of the vacation homes present in this book that have inherent economic advantages over their full-time counterparts, this is a full-time home for two professionals, Gary Mahn and Mary-Ellen Stone. The compromises employed included Mahn and Stone's ability to do painting and landscaping and Gary Mahn's particular talent in finish carpentry, allowing much of the interior finish carpentry work to be executed literally "in-house." The home is built over a crawl space, with one area set upon a slab-on-grade foundation, preempting the ability to have a fully functional basement. The home is heated primarily by the sun and a wood stove with inexpensive-to-install electric baseboard heat serving as a backup.

Beyond these simple cost-saving elements, this home affords the sort of power and presence rare in any home—architect designed or not, large or small, either with or without a large budget. The power present in this demitasse bit of domesticity is facilitated by several simple rules, all of which come under the heading of "keep it simple." A three-part massing is reinforced both in the plan and in all the detailing present. Essentially, two towers "bookend" a central low building mass. These towers have identical sections and are formed, respectively, by a single bay to one side and a double bay opposite. Their flanking presence has a vertical emphasis formed by their extraordinarily attenuated knee-braced roof overhangs and is accentuated by brightly colored trim and window casings.

The central piece is inherently subordinate with a flat roof and is ground oriented, with a projecting bay of glazed wall dominating the lower-level ambience of the home's exterior. The three parts of this composition respect their relative centerlines via structure, glazing, wood stove flue orientation, and gutter downspout location.

There is a lyric ambiguity as to whether these two towers predominate and contain the central bay or

1

UPPER FLOOR

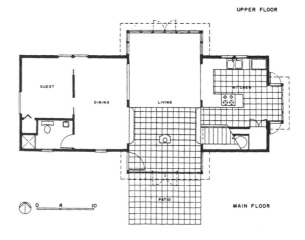

MAIN FLOOR

Figure 1 *Southeast prospect. Nestled in a flattened area in a hilly landscape, a small-scale juggernaut expresses its vital presence in the sunshine—materials, colors, and detailing glow in the sunlight.*

Figure 2 *Floor plans. A "tower" of kitchen under a secondary bedroom, a subordinate gasket of living space with circulation and bathroom-laundry on the second level and a two-bay dining/guest bedroom/bathroom surmounted by a full-width master bedroom form a simple three-part construction. Each element of this triad has special properties. Note that the entry occurs amidship at the lower transitional space that serves as a solar gain area, with overt extensionist desires present with the glass wall and paving pattern blurring inside and outside distinctions. The living area then projects forth out into a descending landscape beyond with a wood stove set as a sentinel amid all the circulation and glazing.*

2

3

4

whether the central bay's presence has the power to slice through the stoic presence of a dominant gable-roofed building form. These moves are not inherently expensive, and in fact, all the subordinate articulations implicit in these basic massing moves have an eye toward economy through the use of standard materials and detailing. The attenuated roofscape is formed by simple dimensional lumber. The extended presence of the central glazed bay is formed by a simple cantilever off of the line defined by the bookends, and its floor-to-ceiling glazing utilizes stock glazed garage door panels set vertically. The predominant vertical siding used is not top-grade clear wood but rather a "tight knot" specification. Simple standard trim details abound throughout the entire house and are made special by the aforementioned intensity of the color palette chosen. A straight-run stair takes up a minimum of space and uses basic railing and trim details. The tight 17-foot framing bay allows for clear span 2 by 10 joists 16 inches on-center, which can accommodate inexpensive cathedralized ceilings on the upper floors with the short span allowing for a single 6- by 10-inch ridge beam for central support.

Figure 3 *Dining area/living area/kitchen. The interior of the house is cross-referenced by a multitude of axes and is enlivened by level play as the cross-axial living, entry, and dining areas are set between kithcen (background) and dining (foreground). Colors and inexpensive light fixtures and materials help to interweave and enliven a series of small spaces that gain grandeur in their coincidence.*

Figure 4 *North elevation. As seen from the downhill side, the three-part harmony of this project is obvious, with the single-bay tower (left), double-bay dominant building (right), and recessive central slot between. Whether the slot is a slice that interrupts a consistent context or a secondary element that is squeezed by two bookends is irrelevant. The interweaving lines of material, shapes, and forms present visual zestiness seldom seen in homes of this size. Note how roof structure, windows, and gutters are coordinated, as is the centerline of the expressed woodstove flue, providing counterpoint to the subordinate flat roof of the connector.*

Figure 5 *North, downhill. The east tower celebrates its ascendence with lighting, materials, and detailing as well as with windowscaping celebrating the leaders. Note the cantilevered living room glazing to the right.*

5

Figure 6 *Entry, southerly glazing. Inexpensive garage door glazing is innovatively used here as a glazed partition maximizing solar input into the home with deck space above providing an added benefit for the bedrooms above. Note the expressed woodstove flue set between the roofscapes and the extraordinarily attenuated eave forms.*

Figure 7 *Windows-eaves-stair. Trim, muntin and mullion patterns, knee braces, rafters, materials, paint, and joinery all coalesce to make a wonderfully conspired array of structure and material. Much of the interior trim was done by the owners, and the tender, loving, care evidenced in all the detailing makes simple alignments elegant and possible awkward transitions delightful.*

6

Functionally, the home offers a straightforward approach that dovetails perfectly with the aforementioned massing. The central bay harbors a south-facing solar-heat-generating sunroom and woodstove area that progresses into a living area opening up to a backside creek. The smaller tower has the kitchen and stair on its first floor and a guest bedroom on its upper floor. The two-bay tower has a first floor composed of an additional guest bedroom and bath and a relatively large dining room designed to share space with the living room, with the master suite and laundry set above. The relatively diminutive master bath is mitigated by the use of an in-bedroom sink (a relatively common feature in another era). Although closet space is relatively limited, the master bedroom itself is a generous 17- by 18-foot space, replete with cathedralized ceiling and glazing on all four walls. A cross-axial relationship is set up between the kitchen, living, and dining room via the use of aligned openings between these spaces. Upstairs, the central slot has a greatly recessed heated and finished space accommodating a hallway and the stair. Flanking this diminished finished space are two generous decks.

This building's power is related to its unapologetic manipulation of scale and space and honest use of materials. It evidences the best sort of innovation for the average housing consumer, a spirit that strives for an invigorated ambience rooted in the knowledge of technology. Clearly the presence of an owner/finish carpenter benefited this entire project as virtually all the joinery and materials used have a commonsense elegance that defies adequate written description.

As much as any project in this book, this sweet little home emphasizes the joyful embrace of the possible over the pessimistic. There are many reasons not to build, not least of which is the uncertainty of the final cost. Additionally, and scarier for most Americans, is that it is not possible to walk into a showroom and "test-drive" a prototype of any custom-designed home. Lastly, the issue of timing must be considered. Most people simply cannot afford to build on a cash basis and must take out a loan to build their dream, and loans often necessitate having equity in an existing home. Absent that, rent must be paid while the cost of a building mortgage is absorbed, so timing has enormous economic impact as well.

In all these areas of legitimate fear, small houses in general (and this house in particular) can overcome many practical difficulties. The smaller the home, the more inherently limited its budget. The smaller the home, the more readily its form and spaces can be effectively apprehended prior to building. Lastly, the smaller the home, the shorter the construction schedule, easing that anxiety as well. Given the simple compromises described earlier, the Stone/Mahn house is a home without effective compromise for the occupants. It presents just the sort of American dream that can be attained by a far greater segment of our society than most "experts" acknowledge.

7

"Make No Small Plans"

A tiny home seems to have a sense of manifest destiny.

LIKE most young couples Allan and Julie Shope wanted a home of their own. They had a leg up on this proposition since Allan is an architect, and in 1983 he was on the edge of having a career explode into national prominence (along with partner, Bernard Wharton, whose house is also featured in this book).

When Allan and Julie Shope began their quest for a home, they had not begun a family, and their interest was limited to staking out a site for a permanent residence that would be their home for an indefinite future. Realizing that they had a paucity of funds, they downsized their dream house to become a 500-square-foot outpost, the intention being that their first construction would serve as a "guest" house prior to building the "real" house. But intervening children and a lack of funds to build the "real" house prompted the guest house to become the real house, and five years after their 500-square-foot jewel box cum one-bedroom home was built, an addition of almost twice that size was added to accommodate children and a "real" kitchen.

The original Shope house was widely publicized to laud an architect whose distilled aesthetic was artfully expressed in a tiny, almost symbolic, form. However, it is impossible to fully appreciate Shope's house and design without some knowledge of Shope himself. It is said that if sharks

---

S T A T S

PROJECT NAME AND LOCATION:
Shope Residence,
Greenwich, Connecticut

ARCHITECT:
Shope Reno Wharton Associates

COMPLETION DATE:
Main house 1985; Addition 1988

TOTAL HEATED SQUARE FEET:
1,300

PERCEIVED SQUARE FOOTAGE:
1,615

CIRCULATION-TO-TOTAL-AREA RATIO:
12 percent

BEDROOM-SPACE-TO-TOTAL-AREA RATIO:
41 percent

GROSS COST:
$130,000

COST PER SQUARE FOOT:
$100

DURATION OF DESIGN PROCESS:
Four months

DURATION OF CONSTRUCTION:
Two years

Photos © Durston Saylor.
Drawings by the architects.

---

stop swimming, they die—and it might be said that if Allan Shope stopped building, he'd feel that he was as good as dead. All the elements that you see in the depiction of this house were either built directly by Allan Shope or fully conspired and installed by him and Julie. This intensely productive attitude allowed for an extraordinary amount of amenity to be built for a relatively small budget (the house depicted is a 1,300-square-foot plus, three-bedroom, two-bath house built for approximately $130,000). Allan orchestrated the barn-raising-style erection of the addition to his home by bringing in dozens of friends and neighbors to assemble carefully prefabricated elements that he had been building for three months before. Thus, if the dollar value of the sweat equity were put into this building budget, the home would have needed at least two and perhaps three times the funding that it has had to date. Shope is an architect who truly puts his muscle where his pen is, building as well as drawing. Furthermore, unlike so many architect-owner-builders, he actually finishes what he starts.

In analyzing the house at this stage of its life, it is essentially a three-part harmony: the jewel box starter home, the extraordinarily attenuated kitchen-connector, and the rakish, angular children's wing, a chiseled form as

1

2

3

LIVING ROOM

KITCHEN

BATH

BEDROOM

BEDROOM

Figure 1 *After. Contrasting the "parent" building, which had a levitated eave line with vertical projections breaking the eave rake, the "child" building is just a horizontal construction with a lower-than-normal eave and out-scaled dormers set within the context of an outsized roof plane. Whereas the parent building was axially symmetrical along its ridge line, the child wing has its forms symmetrically organized perpendicular to its ridge line. The parent building is layered horizontally with an open first floor with bedroom-bath space set above. The child wing's raked form is heavily subdivided vertically into bathroom, minor bedroom, and major bedroom spaces with the subdivisions adapting to the exterior form. Whereas the parent building was set directly and unapologetically upon the earth, the child building is levitated above the rocky terrain. Between these radically differentiated forms is a symbolic umbilical cord of glazed kitchen-hall connector.*

Figure 2 *Before. This is the entry prospect of the house with the light well addressing the stairwell with the penultimate focal point.*

Figure 3 *Floor plan. The original home (left) was radically extended via an attenuated kitchen (amidships) tethering the original house form to a new two-bedroom addition (right) intended to house the occupant's three children. This extraordinary linkage allows two disparate forms to coexist and its unique function of corridor-cooking space was necessitated by the interpretation of a local zoning ordinance. A future addition may well be set to the lower-right-hand corner of this plan view.*

Figure 4 *The original home. A vertically expressed assemblage of traditional shingle-style elements set in bold exaggerated terms: the tower to the right accommodates a fireplace flue, and its counterpart (left) is a light well servicing a stairwell. A completely open floor plan has windows regularly set about its perimeter; these same windows are utilized for all other aspects of the house. Ventilation is accommodated via skylights set upon the roof form. A small box is thus radically attenuated and perforated.*

Figure 5 *Living room. A centered space with carefully crafted light fixtures serving as focal points.*

4

rooted to the earth as the original jewel box seems to rise above it. Shingle siding and extraordinarily crafted eave trim and undersides are common to both homes as are the essential geometries employed. But in adding onto his home, Shope has changed a "statement" into the beginnings of an ensemble, which at some point might see a three-story tower evidence itself, moving the kitchen out of the connector, providing guest sleeping space and perhaps even a garage and metal-working shop.

The pragmatic lessons in this house are many. Built on a ragged hilltop of rock amid fully matured trees, both home and addition have no basement, the addition being set on piers and the original home being set directly on top of the rock itself. There is an extraordinary attention to gathering light, either directly (the connector) or indi-

5

6

rectly (via the chimney/stairway/light well of the original jewel). The spaces defined by Allan Shope are extremely simple and gain an extraordinary presence and power by the unapologetic use of trim, the baring of structure, and the use of light fixtures and windows not only as conveyors of light but as the focal points of visual focus from within the home.

Beyond these aesthetic and constructivist lessons, the Shope house evidences the very best sort of ongoing and fluid master planning that can allow small homes to adapt to family requirements. Having started out as a "double-income, no-kids" couple, the Shopes now have three young children (and plans are afoot for a fourth!). Thus the tiny kitchen of the guest home had to become the attenuated 60-foot-long kitchen of this intermediate version. Lest the reader think that the Shopes combine rollerblading with cooking, it should be noted that this elongated kitchen was in fact the vehicle by which their floor plan could be approved by the local zoning board. Originally, this architectural tether was intended to be nothing but a gallery for Allan's gun collection, but the local planning board saw a long corridor space without a function and assumed that the architect was planning to provide a separate rental unit in a district that allows for only single-family residences. By conceptually removing shotguns and physically installing cook tops, sinks, and a refrigerator, Allan Shope was able to convey the seriousness of his desire to create a legitimate single-family home despite the attenuated connector joining the two main forms. A future addition will accommodate a more normally shaped kitchen, but until that time it is this unprecedented functional accommodation of kitchen and corridor that make this intermediate housing form unforgettable. Highlighting this oddball form, all the kitchen cabinets (made by Shope, of course) came from one huge white oak log (harvested by Shope, of course).

Despite the fact that this is a master-planned home, it is not hamstrung by a preconceived, straitjacket definition. Its evolution has more to do with a mind that never rests and hands that are seldom without productive activity. It is this "can-do" spirit that is so starkly evident in all the unapologetically vibrant and almost innocent shapes, details, and intentions of this ever-changing house form. When most people think about homes, large or small, they see the limitations of the walls, spaces, and shapes. When Allan Shope thinks of these things, they are a kinetic, ongoing ensemble of elements that are actively being choreographed by his mind and hand.

It's the lesson that buildings can be evolutionary, adaptive, and responsive to our needs that make this home design a powerful image for anybody thinking about small-house design. The word *small* connotes a diminishment of long-term goals and the confinement of home and hearth, but in truth, the more rigorously designed, tighter, and more efficient a home is, the easier it is for it to be retooled and reconsidered for different uses.

Figure 6 Master bedroom. Set amid ventilating skylights, an axially oriented room has its spatial termination in a double-height clerestory light well glazed with the prismatic windows of Shope's design that serve to refract moonlight. Note the distinctive nature of the natural wood collar ties set in the context of the simple angled sheetrock ceiling.

Interweaving Intentions

Prosaic materials, familiar shapes, and extreme budgetary limitations combine with aesthetic theory to create an evocative presence.

ROBERT Bast is an intriguing architect. His practice is set in rural Vermont, and he has a great deal of experience as a structural engineer as well as being a licensed architect. At first blush, the homes he designs appear to have their genesis in the most obvious commonsense building practices, forms and detailing having more to do with the rule of thumb than the rules of geometry. But on closer inspection, it is clear that these homes have a depth of character and design intent far more complex than any home effected with "by guess and by gosh" engineering or the folk art sensibilities of a typically undesigned Vermont farmhouse. Bast employs organizing principles that have more to do with geometric abstraction than with bucolic prototypes. He explicitly utilizes the generically abstract "golden-mean" proportion, perspectival alignment of walls and rooms, rigorous structural engineering as an organizational influence, and an obsession with house forms that evolve as they progress from façade to façade. When these subcutaneous influences are combined with the more common concerns of scale, proportion, function, and environmental fit, the bucolic-based cladding employed is revealed to be merely sheep's clothing surrounding a wolf of high-art intent on the part of the architect.

STATS

PROJECT NAME AND LOCATION:
*Bloomhardt House,
South Alburg, Vermont*

ARCHITECT:
Robert S. Bast, Architect

COMPLETION DATE:
1991

TOTAL HEATED SQUARE FEET:
1,213

PERCEIVED SQUARE FOOTAGE:
1,368

CIRCULATION-TO-TOTAL-AREA RATIO:
11 percent

BEDROOM-SPACE-TO-TOTAL-AREA RATIO:
.30 percent

GROSS COST:
$56,000

COST PER SQUARE FOOT:
$47

DURATION OF DESIGN PROCESS:
Three months

DURATION OF CONSTRUCTION:
Six weeks

Photos © Robert S. Bast.
Drawings by the architect.

In Ted and Carol Bloomhardt, Bast found clients with a life-style equally as idiosyncratic as his design outlook. The Bloomhardts are both pilots, and they had located a site that not only had a view of Lake Champlain but was also adjacent to a grass airfield. The owners could fly right up to the back door of this second home in their relatively antique plane with their young daughters, Elizabeth and Natalie, aboard. The lot had a somewhat narrow width, but a small home can use a reduced footprint to "ease the squeeze" of abnormal lot configurations.

As you might expect, this young family does not have a large quantity of money to spend on a second home, and in fact, at $56,000 and about $47 per square foot, this home represents one of the very best values possible in a custom American domestic construction in the waning years of the twentieth century. Utilizing standard materials helped, but Bast's emphasis on structural efficiency was critical. This structural obsession is directly keyed to his alter ego as an engineer. This obsession had an additional benefit. Whereas the normal length of construction for homes in this book is anywhere from five to eight months (or more), the basic construction of this home took all of eight weeks. Although the interiors are owner finished (and thus forever trending toward completion),

Figure 1 *East view. The gable-roofed bedroom cleanly incises itself within the dominant roof form.*

Figure 2 *Floor plans. A variety of latent geometric organizers can be seen in these floor plans. Essentially a square has one side skewed (left), another agglomeratively added onto (bottom), and another octagonally added onto (right). Within the context of these perimeter permutations, an entry that is central to the agglomerative extension centers the entry point upon a wood stove which is perspectively enhanced via the dropped, canted beams set within the living room. The house is divided into three distinct areas with serving spaces set to the bottom of the plan (kitchen, half-bath, storage, and stair), public spaces set to the top of the plan, and a large-scale screen porch to the right (each functional distinction having a geometric indicator). On the second floor three bedrooms pirouette off the stairway-bathroom side of the home, and subordinate roofs fall away from the square plan generator. Each bedroom space has a different orientation and shape.*

1

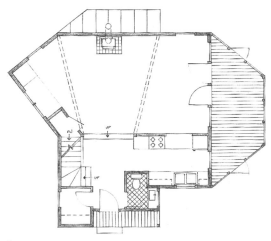
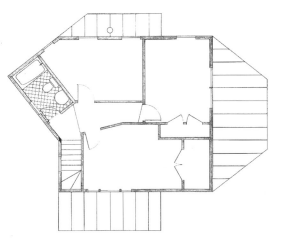

2

3

this is an extraordinary accomplishment. Although there was an anticipation of ledge, it was not encountered, and a full basement was afforded, avoiding expensive time-consuming blasting or chipping out of bedrock.

The architect's working drawings for this project reflect the dual identity of a home designed with deeply abstract intellectual underpinnings that simultaneously evidences an intimate knowledge of the most generic details imaginable. There is a paucity of notes and almost no large-scale details. The drawings appear to be rendering a home that has already been built, perhaps because of the fact that the myriad formal moves simply extend a basic system of detailing that acts as a design determinant. When all detailing is consistent and home brewed, there are few special conditions to describe. The architect's latently esoteric gestures are made almost poetic in their store-bought, off-the-rack applications. At first glance, it is hard to reconcile the "funky" bucolic qualities of this house with the expressed intent of the architect to manifest abstract geometric notions and convoluted massing permutations, but a closer look evidences some intricate underpinnings to the intellectual intentions. The entry door, set to face the adjacent airfield, is axially located to the wood stove at the opposite side of the house, and the angles of two splayed dropped beams are set to coincide with the point of entry. A

4

Figure 3 North elevation. The beveling westerly wall spawns a shed that accommodates both a wood stove and outdoor access to the basement. Resonantly beveling the porch (left) continues the subordinate shed roof extensions that extend from the first floor of the house while windowscaping is keyed to the dormer or roof centerlines or is randomly applied. Note the use of knotty trim and siding as part of the cost-containment strategy of this house.

Figure 4 Entry, south. A simple shed roof form centers on the dominant roof peak, a peak that either spawns or collects the permutational angling roofs set to both sides of the home.

Figure 5 West elevation. The one antireferential element of the home is the three-dimensional result of the consistent dominant gable roof form and skewed plan perimeter interacting with each other. This is one façade that has no centered elements and is unabashed in its random meanderings.

5

Figure 6 *View from a screen porch. The rolling landscape cascades away from the primary view-embracing aspect of the house—the beveling screen porch.*

6

secondary threshold is set between the entry steps and the first-floor half-bath, and a tertiary threshold is present at the two columns that accept the ends of the splayed beams mentioned earlier. These columns frame a second two-step drop into the living area, a living area whose basic shape is keyed to the golden-mean proportions mentioned earlier.

This living area has one corner angularly "cranked" at an angle that's reflected by the octagonalized porch at the other end of the living space. The stair is set to an exterior corner and ascends to a second-floor corridor that is subtly splayed to mitigate the sense of constriction implicit in a tight floor plan. From the master bedroom there is a full view of the airfield, and two relatively large additional bedrooms are oriented in a pinwheel fashion.

Appendages are set about the perimeter of this house, either attenuating or generating roof geometries or simply serving as subordinate counterpoints to the overall massing. The front entry porch is in the form of a traditional lean-to centered upon the front door, which in turn has the master bedroom window array centered upon it, which in turn centers on the major roof ridge. The octagonal screened porch mentioned earlier addresses the water view. The porch's roof form is a simple chamfered extension of the dominant roof plane set by the central ridge mentioned earlier. Contrasting this extended roof plane is what appears to be an incised dormer slicing into the backside of this overall roof plane. A careful bend in the roof is set at the intersection between the horizontal eave line of this semidormer into the large-scale roof plane noted earlier; this bend allows for headroom on the first floor. On the side opposite the entry, a subordinate lean-to roof form accepts the wood stove flue pipe while at the same time affording a covered access to the basement and allowing the angled roof plane to extend its presence to the first floor. On the last façade the dominant roof plane of the master bedroom/entry façade simply extends to form a triangular roof whose shape is determined by the "cranked" end of the master bedroom. The low point of this triangulated roof is well below head height and is set to the backside of the second-floor bathroom's tub and shower array location where head height is not needed.

If these formal manipulations were based solely on some abstract idea of volumetric play or aesthetic preconception, the result would be an affected building whose arbitrary basis for design would stand in unhappy contrast to the nuts-and-bolts character of the construction and finishing. But it is the clarity afforded by Robert Bast's structural engineering background that allows his abstracted conceptions of space and form to be manifest with a minimum dose of affectation and a maximum dose of common sense.

It is a happy coincidence that the combination of high-art sensibilities and technological insight that form the core of Bast's design outlook are steeped in the presence of a rural constructivist aesthetic. The implicit ascetic qualities of low-end construction have a remarkable resonance with Bast's abstract outlook, given its lack of stylistic pretense.

Just as early twentieth century Modernists sought to defrock the high priests of historicist aesthetics, it can be said that Bast has endeavored to declare that the emperors of Post-Modernism have no clothes. There is always an evident awkwardness involved when those mimicking commonsense building forms and details utilize those details in ways that are ultimately disingenuous, affected, stilted, and decorative rather than evidentiary of an innate understanding of their latent intentions and possibilities.

The Bloomhardt house can be appreciated on a variety of levels. It is as familiar as any clunkily evolving roadside farmhouse. When focused upon with a clear head and thoughtful eye, the building begins to become animistic. In another light it has a stark haunting presence. All of this at $47 a square foot!

Temple to a Great View

An amazing site is controlled by a simple home.

S T A T S

PROJECT NAME AND LOCATION:
*House in Rutherford,
California*

ARCHITECT:
Anderson/Schwartz, Architects

COMPLETION DATE:
1987

TOTAL HEATED SQUARE FEET:
1,500

PERCEIVED SQUARE FOOTAGE:
2,049

CIRCULATION-TO-TOTAL-AREA RATIO:
11 percent

BEDROOM-SPACE-TO-TOTAL-AREA RATIO:
47 percent

GROSS COST:
$350,000

COST PER SQUARE FOOT:
$230

DURATION OF DESIGN PROCESS:
One year

DURATION OF CONSTRUCTION:
Two and a half years

Photos © Michael Moran.
Drawings by the architects.

THIS is a story about families, and working within a master plan. It is also a story about how an architect kept both in perspective while building something that is a gift to the world.

Ross Anderson is a New York City architect who had had a solid 15 years of professional experience prior to his being called upon by his parents to help them build a family compound in the hills of Napa, California. His parents had seen three children grow up and leave the nest. They knew that the only way that they could regularly see their children and grandchildren would be to create a siren song of amenity and accommodation. Fortunately, they had a son with proven abilities as an architect who, in turn, has proven himself in this house to have a keen sense of perspective when it comes to getting the best "bang for the buck" given the inherent budgetary limitations in designing both a second home and a home built on a difficult site.

Many of the homes that are focused upon in this book are second homes, that is, homes that need not have the functional versatility of a primary residence. However, all the homes in this book, whether they are occupied full or part time, hopefully evidence the sort of value judgments that can be applied to any home on a tight budget or they have idiosyncratic design requirements or they are built on a difficult site situation. This project had all of these relatively problematic aspects, and the seeming simplicity of the ultimate design product belies the extraordinary level of skill and thoughtfulness applied to overcome these problems.

In the Andersons' quest to create a beacon for family coalescence, they found a remarkable 20-acre site on a hilltop overlooking the sweeping panoramic beauty of the Napa Valley. The inherent bucolic poetry of this situation effectively masked the problematic aspects of building something that could be sited to receive the views. First, access by car was possible only at the base of the steeply sloping hillside that provided the beautiful view. Second, because California is a land of earthquakes, mud slides, and brush fires, both the foundation and the wall structure of this home needed to meet the seismic and flammability criteria ever present in California construction. For example, the exposed surfaces (especially the terne metal roof) have a capacity to shunt wind-driven incendiary sparks, which could prevent the house from "going up in flames." Whether by code or common sense, any home design in this context needed to respond to these relatively drastic design criteria.

Last, this was not a home simply for this or the next generation; this is

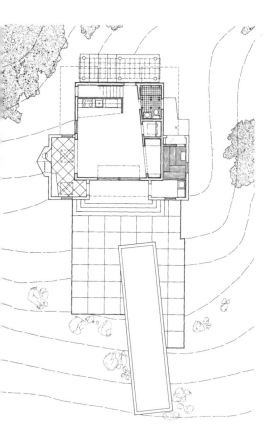

GROUND LEVEL PLAN

SECOND LEVEL PLAN

THIRD LEVEL PLAN

1

2

Figure 1 Floor plans. A simple rectilinear shape has two "book end" single-story extensions: to the left an inglenook-backside entry, and to the right two spaces that are only accessible from the outside—a bar addressing the pool and a sauna addressing the back. The central house form allows for a bathroom on the first floor, at the upper-right-hand corner, with storage space and reading nook-daybed all combined behind a perspectively canted wall with the simplest of strip kitchens combined with the entry stair set to the other side of the entry. The entry is centered upon one of the windows forming the large-scale fenestration addressing the view. The shady north-facing entryway is set below the further sunscreen of a trellis. Note that the underside of the stair is used for storage. A canted lap pool juts into the landscape and is received by the house via a large-scale patio that addresses the elevated central slot formed by the three plan elements. On the second level a simple half-bath is set in the same slot as the stairway for the project, and two identically sized bedrooms have fixed beds addressing the view (their elevated status allows for a section manipulation over the main window addressing the view downstairs). The twin additions afford an inaccessible roof with skylights in it to the left and a terrace addressing the right-hand bedroom. The top level is simply an open loft to accept overflow sleeping accommodation. Note that this loft is open to the stairway set at the second floor, thus allowing the north-facing window a dimension not possible before the floor continued to the perimeter wall.

Figure 2 The view-addressing façade. Semidetached, single-story masonry bookends and a semifloatational roofscape create a soft central portion of the building mass designed to receive views and focus attention. The canted pool can be seen in the foreground, providing a dynamic subordinate landscape element, kinetically arrayed and gathered in by the central void of the home. Note the variety of materials used, from concrete block to vertical siding to standing seam roofing.

3

a project that will, it is hoped, span many generations. Thus any home built would have to have the capacity to expand. Rather than design a half-loaf scheme that needed subsequent revisions or additions to become whole, Ross Anderson decided to stake out the first part of a large compound with what would ultimately become an outbuilding. This approach brought the project a new level of control and regulation. In the applicable zoning laws, buildings deemed to be guest cottages needed to have their total square footage limited to 1,500 square feet. It is remarkable that such an evocative and inherently positive building resulted from these limitations. Indeed, this house, as much as or even more than any other project in this book, dispels the common conception of a small house as cute or simply diminished in its possible aesthetic or functional effectiveness.

To do anything but worship such a spectacular view would be a mistake, and in creating this 1,500-square-foot, three-bedroom home, Anderson did his best both to recognize the view from within (virtually having all spaces look out to the extraordinary prospect) and to have the house self-consciously present itself as a focal point in the landscape for others to view. Symmetry is employed for the hillside façade, a symmetry effected by simple massing moves rather than subtle trim or material changes, responding to the extraordinary distance from which this building can be seen. The other three façades of the house are kept simple and subordinate to the double-hipped pyramidal roof that vertically caps and focuses the entire building.

Given the rough terrain, site development was quite difficult, and the boldest gesture of site development was the extension of a lap pool projecting from the focal point of the façade—a linear element dynamically skewed from the central mass, thus creating a sense of a site-related feature tethered in by a nobly centered artificial

4

5

Figure 3 *The view as seen from inside. A seating nook-daybed (left) creates an intimate space in the context of an out-scaled window, a window whose overall shape manifests itself by the insinuation of a raised platform bed, allowing the ceiling to rise at the window. The extraordinary view of the valley below can be well appreciated in this photograph.*

Figure 4 *Section. A three-story construction has its entry (right) set to address the views through the main living area of the house with the view framed by a window whose height is aggrandized via the use of a second-floor built-in bed platform, which facilitates the local elevation of the ceiling plane. The middle layer of the house is given over to two bedrooms with the upper open loft area designated for overflow sleeping. Special relief was provided to this space by the use of two subordinate dormers. The building is set on the downside of a slope with the lap pool set below the main floor level, both accommodating the natural contours and mitigating the built-up terrace-pool's imposition on the bottom edge of the view.*

Figure 5 *Lap pool. Jutting into a seemingly infinite landscape, this landscape element is both graphic and formal: graphic in the considered application of the patio grid set to be violated by the linear imposition of the lap pool and massive given the stripped and/or bared concrete shapes and the three-dimensionalization of the aforementioned grid to return to the slightly lowered level of the concrete pool.*

object. This starkly simple pool becomes the counterpoint to the carefully articulated, multimaterial mass of the house.

Materials play a crucial role in this project in two ways. First, a wide variety were used—from concrete block to painted plywood to terne metal as well as exposed concrete, board-and-batten eaves, and simple trim. Second, the materials used were coordinated by being unabashedly stock store-bought products celebrating innovative application rather than custom craftsmanship. This approach of artfully using prosaic materials can also be seen in the large-scale detailing of the home's interior, where clear-finished plywood and unfinished concrete block interweave with galvanized sheet-metal details and precast, tinted-concrete elements to create a sense of carefully designed spaces derived from relatively stark materials.

It is in the inventive but unapologetic use of the quasi-industrial materials that the home gains a wonderful sense of domesticity. A good example is the clever use of a real firebox—one made of concrete and firebrick. Its inherently cheap components allow the use of a large Rumsford fireplace configuration (an eighteenth-century design employing a very shallow firebox with a very broad opening to facilitate the ability of a fireplace to radiantly heat a house). This use of materials is in contrast to the even less expensive prefabricated sheet-metal fireboxes that often have a relatively small opening and provide heat via convection (employing appliancelike grilles on the front of the firebox). This would seem to be an exchange of money for amenity (as masonry fireplaces are always more expensive than their prefabricated counterparts), except that Anderson has bartered a prefabricated metal flue (versus masonry) to both diminish cost and provide a light counterpoint to the home's overall heavily centered and solid exterior.

This cleverness of detailing can also be seen in the accommodation of the outsized central window, the focal void in a façade set amid four simple massing elements to quietly dominate the landscape from without and embrace the view from within. Flanked by two concrete block boxy bookends and capped by the aforementioned pyramidal roof with attenuated eaves, the central plywood "shaft" of the home has a relatively huge opening that accepts the similarly huge presence of the landscape into the home's interior. When designing small homes, large-scale window openings have implicit problems given the fact that economy and efficiency often mean that floor levels are left continuous, thus preempting the double-high space to accommodate large-scale windows.

Additionally, this particular home was subjected to a 35-foot-height limitation and needed to fit three bedrooms (one of them having the capacity for several occupants) within that code-compliant envelope. Given the desire for density of accommodation and the need to respect the 1,500-square-foot limit on space, one might suspect that accommodating a window of this size would be highly problematic. However, Anderson utilized raised bed platforms in the two second-floor bedrooms not only to gain a better view for those who are bedbound but to provide a miniclerestory space, allowing this focal window to fully flesh out its desirable size.

The interior organization of the home is deceptively simple, with the first floor given over to public spaces—one backside corner to a kitchen-stair combination, the other to bathrooms on both floors. The flanking concrete block bookends mentioned earlier accommodate an inglenook on one side and a sauna and laundry on the other. Additionally, the line of the bathroom core, mentioned earlier, extends on the first floor to form storage and part-time daybed for overflow sleeping. It can be said that virtually all the spaces worship the view and are meant to enhance a sybaritic sensibility of rest and relaxation and a simple accommodation of human get-togethers.

Figure 6 (opposite) Inglenook. Concrete block and simple precast concrete elements contribute to the design integrity in the careful alignment of the mortar joints and the careful application of steel appointments and the thoughtful insinuation of openings with one window being deeply recessed (right) while its counterpart is set tight to the inside face of the wall (left). A deep-welled skylight allows top-lighting to preempt any sense of "bunker." This inglenook also serves as the main transition between the patio and pool and the main living area.

The laundry is accessible only from the outside, perfect for use as a postswim changing area. Similarly, the sauna and outdoor shower have indirect access to the interior of the house—again, perfectly acceptable for a fair-weather home. The grotto cum inglenook mentioned earlier is set into one of the tight concrete block bookends and is overtly cast as an incidental element rather than a focal point in the plan. The kitchen is of a simple strip configuration without a "real" refrigerator—again, perfect for barbecue and part-time occupancy. The second floor has two bedrooms nestled to the view and a backside bath. The third floor is an open loft for overflow sleeping accommodations.

A rear trellis affords a shady area for internal contemplation or reading, worlds away from the extraordinary views and south light of the proudly projecting, valley-oriented side of the house. Additionally, there is no full basement—just a crawl space—nor is there an attic as there is no need for accommodation of storage in a building that is to be occupied only part-time by a changing population.

All in all this is an extraordinary combination of clearheadedness and intricate interweaving of materials and shapes. In a rolling sea of foliage, this house provides an anchor to windward for a typically scattered American family. When the winds of career and personal predilection have cast family members out into the world, this anchor will tether the family back to a situation that has more than the simple rewards of home and hearth but affords the exhilaration of a building that celebrates the landscape it sits in and has overcome the now-unseen obstacles in the path of its realization.

Figure 7 (opposite) Loft. With insulation set atop the sheathing exposed in these pictures, an extraordinarily simple double-hipped roof with flanking gable-faced dormers is given structural zest via the connection of the dormers' ridge plates as collar ties. A low knee wall height is mitigated by the aforementioned dormers. Note the use of generic wire mesh as a barrier to the open stairwell (lower right).

Setting Sail

Nautical aggrandizement energizes a tiny house.

SITES set on salt water are often tiny, as is this 42-foot-wide by 98-foot-long lot in Seaside, Florida, which is one of the most aesthetically regulated communities in the United States. This community, as designed by Andres Duany and Elizabeth Plater-Zyberk, lays out tiny lots in a tight street configuration with regulations governing the building materials and the geometric possibilities that can be employed. This is also a town of small houses designed by architects from all over the country. Among the award-winning wee houses, this three-bedroom 1,540-square-foot house stands out like a flagship in a large fleet of tiny boats.

This home was originally built as a spec project and therefore had the further imposition of a profit motive in its conceptualization. The firm of Cooper Johnson Smith Architects has designed dozens of homes in this coastal community and has never let the rigors of the aesthetically determinate zoning code nor the possibly problematic aspects of for-profit building limit their outlook.

What makes any home affordable, whether built for profit or not, is an essential knowledge of how construction can be executed to maximize impact and minimize cost. In this particular case the zoning code demanded that an 8-foot reduction from the maximum allowable building width be obtained at the second floor of any project, thus creating an inherent upper-level porch or patio. This recessive second story determined the fundamental structural bearing lines for the house. Cooper Johnson Smith wrapped this central home with a fairly fluffy plinth below, capped it by an aggrandized eave and finally punctuated it at its apex by a lyric widow's walk. This layered approach could have been cacophonous had there not been a nautically referential aesthetic imperative to bind all the building's elements into a singular mind-set. A complementary (and code-compliant) palette of materials was consistently used and reinvented throughout the entire project. Additionally, Cooper Johnson Smith used innovative planning to allow for subtle spatial expansion to occur where needed while keeping the lean ship-shape ambience intact. Three bedrooms and three baths plus a laundry on the first floor can widen out within the first-floor plinth. This base of space is crowned by a completely open living-dining space. Set as an interior pavilion, an isolated freestanding kitchen-stair core is scaled to subdivide an out-scaled space while allowing its maximum impact to remain in force.

In effect, this is a horizontally and vertically layered composition providing a main path of circulation to bypass the first-floor bedrooms and aspire directly to the open second floor. There is a third level set over

Figure 1 *Entry/front. A layer cake of line, space, and material, this nautical composition provides multiple formal readings. The essential enclosure relates to the central (and simple) gable-roofed mass, a mass that has its roofscape attenuated by an extraordinarily extended knee brace eave line. A secondary perimeter of construction both forms the ceiling for a wraparound veranda on the first level and supports the second-floor balcony that surrounds the central building mass. Note how the entry door (with its overtly nautical window) is set within a subordinately roofed vestibule space. The apex of this light-hearted construction is celebrated via flags and the overtly nautical steel pipe–derived cupola. All the visual activity is carefully metered by the use of consistent vertical and horizontal lines and has simple commonsense structural logic—not unlike the naval architecture it emulates.*

Figure 2 *Floor plans. Ground floor plan (left) evidences two points of entry. To the lower left is the front access, four steps up to a front porch which in turn leads to an open stairway, which addresses the second-floor living areas. Around the corner to the right is the "private" entryway, set to a hallway that links three bedrooms and a back stair. Note that the front bedroom and one of the rear bedrooms have their own baths, and the third bedroom has access to a bath that is potentially shared by those coming in from the beach. The laundry is set to this hallway as well. All three bedrooms have corner exposure and ample closet space for a second home. Note that there is a privately accessed rear porch with a spiral stair allowing access to the upper floor and direct access to a shower from the beach. The second-floor plan presents all four sides of its space to the views presented by its lofty presence via an open porch with most of its area covered by the extraordinarily extended eaves set about its perimeter. The actual front door of the house is set in an alcove to the left with the living area set to one side of the open space and the dining area set to a radial bay at the backside. Amid this large open space is a kitchen and stair ensemble with one stair going up to a loft and its counterpart descending to the bedroom floor below. The loft plan shows the space that is set above the kitchen, which in turns allows a ladder stair to ascend to the rooftop loft-cupola.*

2

1

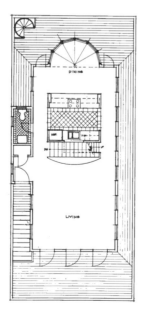

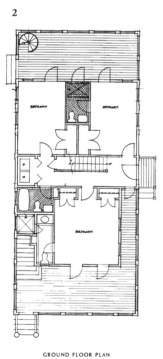

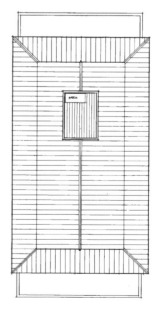

GROUND FLOOR PLAN   SECOND FLOOR PLAN   LOFT PLAN   ROOF PLAN

3

Figure 3 *Backside. The central building mass, with its celebrationally attenuated eave form and wraparound deck-balcony skirt, has a placid bow window slipped between its horizontal layering to accommodate the dining room. Proudly perched upon the roof is the widow's walk/cupola. Unapologetically jaunty flags further express the building's naval influences.*

Figure 4 *Living room/loft. An out-scaled space evidences a great deal of layering and structural simplicity. Beyond the built-ins is the open stair which ascends to the bedrooms. Yet another nautical element—a ladder stair—ascends to the central perch of the loft, which in turn has a ladder stair ascending to the cupola above. Note the stiffening ties, upper left and upper right, which stabilize the long walls of this room and the flattened central portion of the ceiling-scape which in turn facilitates the use of collar ties, preempting the need for visually interruptive beaming or truss work. The central void in this interior wall allows for an axial orientation through the kitchen and onto the dining area. Note how inside and outside materials mesh and the use of hardwood flooring throughout the dining area.*

the interior pavilion: a loft for overflow bedroom space set to overlook the double-height living area. Access to the rooftop/cupola/widow's walk/pavilion is available from this loft. The secondary means of access to the two main public floors is an interior stair set to a first-floor central corridor, which in turn can be accessed by those "in the know" from an unseen door set around the corner from the grand and public stairway leading to the ascendent living room.

As with most all waterfront projects, this design maximizes views in all directions, and because it is in a southerly clime, covered porches provide a shaded vantage to accept these views. These porches are accessed from multiple points within the house. Because of their open planning, they serve as a tertiary level of circulation, and in fact, a spiral staircase is used to connect the first and second levels of these verandas as well. Given the absolute code-compliant definition of the building's perimeter and vertical volume, the architects have sought to provide an extraordinarily playful evolution of the given materials and dimensions. In its salute to nautical architecture, the architects avoid a Disneyesque caricaturization by the careful simplification of certain details (the plinth) and sophisticated aggrandizement of others (heavily expressive knee braces around the extended roof eave over the second-floor terrace). Rigorous planning has also allowed for bathrooms and the kitchen to mimic the "heads" and "galleys" of their seagoing counterparts, thus freeing common and public spaces to appreciate the views that are present from virtually every angle that the home addresses.

A classic combination of materials is used on the interiors, with wide-board tongue and groove paneling for all surfaces and the celebrational use of a light pastel color palette. It should be noted that there are ample shading devices in addition to the eave overhangs utilized throughout and that all windows are operable with many set at a high clerestory level to allow natural ventilation and shading to compensate for the possible hot summer months of Florida weather.

Although flags, cupolas, and a jaunty countenance are an overt inference of a naval bias, it is the subtle planning and commonsense structuring of this project that allow it to aspire beyond its theatrical presence. It is often all too easy for architects of small houses to pick an image and build a house to contour to it, in this case a boat. To make any image transcend its origins, there has to be a knowledgeable sense of a home's true size and the possibility for architecture to be inventive via contrast. This home truly goes beyond the possible limitations of its code name "Land Yacht."

Figure 5 (opposite) Dining room. A faceted window array provides ample visual connection to a fairly limitless view. Note that the wall of the second-floor porch prevents unwanted visual intrusion of the second floor from those who might come close to the home's perimeter.

Choreographed Coincidence

A Maine retreat affords many lessons in subtle expression.

Young architects are often tempted to vent their collected aesthetic bile when given the opportunity to design a home. Fortunately, there are those who eschew the temptation and instead provide the sort of clever insight and inspired application of simple truths that can make a small house an ongoing delight.

This particular project had a host of limiting factors. Whatever was to be built had to avoid the view-ways across the site from a neighboring church. It was a coastal site, and therefore any new construction needed to be set at the appropriate distance from the floodplain. Additionally, there was an existing home set directly at the water's edge, and this house had to in some way relate to it. Last, groves of trees were flecked across the landscape, and it was desirable to weave the house into that context without interrupting it. The overarching aesthetic mind-set reflected in this home was its integration with the antique fishing village that it views and that views it. Neither the owners nor the architects had a desire to reinvent this little world or get shock value in a dissonant display of self-perceived genius. Instead, what was created by two young architects, the brother and sister team of Garrett and Martha Finney, was a home remarkable for its interwoven progression and subtly expressive massing and detail.

S T A T S

PROJECT NAME AND LOCATION:
*An Island House,
Penobscot Bay, Maine*

ARCHITECT:
Garrett Finney and Martha Finney

COMPLETION DATE:
1992

TOTAL HEATED SQUARE FEET:
1,700 (unheated)

PERCEIVED SQUARE FOOTAGE:
1,983

CIRCULATION-TO-TOTAL-AREA RATIO:
11 percent

BEDROOM-SPACE-TO-TOTAL-AREA RATIO:
28 percent

GROSS COST:
NA

COST PER SQUARE FOOT:
NA

DURATION OF DESIGN PROCESS:
Six months

DURATION OF CONSTRUCTION:
Ten months

Photos © Catherine Bogart.
Drawings by the architects.

The most successful projects in this book evidence an architect's capability to simultaneously embrace a site's inherent sensibilities and a client's idiosyncratic outlook. This project seamlessly slips into the site, and the house reflects a melding of the client's desire for fit and the architects' desire to evidence ingenuity in a way that elicits delight from a closer look rather than surprise (or terror).

This is a three-bedroom, two-bath, 1,700-square-foot home. Rather than be cowed by the client's desire to be stealthy and subtle, these young architects saw the possibilities present in the neighboring village's traditional building elements—open-eave detailing, clapboard siding, standard roof pitches (12-in-12, 8-in-12, 6-in-12), generic window types (mostly double hung)—and "tweaked" all of these givens into a quietly progressive array of forms. This house maintains its sense of itself while affording an enormous amount of quiet creativity within the context of a familiar form and time-proven materials.

This home is a good example that the use of the familiar need not be an architectural "sellout." Similarly, it also disproves the myth that young architects are incapable of doing anything that is not wildly impractical and expensive or, conversely, kowtowed and xerographic in its origin. In short, there is a deftness of hand and clarity of insight that belies the age and experience of these young

1

Figure 1 *East, staggered façade. The various building components evidence themselves from main stoic mass (right) to intermediate gasket to subordinate gable roof onto the tail-end spaces of the back door and study at the far left. Trim is manipulated to be normative at the main band and to become progressively more minimal as the mass articulates into subordination to the left. Note the inexpensive latticework that obscures the simple pier foundation.*

Figure 2 *Floor plans. Five distinct bays of construction can be seen, with four of them registering to the aligned right-hand wall, an alignment that allows the formal entry deck (right) to be a proud projection. The minor "back" door can be seen at the upper-left-hand corner. Spaces progress from the top down with the most private (a study) to the back door and bath through the kitchen onto the stairwell and finally to the living and dining room at the bottom. On the second floor, a master bedroom stakes out the dominant corner (lower left) with a secondary bedroom (lower right) and a sitting room/guest bedroom at the top. The central bathroom is set above the kitchen, providing an efficient plumbing layout. Note how each space with the exception of the bathroom has at least one exposed (and windowed) corner.*

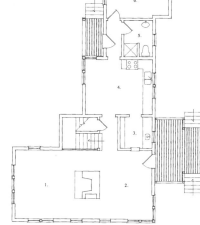
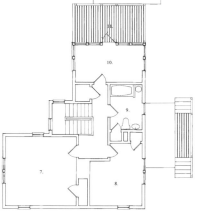

2

Figure 3 Aligned façade, west, formal entry. A variety of roof forms and windowscapes register to a common façade. Windows occasionally orient to corner positions (left and right) and center on roof forms or roof breaks (upper left, lower right). The entry porch is accessed on both sides by stairs, and this bilateral access is indicated by the light cantilever at both sides of the roof. Note the widened rafter spacing at this small span roof versus the tighter spacing of the longer span of second-story roofs above.

Figure 4 Site plan. An existing home (lower left) is set on the water. The new construction (upper right) is set to the existing trees and is oriented to avoid impeding the view of neighbors (to the upper right). The diagonal orientation of the house allows for water views from two sides.

3

designers and most assuredly evidences the role good architects can play in the creation of homes that are delightful rather than benign.

The Finneys made some simple moves that evidence a clear and present inventive mind-set. Whereas most of the homes in the United States gain complexity by an additive process, as over time a variety of additions simply bud forth from the "parent building," this is a home that was all built at one time but has had the sense of quirky and expressive addenda stepping out from a "starter" home. Essentially, this is a five-part house with the main building being set with its long dimension facing the water view. The next layer is a pantry-stair followed by a kitchen followed by bath-rear entry followed by a computer room at the caboose of this little architectural freight train. Elaborating upon all of these subordinate forms are two entry decks. A single, built-all-at-once home thus replicates the logic of 100 years of building evolution where a small outpost of civilization (often a summer cottage) had an ell added to it for a summer kitchen and progressed to a further extension of the ell to allow for plumbing, and followed up with additive porches to ease the joints and provide access. Having said this, it might be that a disingenuous antiquity could have crept into this design. Nothing could be further from the truth.

SITE PLAN

4

There are continuous clues of crisp reinvention present at virtually every corner of the house involving the combination of windows with eave lines, the creation of relatively stark corner window glazing, and the ability for eaves to vary in size while maintaining identical detailing. Siding similarly has its spacing altered while maintaining identical material type and finish. But the single most recombinant aspect of the entire project is the long and unabashed axial relationship between all five spaces previously mentioned. This axial relationship allows for spatial definition in the kitchen, subdividing cooking from eat-in space. This axis also locates the central fireplace,

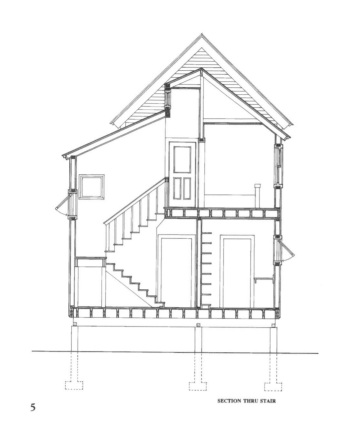

5

SECTION THRU STAIR

6

7

Figure 5 *Section. Taken at the stair, this view allows the apprehension of the multiple eave and roof "tweakings" from the considered misalignment of the stairwell windows (left) to the manipulation of the roof angles from shallowest over the stair to a middling angle above the bathroom (upper right) to a traditional 12-in-12 peak beyond. There are a multitude of ceiling heights and types present as well, from a clerestory window at the second-floor hallway to relatively tight height at the second-story bath to a simple angled shed underside over the stair to thoroughly normal height over the pantry (lower right). This section also evidences the inexpensive foundation utilizing simple piers bearing on consistently aligned beaming.*

Figure 6 *Stairway, axis. Trim components are manipulated to create out-scaled balusters and handrails (left) and relatively passive trim in other areas.*

Figure 7 *Entry prospect. The simple shed roof with cantilevered ends off of two simple posts provides a quiet layered transition between most exposed (left) to covered (right) and finally transitions into the building envelope. Note the subtle differences in the exposed rafter tails to the upper right.*

8

Figure 8 Details. *As seen on the west façade, trim elements, window placement, and other details conspire to quietly animate what at first blush may be seen as a predictable construction. Note the consistent dimension of wrapping trim and the differing depth of exposed rafters. Note also the ornamental gable rafters seen at the far left. Note the subtle difference between the tighter clapboard spacing for the smaller building component to the left than that of the main house mass to the right. Note also the considered attachment of the center window to the outsized concave corner trim and the equally considered misalignment of windows left and right. Finally, note the only overtly ornamental aspect to the home's interior and exterior, the chimney, which has an intriguing combination of corbelling in a lightly untraditional fashion.*

Figure 9 Firebox. *The one element in the home that is overtly irreverent, utilizing standard brick and custom stone, this central spatial divider has its mass aggrandized laterally and its flue minimized vertically to allow maximum connection between living and dining spaces. The right-hand stone support of the fireplace arch has its side canted and its height reduced just enough to announce its dissonance from its counterpart to the left. Note the baseboard trim treatment.*

9

thus allowing the formal dining area to be separate from the living area. As with all good axial schemes, there is a definitive cross axis where the overtly public front door is set to one corner of the main living space and helps orient the entrant to dining, living, and stair spaces.

The home's massing is just as interweaving and lightly expressive as its planning. In creating a dominant water-facing mass, the Finneys have then set the rest of the house's progressive massing to play off of its stoic simplicity, involving a counterposing roof set over a summer porch, and effectively acknowledged the intervening stair and second-floor bathroom space with a lower pitched roof. In aligning the water-facing sides of this home to form two unbroken flat planes, they've allowed the backside to be a conscientiously soft "underbelly" of progressively developed perimeter. In short, there are a wide variety of roof forms here, all relating to the functional distinction within them.

The leavening of the semitraditional rulebook, as seen on the exterior, has a greater latitude for expression on the interior. Virtually every trim condition has been carefully considered—most delightfully where the normally butted or mitered corners of baseboard trim have a vertically expressive corner piece creating a proud corner where often a subordinate linear transition occurs. Similarly, in the staircase the most normative of handrails become generative of an out-scaled vertical screen of larger balusters that extend from stair stringer to ceiling underside. These out-scaled balusters are then "gripped" by traditional ceiling trim which is normally set between ceiling and wall. Similarly, in and around all windows larger-scale lintels of header trim quietly reach over and around and serve as connective tissue between windows that most normally would have been set up against each other in an unconsidered carpenterly construction. Most intriguing of all these elements is the relatively exuberant hearth that uses granite appointments in an oddly woodworkish manner. Light inflections of the granite detailing help engender a sense of the ever-present designers' hand.

Quietly unrelenting innovation can take the simplest of structural systems (light-frame wood construction set on a very standard concrete foundation) and create something that is memorable for its subtleties rather than for its grand reinventions. Noble failures due to creative excess are still failures—gentle successes, by clever and subtle invention, are still successes. The simple lesson to be learned in this case is that success is always better than failure.

The First House

Compositional balance on a common axis.

S T A T S

PROJECT NAME AND LOCATION:
Reed House, Everett, Washington State

ARCHITECT:
*Robert B. Reed of Bayliss Brand
Wagner Architects*

COMPLETION DATE:
1993

TOTAL HEATED SQUARE FEET:
1,741

PERCEIVED SQUARE FOOTAGE:
2,362

CIRCULATION-TO-TOTAL-AREA RATIO:
8 percent

BEDROOM-SPACE-TO-TOTAL-AREA RATIO:
17 percent

GROSS COST:
$135,000

COST PER SQUARE FOOT:
$77.50

DURATION OF DESIGN PROCESS:
Six weeks

DURATION OF CONSTRUCTION:
Eight months

Photos in Figs. 1 and 7 © Michael Ian Shopenn
and in Figs. 4 and 6 © Robert Reed.
Drawings by the architects.

WHEN Robert Reed designed this home, he was an intern architect. The modifier *intern* before the word *architect* defines those who have not had a chance to take the licensing exam but have in fact graduated from school and are hard at work in an apprenticeship position. Robert Reed works for the architectural office of Bayliss-Brand-Wagner in Bellevue, Washington, and in this early stage in his career he found a vehicle for creative expression in the design of his own home. He and his wife Rhonda are typical of late twentieth century professional American couples, working in their respective careers to get to the point where they can have the time, resources, and mind-set to start having children.

Building homes at this time in the century is just not as simple as it once was. The psychosocial downsizing of the American Dream mandates a "reality check" for our homes, and we might do well to look back to the roots of our domestic accommodations. The relatively tiny size of classic American housing prototypes (the bungalow, row house, or Cape) was the norm until after World War II.

Despite the values of retrospection, no reduction in house size can overcome the realities of late twentieth century building. Beyond the increased cost of using ever more precious wood-based building materials,

the reduction in land available to build upon around urban centers has imposed a concomitant reactionary governmental overview of site development that was unprecedented prior to this generation of housing consumers. On this particular site the required setbacks from a modest stream along one corner of the project rendered more than 50 percent of the entire site area "off limits" for the imposition of any building's footprint. Additionally, although the vast majority of height limitations in this area were set at between 30 or 35 feet, this particular zone called for a 28-foot-height limit, thus reducing the vertical dimension that could be obtained. Other than these impositions, this is a relatively benign site involving a slight grade and a more or less regular, four-sided lot configuration.

Beyond governmental and geographical limitations there are new financing regulations that need to be dealt with as well. Because this was their first home, Rhonda and Robert Reed had to finance the purchase of the lot itself, and to obtain this financing, they had to convince a bank that what they were proposing had adequate intrinsic value to justify the risk the bank would be taking in underwriting their efforts. Given the fact that Robert Reed is an intern architect, this meant that nights and weekends had to be devoted to this

1

AIN FLOOR PLAN

PER FLOOR PLAN

Figure 1 *Front elevation, entry. A simple building form gains scale and presence through the coordinated use of trim and materials. A first-floor plinth of painted plywood sets the window sill line while intermediate banding is set to the second-floor window sill above. Dormers have their gable forms highlighted by trim and their centerlines reinforced by careful gutter downspout location. The simple "cut-in" entry recess will ultimately have a trellis set before it, thus giving a local positive focal point to counter the conspired grandiosity of the chimney flue shroud above. The master bedroom/living room wing is recessive while a voided corner to the right helps provide a sense of formal animation. Note the careful use of window mullions to create subordinate patterning that lends a richness to the façade and the considered local asymmetries set to contrast the symmetries dictated by dormer locations.*

Figure 2 *Floor plans. The lower level is a study in cross-axial organization and "dense-packing" of the serving areas of the house (bathroom, stairs, kitchen, fixed dining). A cross axis is created at entry between the front door and a window that addresses the stairway, while an unencumbered through house axis is presented between the door access to the covered porch to the right down to the window array in the living room (left). Kitchen, stairs, mechanical equipment, laundry, bathroom, built-in storage, and seating all gravitate to the backside (top) of the house. Given the fact that there is no basement for this construction, the hot water heater and the forced air furnace sit below the stairway and are accessed only by the removal of a fixed panel. A stackable washer and dryer are set into the powder room. Most of the backside of this plan is raised one step up to allow for easy mechanical access and to provide a light spatial distinction between the public areas and the serving spaces. Smaller scale elaborations of space can be seen at the front wall as well where a built-in window seat/fireplace creates an inglenook and a "deep wall"/in/out front wall provides opportunities for built-in storage and closets as well as a recess for the front door. Note the front door has a considered asymmetry to the house in general and to its local recess. On the second floor the central axis is repeated with two suites being created: To the left is a prototypic master bedroom suite with fully vaulting ceiling over the subordinate wing, and to the right two bedrooms feed onto a playroom and have common access to a bath with each space being individually cathedralized and with each bedroom having a dormer-window seat combo. The central slot of circulation has a study set opposite the stairwell, facilitating maximum buffering between sleeping spaces. Note that neither bathroom has a window but is a vaulted space utilizing skylights for natural illumination and ventilation.*

process, versus a more typical scenario whereby a design is either supplied by someone else working a nine-to-five job or pulled from a stock set of home designs.

Obviously, all of these various pressures were met and overcome by this intrepid young couple. Not only were tough questions answered but latent opportunities were aggressively obtained, and thus some valuable lessons can be learned from the final product.

The vast majority of projects in this book have two essential methods for realizing affordability. The most obvious is the reduction of the overall size of the house from our cultural norms. The second widely used method to obtain affordability is the embrace of existing building technologies. Experimentation on a budget is almost impossible unless the designer, builder, and occupant are the same person. The problem with radical experimentation in the context of small-house design is that there is very little opportunity to overcome the "learning curve" given the fact that 99 percent of all the people in the home construction industry have 99 percent of their experience dealing with the simple light-frame construction techniques that this home so nobly evidences. Rather than reinvent the wheel and dabble in structural experimentation, Robert Reed and many other architects in this book have opted to use what standard light-frame wood construction can offer—extraordinary flexibility and implicit geometric properties that when thoughtfully used convey an explicit domestic countenance.

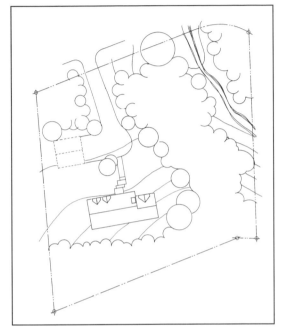

3

In this way this home evidences the most direct path for affordable innovation: the thoughtful application of an in-place, holistic system of construction. If the Reeds didn't need to earn a living, there could have been a devotion of time and effort to actually building their own home, perhaps facilitating low-cost reinvention. But this home gains meaning to the average housing consumer simply because it was constructed by a professional builder for under $80 a square foot.

Given all these now prototypic givens   site limitations, budgetary and time pressures, and the embrace of the standard building technology—this project shows the sort of engaging creativity that affords a multitude of magical moments within the context of a 1,700-square-foot home.

This is not a symmetrical building, but it does have a sense of balance. Balance in this case is evidenced in the considered application of an entry-chimney ensemble that dominates a simple rectilinear building form. There are two flanking formal manipulations: a recessed wing to one side and a void forming a corner and porch to the other. The extended gable shape and its aforementioned manipulations have an implicit axial orientation, following the consistent axis of the ridge line of the dominant form. This axis is evidenced in the interior where it locates spaces addressing the front of the house via an implicit line of circulation down the long direction of the building. This major axis is accessed via the cross axis defined by the entry, chimney, and central stair. Both these axes have their thresholds, pathways, and focal points respected, and there are subaxes present both in the kitchen-dining room ensemble and in the living room. All this spatial openness is structurally accommodated by the use of multiple mini-shear walls present throughout the first floor, efficiently created by the insinuation of plywood set directly to the wall framing and under the sheetrock-finished surface. Functionally, the house is also clearly organized with wet and mechanical spaces orienting to the backside of the house, complemented by the use of built-in storage and the more defined dining areas.

On the second floor the major axis noted earlier is also imposed, with a dose of spatial liberation that can be afforded in almost any light-frame wood construction. Small cathedral ceilings are erected on a room-by-room basis simply by returning an angled ceiling plane on the side of the room that's opposite the exterior wall, using the ceiling plane that mimics the angle of the underside of the roof. The ceiling-scape thus centers the space defined by the floor plan of the room. This house is given even more impact when dormers are incised into the cathedralized ceilings. This vaulting aesthetic is fully fleshed out in the master bedroom suite where the entire roof underside is

Figure 3 *Site plan. A simple site had its house location restricted by the setback from the wetlands and stream (upper right) and has provided for a future garage (left) and has its form set into the terrain.*

Figure 4 *Stair and hall. The 7-foot, 2-inch-high hallway ceiling stands in contrast to the vaulted ceilings used through the second floor, in this case over the stairwell. Note how the stairwell railing pattern is directly keyed to the window mullion-muntin patterns.*

4

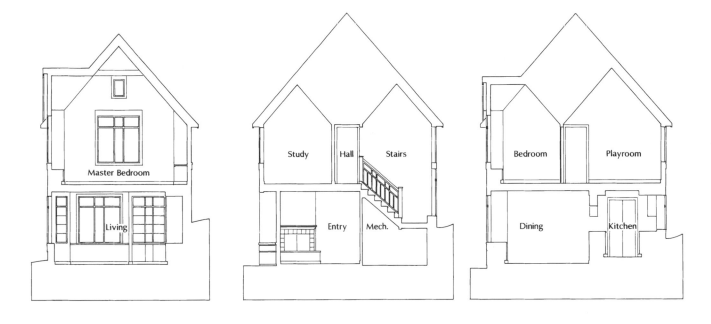

5

celebrated in a "true" cathedralizing effort—an effort that gains a quiet sense of coordinated design when collar ties set in this space to hold the roof together are located to center upon the dormers mentioned earlier. All this vaulting preempts an attic for storage, but built-ins help overcome this limitation.

Some interesting planning elements are also imposed. Two small children's bedrooms both address a large-scale playroom and study area. This suite is fully fleshed out with a bath creating a quartet of rooms separated from the rest of the house by its own doorway. The central stairway has a study-office set opposite it, and the master suite occupies the remaining narrower wing, utilizing bathroom and closet as a separating layer between the bedroom and the rest of the house. The organization of the entire second floor offers parent proximity with privacy via some architectural interventions.

There are also some architectural idiosyncrasies that provide a sense of room-by-room inventiveness. Rhonda Reed has a penchant for storybook referential imagery, fleshed out in this house by the use of an inglenook set upon the entry incorporating seating and millwork. All three bedrooms have a window seat fused with shelving for books and set in the context of the dormers mentioned earlier. Functionally, the relatively small master bedroom closet is complemented by a quartet of built-in shelving units obviating the need for furniture. Bathrooms are windowless, but they have a central skylight and like all other second-floor spaces are vaulted.

As with many small houses on tight budgets, custom windows and millwork were limited to the most important targets of opportunity present within the home. These included the aforementioned inglenook as well as those windows facing prominent views from within and without. Vaulted spaces have relatively expensive (though stock) lighting fixtures celebrating their vertical presence. Aggrandized exterior trim is formed from stock sheet material or catalog-derived trim elements.

Master planning can be seen in small houses in one of two ways. The most literal master planning is expansion and/or reinvention of the home as a family evolves. In this particular case, the Reeds opted for a more calming approach: the creation of a fully functional home with only a few compromises. There were secondary elaborations being left to future funding. Trellises at the entry and side porches were planned for in the framing of the home,

Figure 5 *Sections. There are three different cross sections utilized in this home. The subordinate master bedroom wing (left) is a fully vaulted space utilizing expressed collar ties with a fully open living area below. The entry section utilizes a recess in the front door and directly addresses a stair. Note the 7-foot, 2-inch high central hallway ceiling that also serves as a spring point for the roofscape, responding to the restrictions of the zoning codes placed on building height. The children's bedroom suite section (right) shows the relationship between the children's bedroom and playroom—both with vaulted ceilings—while the kitchen is set to address the dining room via an opening set in the kitchen cabinetry. Throughout all these sections a great deal of built-in millwork has been planned. The home sits directly on the terrain utilizing a slab-on-grade foundation, but its backside serves as a retaining wall as the home is led into the earth from a maximum of about 5 feet (left) to a minimum of 3 feet (right).*

Figure 6 *Master bedroom. Careful location of collar ties celebrates the centerline of the dormer with lighting, built-in storage, and window seats providing the sort of careful elaboration via simple construction techniques that foster a sense of richness that is relatively affordable.*

6

7

and a two-car garage was also accommodated by the siting of the home. Additionally, future computer-telephone modem hookups were provided for in the den and children's study spaces, and built-ins in both the dining room and bedroom were also deferred, but designed into their spaces.

Economics dictated a slab-on-grade foundation (no basement) mitigated by the use of built-ins and a semisealed mechanical room on the first floor. A stacked washer and dryer unit was set within the first-floor half-bath. The flue of a prefabricated firebox was shrouded in shingles (versus masonry). But Reed uses a sheet-metal shroud to obscure the almost iconic sheet-metal thimble present for all prefabricated fireboxes. Otherwise, the configuration of this home could serve a vast majority of American families.

Reed used implications of these cost-saving moves to the home's advantage. It's hard to accommodate first-floor plumbing when a slab-on-grade foundation is used. So he elevated the kitchen and half-bath by a step of wood framing providing space for pipes that also facilitates a light underscoring of functional distinction. The 28-foot-height limitations could have flattened the home's roofline, but Reed set the eave line of the roof to the stock door height of 6 foot, 8 inches. Window heads align to this dimension, and the locally vaulted ceilings spring from it. When the hallway height is kept low as well, a very nice sequence of spatial manipulation eliminates any sense of compromise.

Window muntin patterns, shelving divisions, and stair handrail designs are carefully coconspired to create a fairly rich sense of customization. Similarly, hardwood floors, custom handrails, and extensive use of trims and millwork create a sense of personal accommodation that is rare in a home with these budgetary limitations.

An intriguing aspect of this home is that it is a tangible product of its architect's academic studies—Robert Reed's master's thesis focused on small-home design, and he used the first edition of this book as part of his study. Although books can display the virtues of a design ethic, it is talented architects like Robert Reed who indicate that a happy future is ever present and waiting to be fleshed out in the world of residential architecture.

Figure 7 Axis and cross axis. The axial relationship through the main body of the house to the living room can be seen clearly as well as the cross axis between the front door (center left) and the stairway (right). Note the applied panel to the left of the kitchen beyond which the mechanical equipment is placed. This panel preempts the need for a door that would have been an unwanted visual presence as seen upon entry and has its counterpart opposite the stairwell opening in the form of a dummy panel. Simple flat stock trim is used to delicately outline and highlight various identities throughout the house.

Simply Rich

Light, space, and wood delicately dance in California.

W HEN the children grow up and move away, there is often a great visceral desire for a change of venue. If you are an architect who has spent a great deal of your practice designing homes in one of the most celebrated planned communities in America, that community might be a logical choice for a site for your own home—even though it might come with some aesthetic baggage. Donlyn Lyndon is an architect in the full flower of a career marked by a great number of built projects and written thought. So when he and his wife, Alice Wingwall, needed to decide where to live in the "next phase" of their lives as "empty nesters," it was a question that would not abide a simplistic answer. They chose to build in Sea Ranch, a location where Donlyn Lyndon had helped to shine a bright beacon of light onto the world of housing design that had previously known mostly aesthetic mediocrity and social blunders. (The first house study in this book, "Simply Extraordinary, Extraordinarily Simple," focuses on another element of this community.)

It was in this context that Lyndon and Wingwall decided to build a rich miniensemble of simple parts. The givens were many: Existing viewways had to be respected, a potential view of another house had to be avoided, building geometries and lot coverage were restricted in the Sea

Photos © Jim Alinder.
Drawings by the architects.

STATS

PROJECT NAME AND LOCATION:
*Lyndon/Wingwall House,
Sea Ranch, California*

ARCHITECT:
Lyndon/Buchanan Associates

COMPLETION DATE:
1993

TOTAL HEATED SQUARE FEET:
1,750

PERCEIVED SQUARE FOOTAGE:
2,396

CIRCULATION-TO-TOTAL-AREA RATIO:
7 percent

BEDROOM-SPACE-TO-TOTAL-AREA RATIO:
30 percent

GROSS COST:
NA

COST PER SQUARE FOOT:
NA

DURATION OF DESIGN PROCESS:
Six months

DURATION OF CONSTRUCTION:
Nine months

Ranch Design Guidelines, and there was the "innovation imperative" that almost all architects feel when they design their own homes. There are very few, if any, excuses when an architect designs his own home. When the control of the design is also accompanied by control of the purse strings, design program, and site selection, architects have only one tough critic to answer to—themselves.

Small houses can aspire to be gems in the landscape—dissociative and nobly focal in a raw naturalistic sea of landscape. In this case, Lyndon drew his inspiration from the raw rock outcroppings that perforate an already rough landscape. Since rocks are seldom perfect, the home gestures toward the rough-hewn quality of the multifaceted, semieroded forms with its own lightly complex shaping.

It's not surprising that given Lyndon's track record, this is a building that uses the familiar idiom of Sea Ranch construction: heavy timber construction, redwood planking surfaces, an eaveless raked roofscape, and lateral extension of walls to define space and extend building mass to create a playful subtlety and a surprisingly poignant collection of shapes.

As with most Sea Ranch construction, the structural and surfacing aspects are meticulously defined and rigorously applied. A slab-on-grade

1

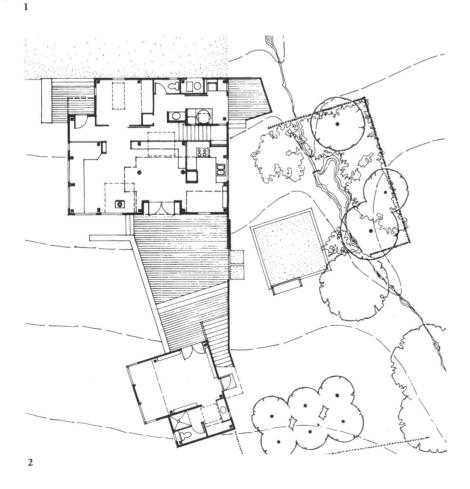

2

Figure 1 *South, private elevation. The raked roof form of the main body of the house (left) accepts the sun while the centered and agglomeratively massed studio (right) sits in contrast*

Figure 2 *Floor plan and site. Two elaborated box plans are linked via a broad south-facing deck. Cars are contained (top) in a motor court, and the house centers its notched entry to the curb cut which accesses the site. Once inside the major longitudinal axis of the house is presented, running from the point of entry up the stairs to a second-floor loft. From that point on a wide variety of subordinate cross-axial relationships occur, utilizing skylights, window orientations, a wood stove, the column grid, and other items to enrich and enliven a rectilinear construction. As with most projects at Sea Ranch, the column structure that supports the building is distinctly separate from the enclosing membrane. The studio-guest bedroom (below) is canted at an angle to facilitate formal distinction from its "parent" building but is married to the "parent" form by the extended wall structure and aforementioned deck. Resonant orthogonal impositions on the fairly wild and woolly landscape in the form of gardens, walls, planting patterns, and so on, help bleed the fabricated into the natural.*

3

Figure 3 *Studio/master bedroom. The benefits of the consistent use of a limited palette of materials can be seen in this small hill of a building. A blank wall is starkly perforated to provide access, and the deck's ascending planes are further extended up to a lofty perch above this simple cube—with saddlebags. To the right, note the attenuated scupper and the voided corner window.*

Figure 4 *Living area. Windows are sized to present an unencumbered view of the landscape while simultaneously responding to the structural grid that orders the entire house. The inside-outside ambiguities of the interior detailing are enhanced by the ability to see through to an immediate adjacent structure (the studio) whose materials and detailing are akin to the interior of this space.*

4

foundation is used, integrated with radiant heating in the floor. In the main house a four-bay alignment of columns allows for only five interior support columns to impose on the interior space. Not surprisingly, there is a paucity of interior walls, with most areas simply being "defined" by exposed structural elements and variations in the ceiling-scape. In such a construction it is not unusual to see multiple interior spatial overlaps involving window orientations, wall alignments (and considered misalignments), as well as the inherent subtleties involved when a very basic system of structure and surface is manipulated to create interior focal points and spatial pinching and releasing.

Axes are present throughout. The coincidence of the wood stove of a bedroom and a hallway between the living and dining areas serves as a major cross axis through the house. This semiformal cross axis counterpoints the long axis that connects entry to stair. Set amid these cross-axial ordinates is a house that lays out spaces on the simple grid defined by its structure into four basic quadrants: living area, dining-kitchen area, stair, and mechanical-bathroom area. Setting above this open plan is a lofty guest bedroom that overlooks the living area and provides a sense of lowered scale in the dining area, appropriate when you consider that most of the time you are sitting in the space below.

Two aspects are used to defeat any sense of monotony when a consistent palette of materials is used in a building such as this: whimsy and scale. The desire for whimsical counterpoint is served by the use of an occasional classical column and ornamented finial. These painted elements set in the context of raw wood provide a sense of relief and intimacy in a potentially blank context. Similarly, scalar variation is provided not only by the obvious space manipulations addressed earlier but additionally by the varying sizes of the perforations of the building's skin where large window walls are created as well as out-sized skylights—all sized in concert with the spaces they address. Additionally, the scalar sweep of such an open building is mitigated by the use of furniture, both built-in and freestanding.

The exterior cladding of the house is also typically simple, involving the exterior "hanging" of the insulation, sheathing, siding, and roofing, and thus allowing the structural skeleton to be fully celebrated within the building. This applied skin is then extended to form an exterior wall and umbilical cord that tethers in a secondary studio building—a pavilion that mitigates the semistark sensibilities of its parent building. Both this studio space and the loft space in the main house accommodate the "empty-nester imperative": They serve as remote sleeping areas for occasional family visitors, while at the same time doubling as spaces for secondary project-orientated use by the occupants. Given their programmatic necessity as bedrooms, this home has a legitimate three-bedroom capacity.

The main house has a classic sawtooth cross section with sex appeal provided by the pulling in of the entry at one corner and the similar pulling in of the focal view-oriented double doors at the backside. This second recess is counterpointed by a modest cap piece, a lantern designed to provide top lighting back lighting as well as passive ventilation.

All wall and floor work is set to be deferential to the dominant structural system, and openings are similarly used to act in concert with the three-dimensional grid provided by the structure itself.

In contrast to the heavily three-dimensional and gridded home, the studio is a model of "budding geometry" where the central space is a semicubic volume and mass with a saddlebag bathroom on one side and lateral extension to the other. The roofscapes tend to marry with the steps that ascend to the upper deck to make a true pavilion set in contrast to the intermeshing structure-skin-space-perforations of the main house.

As with many small homes there is master planning involved, and in this particular case a future garage will be used to define a secondary public space beyond that defined by the two buildings. This space will be set to the north of the main body of the house and help provide additional screening from the south-facing courtyard defined by the two building masses and connective tissue mentioned earlier. In sympathy with the notion that buildings can define "outdoor" rooms, the driveway is treated as a courtyard surrounded by walls.

The danger in small-house design is that the scale of the house won't tolerate complexity. A sophisticated architect such as Donlyn Lyndon can spot that danger a long way off, and it is because of the unrelenting consistency of materials, window shapes, and the trimless quality of the detailing that the house's relatively complex massing and evolving shape is wholly comfortable with itself and with its context. A limited palette of materials and shapes is manipulated to adapt to the functions of the floor plan and the shapes provided by its natural surroundings.

In small-house construction it is tempting to simply create a shell, inhabit it, and call it architecture. But this approach begs the question of depth. Any home has an ethical requirement to fit its owner's idiosyncratic sensibilities, and in designing a home for himself and his wife, Donlyn Lyndon has instilled the thoughts of a focused career into a thoroughly unpretentious but aesthetically rich ensemble of structure, space, and light.

5

Figure 5 *Interior view. Dining area and stairway and loft bedroom-den above are spaces defined by a variety of architectural elements, the most dominant of which is the unabashed framing system evidencing straightforward attachments and a clear organizing grid. A secondary system of attenuated wall surfaces form a low wall to provide distinction between the main axis of the building, terminating in the stair (left) and the dining room—a system that in turn gains a more completely separating and enclosing presence in other areas. The uniformity of raw wood is complemented by the occasional inflection of semitraditional details (newel cap, upper left, and salvaged columns). The floor is a simple polished concrete, and trim is held to an absolute minimum. Note the peek-a-boo quality of the kitchen as seen under the ascending stair.*

"The Vertical Dimension"

*The expressed design imperative of a young couple, who conquered
a tight budget with patience and perspective.*

Second homes don't often "play by the rules." In this particular case, the lack of an immediate need for full-time accommodation provided a young couple—Harriette Resnick and Michel de Konkoly-Thege—the time that was needed to build the home they wanted, where they wanted it and at the right price. With two highly pressurized careers as lawyers in corporate New York, and an idea toward beginning a family, this young couple searched the countryside of Long Island to find a building site that would allow them a weekend respite from the day-in and day-out pressures and tribulations of living in Manhattan. They found a lot, in ever-pricey eastern Long Island. They were able to afford it because although there were beach rights, the site was not a waterfront property.

They had seen, firsthand, the house that introduced the first edition of this book, the 1,100-square-foot, one-bedroom, one-bath home of this author. Their hearts soared along with its undeniably vertical presence, but there was an overlay to their positive regard. This young couple had spent most of their free time during their prechild years traveling in Europe and had found the sensibilities of Greek architecture appealing, almost on a visceral level.

When they came to me, they had an intriguing desire—simply to com-

---

S T A T S

PROJECT NAME AND LOCATION:
*Resnick/de Konkoly-Thege House,
Long Island, New York*

ARCHITECT:
Duo Dickinson, Architect

COMPLETION DATE:
1993

TOTAL HEATED SQUARE FEET:
2,100

PERCEIVED SQUARE FOOTAGE:
2,639

CIRCULATION-TO-TOTAL-AREA RATIO:
6 percent

BEDROOM-SPACE-TO-TOTAL-AREA RATIO:
28 percent

GROSS COST:
$200,000

COST PER SQUARE FOOT:
$95

DURATION OF DESIGN PROCESS:
Three years

DURATION OF CONSTRUCTION:
Nine months

Photos © Carol Bates.
Drawings by the architect.

---

bine the vertical zest and positive presence of our own little house in Connecticut with the equally clear and poignant aspects of Greek folk architecture. Not to be confused with the classical variety, this is an explicitly unarchitected, but somehow quite compelling and thoroughly pragmatic aesthetic.

Implicit in their twin desires was a composite palette of materials. A fully wood-shingled exterior would sustain aesthetic interest and at the same time be highly durable in a northeastern climate (and needless to say, wood shingles on Long Island have a remarkable history). The interior would have large white surfaces combined with overtly hand-crafted and often bright blue appointments—à la the Greek folk style.

There was a list of functional desires—an almost prototypic three-bedroom, two-bath, second home wish list involving a large common area directly connected, both visually and functionally, to a fully fleshed out kitchen (both Resnick and de Konkoly-Thege use food as a socializing and artistic hobby). The three bedrooms were to be commodious, each one easily accepting two people.

While this is not a unique scenario, the lessons to be learned from this project are those that often go unseen in an analysis of a built product. Having been together for well over a decade when they conspired to exe-

Figure 1 *Entry prospect. A simple shape spawns extensions (cantilever and dormer to the right) and attachments (entry roof and deck). Enigmatically located windows at the gable face are set too high to allow visual intrusion and are located to reinforce the latent vertical thrust of the chimney flue, revealed only past the barge board line.*

Figure 2 *Floor plans. A simple plan perimeter is subdivided with out-scaled living spaces to the left and heavily subdivided serving spaces to the right. Note the cross-referential patterning of the windows and the central, ceremonial fireplace. The kitchen is fully formed with generous counter space and storage capacity. A guest bedroom is nestled for maximum privacy to one corner of the plan while a commonly accessed full bath stakes out the opposite corner. Note the outdoor-oriented storage—a compensatory gesture for the lack of a garage. Do note, however, that there is a full basement for this project.*

The second floor evidences a similarly simple plan perimeter with the slight articulation of a 3½-foot cantilever to the bottom of the plan facilitating a full-capacity children's bedroom. A common second-floor bathroom has a sequestered toilet-tub-shower space and two sinks to help relieve congestion, and the master bedroom has enough space to facilitate one occupant's desire for paintings (upper-right-hand-corner). Note the considered nonalignment of the stairwell and fireplace.

1

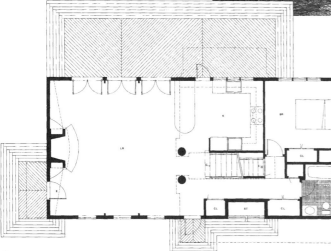

2

cute this home, this couple had not as yet taken the plunge into bearing children, with all its concomitant transitions and anxieties. A second home is definitely on the third level of importance behind building a family and constructing a career, and the schedule responded to these priorities. Another lesson to be learned is that the application of a firm and unrelenting focus on costs can be maintained over a long-term design and build schedule.

So it was with a sense of master planning and budgetary constraint that the design process began, manifest in three preliminary designs, all respecting the subtle design influences of a relatively benign site, namely, two undeniably powerful pine trees and an almost inexplicable minimeadow of grasses set to one edge of the site. No sooner was this preliminary exercise begun than Harriette became pregnant with their first child. Needless to say, Mother Nature preempted the course of timely building.

Once the sense had been reached that their lives were back in control again, design development proceeded with an eye toward obtaining a "real" sense of what the budget would be for the home that they wanted. The simplest house form of the three presented best reflected the home's twin inspirations. Within several months a comprehensive budget-bidding exercise was obtained, and the resulting numbers meant either building less house or providing more money. The latter was chosen, and time was taken for funds to be marshalled. During this lull the Resnick/de Konkoly-Theges learned they would be graced with a second child, and the finalization of the design was again pushed back for more important events. It was only after their second child had been born that a finalized set of drawings could be prepared and sent out to bid, and it was only with the obtainment of the very last bid that it was revealed (after much anxiety) that a budget at or about $100 a square foot could be achieved (a relatively remarkable result for an architect-designed, custom-built home in this affluent area). Although the design process took almost four years to execute, the building process proved more expeditious, and after nine months of construction a "dream house" was made real.

The resulting 2,100-square-foot house has a simple base shape with some careful manipulations inside and out. The central drive to manifest "the vertical dimension" (as Michel de Konkoly-Thege put it) was effected in several simple gestures. The first is the symmetrical gable form of the house, utilizing a 12-in-12 roof pitch with a full two-story height set below it. Since a cost-effective two-bay floor framing was used, resulting in a 24-foot overall width, a vertical presence was ensured. That first blush of verticality is echoed in the dominant window forms that grace the double-height living area.

3

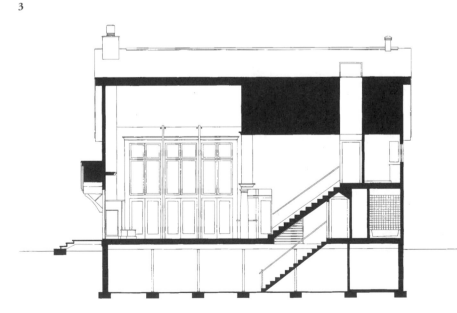

Figure 3 *Section. Set to the centerline axis and front door, the sequencing of spaces from maximum height at the living room to the transitional stair ascending to the top-lit landing and finally the subdivided wet spaces to the far right evidences a very simple plan and section organization. Note the full basement and the single bearing line down the center of the building, promoting economy and ease of construction.*

4

Figure 4 *South, front. A study in the coincidence of vertical, horizontal, and raked lines set in the context of a simple flat plane. This elevation evidences graphic, formal, and material qualities utilizing angular interest at the peak and curvilinear embrace at the entry. Note the use of synthetic stucco as an aggrandizement of the eaves and entry overhang—a cheap material that gains stature in this context.*

Spatially, the house progresses from most open to most defined over its length. As a long entry walk is traversed, a cottage transforms into a dominant presence, and the relatively huge living area is immediately encountered upon entry. There is no axial focus for this entry sequence, but a series of foci, from overtly vertical windows to a carefully crafted stairway ascending to a top-lit hall, to a semi-"grotto" kitchen (remarkable for its unapologetic blueness), to a thoroughly out-scaled window array accessing a simple plinth of porch, and finally this rotating series of spatial and architectural events is resolved in the central fireplace mass—the lone recentering device that serves to anchor the home's perception from inside to out. A subordinate back hall filters back through to the first-floor laundry, a full bath, and a guest bedroom, forming an ever more private sequence of functions.

Upon ascending the relatively large staircase, a secondary vertical exclamation point is realized—a full-story-height, skylit lightwell, lifting any sense of ceiling away from the top of the stairs and providing a distant point of light seen upon entry. Flanking this central stair is a bedroom large enough to have sleeping space and studio space for Harriette Resnick's painting and a bedroom large enough for two children (fortunately, two boys). Set between the sleeping spaces is a common bath, with a segregated toilet-tub area for multiple occupancy. A structural and formal move was necessitated by the dominant character of the out-scaled living area absorbing fully half of the available second-floor space. The children's bedroom had to grow, and this expansion was made via a simple, inexpensive cantilever. From the outside this floor and roof projection is resolved by a secondary focal point in the form of a dormer, giving primary spatial relief to the descending extension of the dominant roof form.

The interior of the home is marked by relatively uncompromised use of materials despite the project's low cost. Wood floors are set throughout almost all the spaces on the first and second floor, custom tilework is present in both bathrooms, and the kitchen and stair evidence skilled finish carpentry and the use of high-quality materials. The use of custom columns and expressive trim throughout the large living area complements the semiexterior scale of this space. The standard zero-setback metal firebox is covered in custom-crafted slate, and the 8-foot-high mahogany front door is again scaled to the relatively mammoth proportions of the room it services.

Figure 5 West, deck. An out-scaled window wall has its pattern bled into the remainder of the façade via considered spacing with secondary centerlines of kitchen windows, trellis, master bedroom windows, and guest bedroom windows and painting-oriented master bedroom windows finishing up the linear sequence. Note the directly cantilevered wood trellis that provides a threshold from the out-scaled deck into the kitchen area. Overtly intended to capture the setting sun and address a minimeadow, the out-scaled living room windows do need solar control given the intensity of midsummer low-angle sunlight.

Figure 6 (opposite) Living room and fireplace. A grand, open space celebrating verticality and linearity, this room ultimately worships the central firebox as a positive presence, but this photo's point of outlook (the stair) is a primary focus upon entry (note entry door to left). Note the flared sheetrock coincidence between flue and ceiling and reciprocal tie rods and stays—painted bright blue. Note also custom turned columns and trim utilized throughout.

5

On the exterior, a variety of trim details, surface treatments, and demiarchitectural elements enliven a potentially stark box—both to attract and to sustain interest. A cantilevered trellis addresses the kitchen and uses stock framing lumber made special by its considered construction and lightly arced geometry. Similarly, the entry overhang utilizes solid cedar brackets, again using standard materials made special by their shape. The shingled siding has its corners mitered throughout. Lead-coated copper detailing and synthetic stucco are used to aggrandize the upper edges of the construction and the entry overhang. Standard-sized windows are ganged and use custom muntin patterns to repeat an ongoing interplay of cruciform geometries and square shapes, transforming what is potentially unrelenting verticality into a composition that has a visual beginning, middle, and end.

As many projects in this book evidence, there can be extraordinary power in the use of standard framing technologies so easily obtained and applied. The vaulted living space necessitated some serious structural accommodation. Plywood-faced sheer walls are used on the gable walls of the living space, as are buried steel angles and strapping, and small-scale laminated wood pilasters. The cathedral ceiling is tied together via steel tie rods—painted blue for maximum impact.

Although this is a second home, it does have a full basement (a very low cost item given the sandy subsoil) and a full attic over the second floor, and it was sited and designed to allow for expansion—either by the attenuation of the already projecting roofscape mentioned earlier or via the extrusion of the gable form to the rear. In creating a special place out of standard parts that is both affordable now and flexible for the future, this little home presents a positive presence from prosaic parts.

7

Figure 7 Living room, and stair, back door, and rhythmic windows. The negative incision of the stairwell space into the out-scaled living room becomes a singular beckoning element in the context of the rhythmic placing of windows, trim, and structure to the right. Note the consistent use of cruciform muntin patterns.

Figure 8 (opposite) Stairwell. The central primary focus of the living room seen upon entry, this semisculpted architectural event creates a gesture that is both out-scaled and humane, providing a positive presence in a large room while simultaneously making the act of ascent something that is both positive and inviting. Note the use of columns both for structure and to obscure visual access into a back hallway leading to a bathroom and a guest bedroom, as well as the peek-a-boo quality of the kitchen to the left.

Garden Cascade

Evocative massing on a tight hillside site.

I N America, if you want to live close to an urban center and want to build your own home, there are very few options. Either you buy a site that has a nonviable structure already set upon it, tear it down, and build anew, or you build on a site that was considered to be unbuildable only a decade or two ago.

The latter is the scenario in the case of this complex three-bedroom house set on a hillside in Seattle, Washington. George and Leslie-Anne Cone needed a home that provided functional separation between living spaces, guest quarters, and their bedroom, and they wanted to take advantage of the views present from the high side of a tiny urban site just over one-tenth of an acre in size. Given the desire for functional separation in the context of the terrain, they also confronted strict setbacks and height limitations common to almost all heavily regulated urban sites. When they hired Stuart Silk as their architect, it also became evident that the hillside presented foundation problems that needed to be solved with a fairly sophisticated use of concrete pilings augured deep into the hillside. Needless to say, the insinuation of a home into a hillside is expensive, and although this home is remarkable in terms of its ability to accommodate an extraordinary variety of spatial and formal manipulations, the implications of all these

S T A T S

PROJECT NAME AND LOCATION:
Cone House, Seattle, Washington

ARCHITECT:
Stuart Silk Architects

COMPLETION DATE:
1989

TOTAL HEATED SQUARE FEET:
2,750

PERCEIVED SQUARE FOOTAGE:
3,297

CIRCULATION-TO-TOTAL-AREA RATIO:
13 percent

BEDROOM-SPACE-TO-TOTAL-AREA RATIO:
20 percent

GROSS COST:
NA

COST PER SQUARE FOOT:
NA

DURATION OF DESIGN PROCESS:
Four months

DURATION OF CONSTRUCTION:
Eight months

Photos © Michael Ian Shopenn
Drawings by the architects.

moves give this home a cost burden that is mitigated only by the ability of Stuart Silk to make a downsized home perform beyond its spatial limitations.

Rather than be cowed by the inherent site conditions, Silk has dominated them by creating a three-part home: two flanking subordinate bays set to embrace an unabashedly proud central mass that projects vertically to focus attention and provide dominance in a relatively complicated array of building parts. The tripartite massing is reflected functionally as well, with one flanking bay containing a two-car garage at grade, master suite at the middle, and a fairly luxurious kitchen and formal dining area and terrace on the top level. The other flanking bay contains only the formal entry. Typical of hillside sites that are sloping in two directions, this wing begins one level up from the garage elevation and contains a transcendentally vertical space that beckons anyone entering the home up into the relatively celestial third floor. The central bay harbors separate guest suites on the first two floors and has its top level capped by a large-scale living-dining space which has an octagonal view-facing living area and a carefully scaled dining area facing a terrace built into the hillside at the backside of the site.

Each one of the three bays has an explicitly distinct roof form. There is

1

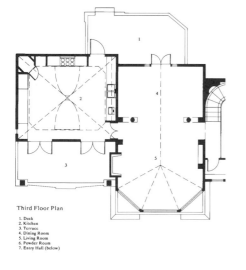

First Floor Plan

1. Garage
2. Storage
3. Bedroom
4. Bathroom
5. Closet
6. Storage

Second Floor Plan

1. Wardrobe
2. Master bathroom
3. Master Bedroom
4. Bedroom
5. Bathroom
6. Closet
7. Laundry Room
8. Entry Hall

Third Floor Plan

1. Deck
2. Kitchen
3. Terrace
4. Dining Room
5. Living Room
6. Powder Room
7. Entry Hall (below)

2

Figure 1 *Floor plans. A three-part construction facilitates accommodation of a steeply sloping hillside site. At the lowest level (top) a garage orients to the street level with a guest bedroom suite and back door/back stair and storage space set completely underground. On the second floor the ever-rising hillside allows the pedestrian entry bay to be realized at the far right. There is a duplicate guest bedroom suite amidships and a corridor set to the next level of the back entry stair. The laundry and a master bedroom suite is set directly over the garage. Note that there is direct on-grade access to the outdoors through the master bath. On the topmost floor the double-height entry bay at the far right has a powder room set to its street side over the entry doors, and the central slot of space is given over to the living room and has its front face pulled back to form an octagonal bay. A fireplace is inserted as well. A dining area directly addresses a backside terrace, providing alfresco dining accommodation. Above the master bedroom suite in the far left bay, a kitchen and formal dining area addresses a view-oriented terrace.*

Figure 2 *Hillside prospect. A tripartite plan gains further enrichment via the integration of landscape elements and formal and material manipulations. The dominant centerpiece has semi-Egyptian rusticated stone corner development, which in turn spawns large-scale planters set at the third level. Trellises at the entry and over a third-floor deck bring the green hillside into the ambiance of the home. Consistent use of stucco helps unify a relatively complicated building mass. Extensive use of walkways and walls helps tame a difficult site.*

Figure 3 *Section. A simple three-bay construction facilitates a great deal of functional segregation. The garage (lower left) has a master bedroom suite set above it and the kitchen set above the bedroom. Adjacent to the kitchen, set above stacked guest bedroom suites, is the living room with the street being accessed via the double-height entry space at the far right. Note the consistent use of arcing openings and dormers to reinforce the centerlines of the roof forms.*

Figure 4 *Site plan and roof plan. A tiny urban site has a fairly radical elevation change set diagonally to its lot lines. Vehicular access is oriented to the lower right-hand corner of the site, as seen here, with terraces and walkways allowing pedestrian access up to the level of the formal entry (far right). Three roof forms correspond to the three bays utilized in planning: A roof arcs over the entry (right), a gable roof transforms itself into an octagonalized street-side roofscape over the living room (center), and a pyramidally formed roof covers the kitchen with a trellis set over the third-floor terrace. Note that there is a dumbwaiter that connects the back side of the garage to the kitchen at the third floor above.*

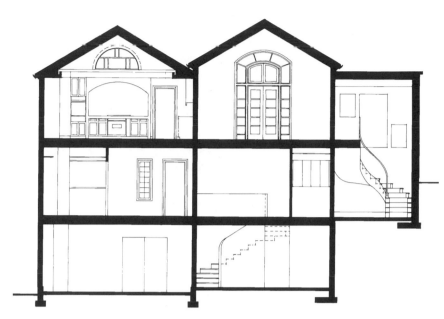

3

4

a pyramidal roof over the kitchen/master bedroom/garage wing, a bowed roof over the entry wing, and an octagonally faceted living room side gable transitioning into a gable-faced rear side of the central bay. Additionally, all three masses have distinctive methods of addressing the ever-changing landscape levels. Obviously, the garage needed to be set to address the street. The master suite at the next level above has a covered walkout to the backside. The kitchen/informal dining area has a walkout to the hillside and is recessed from the front edge of the building façade, allowing for a third-level terrace to have an extraordinary appreciation of the views and facilitate the sense of dominant massing that the central octagonal living room enjoys. The formal entry area has a proud, trellised set of exterior entry steps, and the central bay has a ground-level walkout for a one-bedroom suite, and the aforementioned dining room walkout to a terrace is also shared by the kitchen.

Beyond providing accessibility to the outside that mitigates the spatial constriction implicit in a home of this size, garden elements are interwoven into the fabric of the building façade itself from the vine-covered trellis entry to the entry steps that meander down from it, carefully terraced with plantings, gardens, and trees, to the built-in planters flanking the octagonal living room form and the backside terrace.

In putting the public spaces on the uppermost floor of this construction, Silk utilizes the ability to cathedralize the spaces set below the roof, facilitating a great sense of spatial expansion and expression, especially given the varying roofscapes involved. An added benefit of having a three-bedroom home occupied by a couple is that the guest bedrooms can double as office space, for in-house business activities—a scenario that will become more common in the years to come.

5

    The materials on the outside are quite simple, involving a dominant stucco skin counterpointed by battered stone walls to accentuate the dominant central bay combined with subordinate trellis and entry elements mentioned earlier. Windows tend to reinforce the local center of each bay, and subordinate elements such as railings, low walls, and ornamental figures create a sense of surprise, delight, and power rare in a building of this size.

    Sites that are made problematic by terrain, size, subsoil conditions, or functional requirements need not preclude the ability of an architect to create a memorable building. In this case, all of those limiting criteria were encountered, and it's a testament to the skill of Stuart Silk that he was able to utilize a relatively generous budget in such a way that there is virtually no evidence of these limitations present in the final built form.

6

Figure 6 Kitchen, informal dining. Vaulted ceilings and large-scale openings
to the outdoors and clerestory dormers help create anything but a confined
sense of space in this urban home.

Figure 7 Entry, stair. A sinuous stair beckons those who enter up to the second level, and ascending niches provide intermediate focal points for the owner's extraordinary collection of antiques and art

Houses with Four or More Bedrooms

Extruded Generic

In attenuating the latent aesthetics of factory-built construction, the familiar addresses the future.

IN Europe, architectural design competitions have often been used to point the way to a brave new world of architectural innovation. The idea that the world would be a better place to live if the ever-expanding benefits of technology were allowed to reinvent our lives and enrich our souls is at the core of a Modernist view of the future. In late twentieth century America, however, there is a sense that the ongoing reinvention of our domestic life is not infused with a sense of positive expansionist thinking. The Norman Rockwell vision of the American family as a nuclear entity with parents as a dyad in the center, father working, mother homemaking, with children circling about this binary star in synchronous harmony has become a cultural joke for most Americans. In truth, the economics of the late twentieth century have forced families to adapt in ways our parents could never have envisioned. Beyond both people working to support a family, one parent is often living elsewhere. Children often rotate residences between parents and many people simply don't have children.

In truth, many family structures are fractionalizing and recombining to form new entities that completely befuddle those who would like to categorize prototypes. The Cleavers have given way to the much maligned Murphy Brown. The majority of

women in America today work, whether they are married, unmarried, with children, or without. An increasing number of alternative life-style families are forming households as well, whether gay, or two or more single-parent family households living together, or groups of people formed from special populations living together as families (handicapped, emotionally disturbed, or elderly). Society is changing, and the nature of our housing will need to change as well.

With the explosion of diversity in domestic demographics, it would be easy to assume that the appropriate architectural response would be an explosion of aesthetic variety as derived from the implications of potential occupants' predilections. In a effort to define what our collective housing future might incorporate, *Progressive Architecture* magazine in conjunction with *Decorating & Remodeling* magazine sponsored a competition that elicited more than 600 entries from all over the country. The design program was relatively vague, simply to create a house that would be affordable for any major urban area and accommodate the widest variety of family prototypes.

Those entering the competition soon realized that aesthetic diversity has inherent cost implications that are antithetical to the viability of a housing prototype intended to be

---

S T A T S

PROJECT NAME AND LOCATION:
Double High, Cleveland, Ohio

ARCHITECT:
ABACUS

COMPLETION DATE:
1992

TOTAL HEATED SQUARE FEET:
1,447

PERCEIVED SQUARE FOOTAGE:
2,029

CIRCULATION-TO-TOTAL-AREA RATIO:
15 percent

BEDROOM-SPACE-TO-TOTAL-AREA RATIO:
32 percent

GROSS COST:
$68,404

COST PER SQUARE FOOT:
$47

DURATION OF DESIGN PROCESS:
Three and a half months

DURATION OF CONSTRUCTION:
Five and a half weeks

Photos © Walter Smalling.
Drawings by the architects.

Figure 1 Front. The door seen in this view is
complemented by two others: one amidships and one
at the end of the home to facilitate multiple points
of entry to allow for multiple occupancy types.

Figure 2 Floor plans. A simple elongated rectangle
has single-loaded circulation set to its middle serving
area, an area where a stairway and bath combine
with a central bedroom space to facilitate the use of
the remaining ends of the plan for common space,
kitchen/dining, or a larger bedroom or office space
(far right). On the second floor a similar organization is employed with the exception that the
major living room is set above the kitchen/dining
area. These stacked living and kitchen/dining areas
have a wraparound deck extending their square
footage. This unified, common/public end addresses
the street and is a buffer to the urban scene for the
rest of the house beyond. This simple bar/slab shape
and multiple points of entry on the first floor
facilitate a wide variety of use patterns and possible
additional permutations for this house form.

1

2

built at a cost far cheaper than other architect-designed homes. Most of the entries evidenced the applicability of modularized construction (at least conceptually), but the winning entry was perhaps the most literal advocate of the most generic and possibly aesthetically blank solution—prefabricated stick-built modularized construction. The large-scale limitations of this system are quite simple. Whatever is designed must be subdividable into components that can fit on the back of a truck going down a highway.

The prototypical form derived from the systems employed by the modular home industry is a modified Cape shape where two bays are set side by side with a gable roof formally unifying the two building components.

But in a competition-winning tilt toward innovation, ABACUS Architects (a firm of young partners, Anne Tate, Bryan Irwin, and David Pollack) opted to stack the units vertically and extend them linearly, creating almost a chicken coop house form. The adaptability of this form to most available lots in undervalued urban areas is obvious. The spatial implications for getting light and air on all sides of the project has an extraordinary appeal. Similarly, the ability to "tack on" additions cross-axially to the linear form has enormous utility both in terms of the adaptability of the construction to different occupancies and the ability of these adaptations to be relatively economical and easily retrofittable. The basic organization of this particular project sought to be adaptable in and of itself. Public spaces are set to one side of the double-height bar, and private spaces could be set to the other, separated by a stairway with the bathrooms in the private wing set between two bedroom spaces (one small and one large). The circulation is inherently single-loaded given the width limitations mentioned earlier, and the upper level of public space is, of course, relatively untraditional given the nature of most prototypic house organizations involving a consistent segregation of living and sleeping spaces on a floor-by-floor basis.

Functional shifts can be accommodated in this home without architectural attention. It can be used by two separate single-headed household families. It can have in-house working space. It can easily be used by unrelated people living together.

This holistic and yet subtle reinvention of house organization is set within a starkly simple form that gains presence via its exaggerated proportions (thinner and more vertical in one prospect and longer and flatter in the other). Complementing this attenuated presence is a two-tier deck made affordable by its roofless quality and open tolerance of rain. Beyond the simple formal exaggerations, a sense of presence is provided by outsizing and downsizing windows to counterpoint the blankness of the building's linearity and in the considered noncentering or rhythmatic locations of almost all window and door configurations.

All of this socially responsive innovation and aesthetic articulation is based on a given system of prefabricated home building: the R2000 System as developed by the Ontario Home Builders Association. This system afforded an amazing capacity for heavy insulation while at the same time availing itself of a fairly easy method for stacking a structure.

All dimensions were keyed to a 2-foot module integrating the standard 4- by 8-foot sheet size of plywood and sheetrock. Prefabricated fasteners were used extensively, and trusses were used for floor joists to accommodate

3

Two Bedroom   Two Module   784 s.f.   Two Family   Three Module   1808 s.f.   Three Bedroom   Four Module   1666 s.f.   Two Bedroom   Two Module

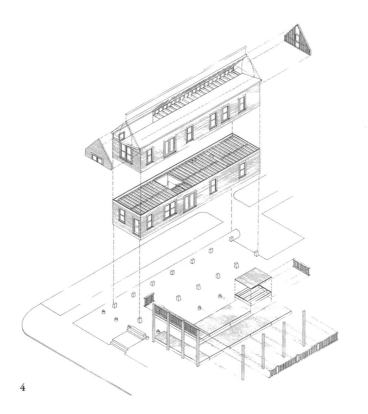

4

Figure 3 The generic qualities of modular construction have a multitude of permutations as seen in these entry façade sketches by the architects.

Figure 4 Construction rationale axonometric. Two prefabricated slabs of construction are set upon a simple series of cast-in-place piers. Roof planes are flipped up into place, gable ends are inserted, and an independent deck structure is wrapped about two sides of one end of the building. It doesn't get much simpler than this.

mechanical systems and provide some of the inherent stiffness required for these components as they are transported and moved about before being set into place. The foundation was a tough budgetary problem with the final result being a grid of concrete piers set to provide maximal support with a minimal need for framing accommodation.

Architects are often called upon to microdesign their projects to fit idiosyncrasies; in this particular case, the architects were called upon to macrodesign their project so that it could respond to the resident's life-style without their direct input. Although this might seem to be anathema to the tradition of custom home building where client idiosyncrasies have direct response in built form, this project evidences the best hope for the vast majority of housing that is built in America, housing footage priced well below $60 per square foot.

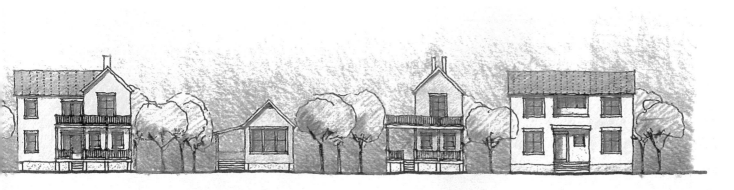

Two Family Four Module 1848 s.f   One Bedroom One Module 588 s.f.   Four Bedroom Two Module 1624 s.f.   Four Bedroom Four Module 2016 s.f.

Because of the adherence to this economic imperative, it can be said that the creativity employed in this project has a poignancy and power that no "genius-based" visionary project could ever have. Although this house has no claims to aesthetic futurism, it does represent the future of the vast majority of single-family residences that will be built over the next century. Given the demographic shifts that are under way, defining a set of life-style patterns applicable to most Americans over the next several generations is problematic. Until those patterns are defined, explicit fine-tuning of prototypical housing units will be impossible for a growing segment of our population. Unless there is a radical change in the prospects for large-scale economic growth, development, and family prosperity, houses of this size and simplicity will become more the norm in our communities, as they were in the century before this one.

If left to those without an aesthetic vision and innovative spirit, these homes will simply be warehouses for humanity, cubbyholes for the spirits and souls of our families and ultimately for our nation. If we have the courage to reinterpret, reinvent, and reflect our cultural shifts in the architecture that accommodates them, there is a future where buildings and families can be in sympathy rather than in conflict. ABACUS Architects, *Progressive Architecture,* and *Decorating & Remodeling* have taken a lead and shown a path. It is up to those who evaluate this house and others like it over time to determine whether or not this methodology has a potential for ultimate success, or whether, like many other projects intended to point to a new and better way, there will be a sense of good intentions without practical application.

It is the sense of this book that the more flexible and generic building technology can be applied to special needs, the more useful and inspirational small-house architecture can become to anyone who cares about the centerpiece of a family's physical environment—the home.

Figure 5 *(opposite) Installation, erection. Rather than the archetypal "double-wide designation," this house has been intentionally labeled "double-high." Needless to say prefabrication can lead to added affordability (if redundancy can be achieved).*

Grounded Ascension

Time and ingenuity overcome a tight budget.

WILLIAM Maclay has an architectural practice located in rural Warren, Vermont, a town replete with urban expatriate architects. This fertile environment fostered the formation of the Yestermorrow School, one of the primary institutions advocating the design-build method of house fabrication, where highfalutin aesthetics are combined with the down-and-dirty reality of framing techniques. The school also deals with budgetary realities in a program designed to allow students to gain enough knowledge to build their version of the American Dream. Maclay has taken the baseline reality of Yestermorrow's message (often from his role as a teacher at the school) to heart with a home set on the property of his extended family's summer residence, a piece of land addressing the Oyster River.

Someone once said that there are three qualities to everything confronted in life: "good," "fast," and "cheap"—the caveat being that you could only have two of these qualities at any given time. If something is "good" and "cheap," it precludes the ability to be "fast" in its realization. Seldom has a project evidenced this reality better than the Crow's Nest house designed and more-or-less general-contracted by Maclay.

The project started with only enough funds to complete the building's shell ($60,000 given by one

STATS

PROJECT NAME AND LOCATION:
Crow's Nest, Chatham, Massachusetts

ARCHITECT:
William Maclay, Architects & Planners

COMPLETION DATE:
1991

TOTAL HEATED SQUARE FEET:
1,760

PERCEIVED SQUARE FOOTAGE:
2,180

CIRCULATION-TO-TOTAL-AREA RATIO:
10 percent

BEDROOM-SPACE-TO-TOTAL-AREA RATIO:
38 percent

GROSS COST:
$120,000

COST PER SQUARE FOOT:
$68

DURATION OF DESIGN PROCESS:
Several years

DURATION OF CONSTRUCTION:
Three to four years

family member) and was subjected to complete familial design review, involving numerous people with strong opinions. Not surprisingly the design of this building was done over a three-year period, and the construction, phased to the available funds, took almost four years.

The working drawings evidence this ongoing budgetary squeeze and design evolution. The foundation sheet describes not one but three potential foundation strategies for competitive bidding. An additional loan of $60,000 was fronted by the architect's family to finish and furnish the house and would be repaid by the rental income of the home for the 10-week summer season. Therefore, the occupancy of the home is fairly unique, involving relatively full-time occupancy by a wide variety of people during the fall, spring, and winter seasons, with a complete evacuation of all family members in favor of a revenue-generating tenancy during the summer months.

The "guts" of the building display both a structural efficiency and an aesthetically expressive articulation of post-and-beam technology. The building's skin utilizes extended polystyrene stress panels, a system that combines the high insulating value of rigid foam with the inherent stiffness of its bonding to plywood sheathing. The floor and roof loads in this house are carried by eight

1

FIRST FLOOR PLAN

SECOND FLOOR PLAN

2

THIRD FLOOR PLAN

Figure 1 *South, view side. An overarching gable form has horizontal trim bands corresponding to floor levels. Note the use of simple trim elements to provide a sense of scale and surface relief for this outsized construction.*

Figure 2 *Floor plans. A simple rectangular construction utilizes three basic framing bays with a central minor, narrower circulation bay facilitating the subdivision between the kitchen-dining (right) and living (left) areas. Note that the mudroom to the rear and secondary storage areas help compensate for the lack of a full basement in this project. Secondary elaborations in this project involve the "tartanizing" of the plan, using secondary cantilevered joist extensions beyond the lines of the interior columns. On the second floor three bedrooms and a bath have their end walls keyed to the ever-decreasing space available within the overarching gable form, with the top floor being a lofted study for overflow bedroom use.*

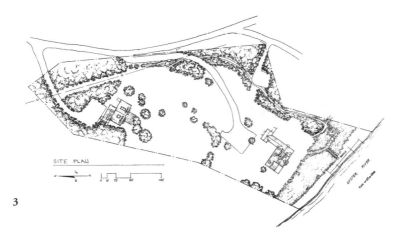

3

6-by 6-inch posts (a remarkably efficient load collection given the floor and roof areas involved). Intermediate framing is accomplished by 4- by 8-inch joists set on 4-foot centers that are set to bear on double 4- by 10-inch beams that in turn bear on doubled 2- by 8-inch "capitals" set to the columns, with each layer set transversely to the other. At the long sides of the structural bay the joists cantilever out to stiffen and support the stressed-skin walls, and at the narrow ends of the construction the doubled beams cantilever to support the floor and the roof. The basic roof structure is remarkably simple, utilizing only two 6- by 14-inch rafters set to the aforementioned column grid. This paucity of structural support is facilitated by the use of continuous 22-foot-long stress-skin panels that are tied into their wall counterparts by the use of a 4 by 8 cleat. In all cases, loads are translated by the use of large-scale through bolts. Beam connections are facilitated by steel flitch plates that are through-bolted to each member.

The home almost mimics the traditional center hall post-and-beam house in its use of its column grid to foster spatial organization. A central narrow column bay of 8 feet is flanked by two larger 16-foot-wide bays. This narrow central bay translates to the second floor as stairwell and open corridor set to subdivide two bedrooms on one side and bedroom and common bath on the other. The top Crow's Nest floor is set to harbor a large open loft bedroom for overflow sleeping accommodation.

This distilled structural approach is mirrored by the similarly simple house form that takes the shape of a broad extended gable, ascending to a full three-and-a-half story height at its apex and descending to a single-story height at its ends. This building shape is often found in middle or late nineteenth century farmhouses dotting the Vermont landscape and has been effectively reinterpreted here by Maclay. As one might expect in a home given over to intermittent use by a varied population, the first floor is almost completely open with dining and living areas separated by a central stair and with one corner of the home given over to a half-bath and kitchen. A simple attenuated appendage accommodates a mudroom-breezeway, and future expansion possibilities in this home are keyed to the extension of this little wing to a future garage. There are even thoughts of future expansion to the east to allow for a family museum or guest suite. These permutations are easily tolerated given the dominant sensibility of the overall built form. The long dimension of the home extends east to west, allowing maximal southern exposure.

Paralleling the simple plan layout, the mechanical systems employed are also quite generic. Large south-facing windows allow winter sun to hit and heat the slab-on-grade first floor, which has a continuous Mexican tile floor. A 30,000-Btu gas unit heater is employed at one end of the house. This home also uses a wood-burning stove as backup to this relatively minimal heating system. The central staircase allows for the easy convection of heated air up through the center of the house into the bedroom spaces. Given the extremely high insulation value provided by the stress-skin panels and the extraordinary efficiencies of the tight plan organization employed, this low-tech multisource heating approach works quite well. In summer months, operable skylights are employed at the third level to provide maximal venting of the interior spaces.

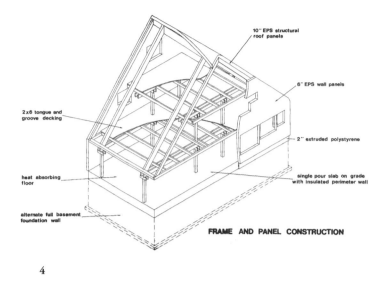

FRAME AND PANEL CONSTRUCTION

10" EPS structural roof panels

6" EPS wall panels

2 x 6 tongue and groove decking

2" extruded polystyrene

heat absorbing floor

single pour slab on grade with insulated perimeter wall

alternate full basement foundation wall

4

Figure 4 Structural diagram. The extraordinary capacity for this structure to collect floor and roof loads into a minimum number of vertical columns is a model of structural efficiency few industrial buildings achieve, and bespeaks the latent strengths of stress-skin laminated wall and roof panels.

Figure 5 Section. The consistent framing dimension of the heavy timber construction helps meter the upper two floors. Note the use of skylights to provide light and relieve space where there are possibilities for "pinch." Note also the use of rounded eaves with dropped gutters and a sympathetically rounded roof peak.

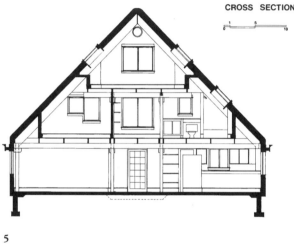

CROSS SECTION

5

The interior finishing of the home is as simple as its structure and shape, with all interior structure, trim, and floor elements being clear-finished and all wall surfaces being painted white sheetrock. Some light fixtures have been integrated into the structure, and some modestly decorous trim detailing is also present, but this building gains much of its power and presence by the celebrated honesty of the structural system employed.

The exterior is similarly consistent, but evidences a bit more aesthetic fine-tuning. The undeniable power of a broad-side gable-end form rising from a one-story base to a three-and-a-half story peak is complemented by windows that are effectively centered upon the dominant ridge line and lightly counterpointed by horizontal banding of attenuated trim boards providing large-scale shadowlines and a tiny bit of shading during the summer. An interesting indication of the properties of the stress-skin roof structure can be seen at the eave and ridge lines where the corners that normally result from multipieced, light-frame construction are now almost monolithic in their structural properties, thus allowing the proud corners of the eave and ridge to be rounded or "eased." This easing of the edges can also be seen in all the edges of the bared-wood structure, vaguely reminiscent of the Arts and Crafts movement but more pointedly indicative of a clear-minded sense that large-scale structural members can be more friendly in a tactile sense if they are seen as smooth rather than as rough-hewn components. There is also a practical advantage during construction when large-scale wood elements do not need perfect alignment with each other.

Implicit in the integration between a large-scale exterior form and a diagrammatically simple structural system is the careful design of the "joints" between the two. The floor planes are held distinct from the angled imposition of the roof structure to allow for expression of the cantilevered frame mentioned earlier. This nonintersection facilitates knee-wall conditions that preempt the sense of squeeze at the floor-wall interface.

Patience and resourcefulness pay off in this home, and an exuberant construction is born of modest means and innovative design. There is a depth of detailing that backs up the raw power of this building's shape and structure, and it is found in the subtle manipulation of familiar materials that humanizes a potentially abstract building. William Maclay evidences the benefits of a clear head and an expressive spirit, a combination that can overcome even the tightest of budgetary limitations.

Figure 6 *Living room, first floor. The structural efficiency of a thoroughly analyzed and carefully implemented superstructure facilitates an extraordinary sense of space within such a small home. Note how the stairway's mass has been detailed to be a subordinate construction within the overarching structural cage.*

Figure 7 *Kitchen-dining. Window sills step to respond to the exterior mass and work well with the similarly clear-finished wood trim to create a lattice of natural linear elements set in the context of simple white sheetrock walls (a material combination echoed in the cabinetry seen in the foreground). This photograph gives some sense of the rolling lawn and view addressed by the home.*

6

7

Figure 8 *Second-floor bedroom. Rafters and beams are combined with lighting fixtures to create a sense of out-scaled structure set within the context of an individual-scaled room.*

8

A Box Filled with Delights

The simplest of house forms contains a large dose of whimsical permutation.

THIS book deals at length with the preconceptions that are evoked by the term *small house*. One of the most common preconceptions is the connotation that the word *small* is tantamount to "simple." The overriding sense is that a small house is relatively more predictable in its concept and realized form than a larger one. This home dispels this preconception. Indeed, this home has a transcendently simple exterior shape with an interior design and intermittent exterior appointments that are anything but simple, predictable, or seemingly rational.

Mark Simon and Trip Wyeth of Centerbrook Architects delight in interplay, whether it is between architectural elements or between the building and those who experience it. In this particular home the duality of the inside-outside interface is extreme. As an object in the landscape, this is an extremely simple form, a squared perimeter capped by an overarchingly extended 12-in-12 pitch roofscape. Flecked about this form are porches and other addenda that seem to be unruly chicks cleaving to or fleeing from the mother-hen house.

The interior of the house incorporates an extraordinary array of rooms that are alternately transitions or destinations, a sequence that uses kinetically abstracted ovals, "cranked" rectangles, or simply skewed spaces, all

---

STATS

PROJECT NAME AND LOCATION:
McKim House, Fishers Island, New York

ARCHITECT:
Centerbrook

COMPLETION DATE:
1988

TOTAL HEATED SQUARE FEET:
2,650

PERCEIVED SQUARE FOOTAGE:
2,908

CIRCULATION-TO-TOTAL-AREA RATIO:
8 percent

BEDROOM-SPACE-TO-TOTAL-AREA RATIO:
21 percent

GROSS COST:
$230,000

COST PER SQUARE FOOT:
$87

DURATION OF DESIGN PROCESS:
Nine months

DURATION OF CONSTRUCTION:
Fourteen months

Photos © Tim Hursely.
Drawings by the architects.

---

bound by the square plan perimeter. There is so little experiential registration between the inside and the outside of this home that once entered, it becomes a fantasy land of spatial permutations, conscientiously conspired to be diametrically opposed to the predictability of its generic container. This is a home to be experienced rather than analyzed. It is deliciously idiosyncratic but not without an extraordinary dose of conceptual underpinnings. In fact, this home has won almost every architecture award that a single-family residence can win, which is a testament to its intellectual integrity as viewed by the architectural community as well as to its overtly whimsical and emotive sensibility.

Its value to this book is that of a 2,650-square-foot house that harbors four bedrooms, two and a half baths, a full kitchen, a separate dining room, and a plentitude of subordinate niches, nooks, crannies, and specialized spaces.

It is a second home in a community of second homes on Fishers Island off Long Island Sound. The entire island was masterplanned by Frederick Law Olmsted in the nineteenth century. This site is set upon a hilly terrain, and code-imposed height limitations and site restrictions allow for each and every home to have a dominant view. Given the slope and these regulations, the seem-

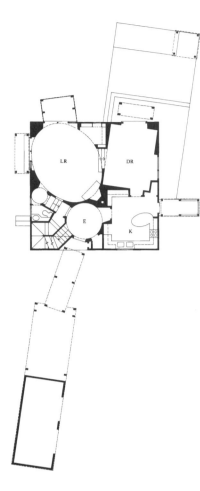

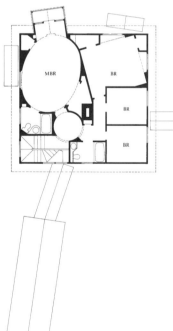

2

Figure 1 *Floor plans. Three distinct but interrelated systems are applied to the planning of this project. The first, and most visible from the exterior, is the square perimeter plan. The first subordinate system as applied to this plan perimeter consists of the overtly (and literally) stick-built exterior elaborations and substructures that form a porte cochere and storage area (bottom), trellises (off the living room and dining room), entry thresholds (off the kitchen and approaching main entry), and follies (on the deck to the upper right). The last system is the jumble of kinetically arrayed spaces that are carved out of a solid mass defined by the square plan, jiggling within its form, or rectified to it—often interconnected with perspectivily enhancing angled thresholds. Resonances occur between the oculus entry and its second-floor counterpart, elliptical living room and its master bedroom counterpart, the dining room below and a skewed bedroom upstairs, and the rationalized-integrated kitchen and the two small bedrooms set directly above it. This hyperkinetic interior articulation has direct and overt coincidental signals in the form of the stick-built substructures mentioned earlier. This interplay is made more or less affordable by the simplicity of the supporting structure employed, relegating the vast majority of the partitions present in this construction to nonbearing status. Note the clever bathroom designs that adapt to the angled impositions and the symbolic elliptical kitchen peninsula presenting a positive form in the context of a rectilinear space in contrast to the living room's void of the building's implicitly solid form.*

Figure 2 *Backside. An extraordinary interplay between a gable-roofed building with an aggrandized eave and delightfully eccentric substructures, each addressing a particular series of spaces set within the building.*

Figure 3 *Entry. Porte cochere (right) and entry canopy (center) animistically queue up to slip into the mother-hen house. Note the distilled and abstracted eave trim and the crisp interpretation of traditional eave brackets. Simple materials are conspired by an abstracting hand.*

Figure 4 *Entry. This centering space explicitly affords a multitude of options and possible directions and presents the sense of an architectural launching pad.*

3

ing effortlessness of this building's mass is all the more remarkable. In fact, full-size mockups were employed to "reality check" the presumptions of the architect as to the final location and massing of the home prior to construction. Given the inherently expensive qualities of building on an island, the price tag of about $100 a square foot is remarkable. This relatively low building cost is facilitated by several factors. The simple perimeter of the construction, a simple support system for all the seemingly "wacky" interior subdivisions, and the use of standard materials and joinery for the trim elaborations all played a role in keeping costs down. Essentially, two simple framing bays were employed, both bearing on one common bearing line. Needless to say, the roof form itself was absolutely generic, and the distinctive pavilions cum porches are detailed in such a way as to allow for relatively low tech construction techniques.

4

The array of appurtenances is made fully palatable by the unrelenting and overarching sense of containment the simple enclosing building box affords. This is an exoskeletal integrity, in which the exterior form exists only in short-term memory once the cubic crustacean's shell has been pierced and the building's interior begins to unfold. Without this memory of exterior definition, the interior meanderings might seem out of control, until its internal consistencies are revealed. On a floor-to-floor basis, the two major spaces formed—living room and master bedroom—reside above each other and share a common oval shape, one skewed from the other but both sharing a vertically expressive and (naturally) skewed porch cum pavilion exterior substructure. Similarly, the connecting stair is set to register precisely to one corner of the house and begins at the rotunda entry and ends at a rotunda that facilitates the joint between the access to the master bedroom and a subordinate hallway linking the three guest bedrooms. Additionally, the kitchen that registers to one corner of the house has its rectilinear fit mirrored by the two demibedrooms on the floor above, while the fourth corner of the house is staked out by a skewed dining room, which in turn is mirrored by the remaining skewed bedroom above. In this way there is a floor-to-floor echo that abets the overall outside-inside dynamic.

This project is well known in the architectural community for its ornamental detailing, which uses simple sticks of standard framing and trim material as evocative semibotanic ornament and distills trim elements that are historically ornamental into abstracted forms—all playfully colored to characterize their lightly idiosyncratic qualities.

Given the contrast of complexity and predictability explicitly interposed in this house, it could be said to be a metaphor for the possibilities involved in the design of any small house. Its gable-faced form is perhaps the most familiar architectural object in the American consciousness. If paradigms preempt innovation, then the design of any home fails to meet their highest potential. In this particular case the potential for expression and permutation is realized in radical fashion, involving extraordinary complexity of spatial and geometric manipulation employing curvilinear, angular, and ornament elements, which in turn utilize color, surface, form, and movement. In short, an almost complete lexicon of experientially evocative architectural features is fully engaged.

It is clear that those who see small houses as implicitly limiting the potential for aesthetic expression are simply blind to the evident truth present in this building. Mark Simon and Trip Wyeth of Centerbrook Architects have maximized these experiential explorations while keeping a clearheaded apprehension of budgetary constraint and a site that has topographical difficulties and historic context. Would that all houses were this blind to their limitations—a blindness that allows architects to see the latent potentials so clearly.

Figure 5 *(opposite) Living room. The living room as seen from the dining room with a clear view through to the living room's entry threshold. This photograph evidences the conspiratorial experiential teasing that makes this home a neverending array of interweaving shapes, spaces, colors, light levels, and sources.*

In View

A tough site becomes an extraordinary experience via a small home.

EVERY cloud has a silver lining, and in this case the silver lining was bright enough to become the genesis for a house design. The cloudy countenance of this site was a 60-foot drop in elevation over the length of a modestly sized lot in the Blue Ridge Mountains of southwestern Virginia. But Washington, D.C., architect Heather Cass saw the latent potential quite clearly. Set at the end of a cul-de-sac, this home has the sort of view that doesn't come along very often— a spectacular setting of miles upon miles of mountain tops that surround the site.

This was to be a vacation home, so the view was an amenity whose appeal overwhelmed the problematic aspects of building on such a steeply sloping site. Clearly, when a site falls away so dramatically, there is little opportunity to seize the landscape for any meaningful use other than as support for the home that is to be built upon it. This might prove problematic for full-time occupancy, but part-time habitation can tolerate such limitations. This home design compensates by creating its own landscape in the form of outsized decks feeding off all levels of the home.

As with all good small houses, this house benefits from a limited multiple-personality syndrome. Given its hillside perch, it's not surprising that

---

S T A T S

PROJECT NAME AND LOCATION:
Martin House, Wintergreen, Virginia

ARCHITECT:
Cass & Associates

COMPLETION DATE:
1992

TOTAL HEATED SQUARE FEET:
3,000

PERCEIVED SQUARE FOOTAGE:
3,895

CIRCULATION-TO-TOTAL-AREA RATIO:
10 percent

BEDROOM-SPACE-TO-TOTAL-AREA RATIO:
26 percent

GROSS COST:
$300,000

COST PER SQUARE FOOT:
$100

DURATION OF DESIGN PROCESS:
Nine months

DURATION OF CONSTRUCTION:
Nine months

Photos © Robert Lautman.
Drawings by the architects.

---

this is a "top-down" design, where the top floor registers to the level of the access road and the rest of the house merely spans the gap between that level and the ground. A clear-headed functional layout allows every formal, spatial, structural, and functional aspect of the home to acknowledge the "take-your-breath-away" view the house beholds. Each level of this home is a study in the meshing of structure and space, using an explicit column grid as an organizing feature. Abstractly, the top floor is essentially basilical in organization with the subordinate flanking pieces and the two doubled-up column spacings creating a "tartan grid" of multiple axial organization.

All these orthogonal organizers are formed by standard dimensional lumber-framing techniques. Functionally, the home is multiply layered both horizontally and vertically with the uppermost central public living area flanked by the interstitial minor framing bays containing stairs on the one side with kitchen, circulation, and inglenook on the other. The extreme bays are occupied by the master bedroom suite set to one side of a gigantic cantilevered deck serving as the outsized view platform to the distant mountainsides. The upper floor is thus an autonomous "house-within-a-house"—providing full accessibility for parents who visit and need wheelchair accommoda-

Figure 1 *Entry prospect. This extraordinarily expressive home uses a wide variety of architectural tools from bared structure to complementary trim to overt to multiaxial orientation and gridded organization to transform a very simple house shape that is both rich and thoroughly responsive to its site context.*

Figure 2 *Floor plans. A gateway entry is seen at the top of this plan with a bridge spanning the descending landscape, accessing a narrow intermediate bay set in the context of the tartan-gridded frame layout. Each bay's inherent dimension and characteristic are revealed in many ways, either by formal expression, columnation, or roof type. In the case of entry, the slot of space is a singular descending staircase with a cross-axially oriented bridge spanning across its slot of space. The left-hand bay houses the master bedroom suite, and the main central bay has the kitchen, living, and dining area. The entry/stairway bay's counterpart is a deep wall of kitchen cabinets, storage entryway, and inglenook, with the master bedroom bay's counterpart being the outsized view-worshipping deck. On the next level below entry, two completely independent guest bedrooms are set in the main bay with an isolated bedroom set under the master bedroom suite. The stair bay's counterpart becomes a shallow deck. The lowest level is essentially given over to storage and basement space dug into the hillside itself with a family room/emergency bedroom set at the bottom level, which addresses a minor deck with steps descending to grade.*

1

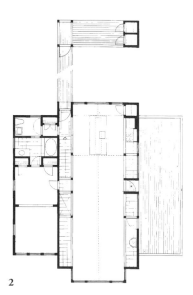

2

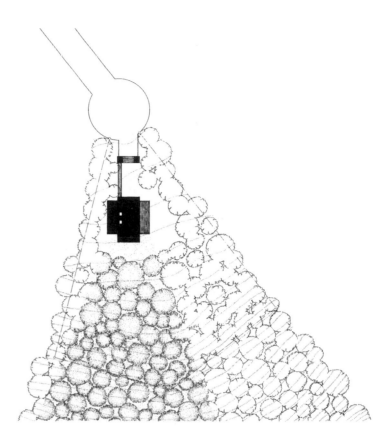

Figure 3 Site. Set at the end of a cul-de-sac, this heavily treed triangular site presented more problems than opportunities for a typical home. By orienting the home so clearly to the view, the home reinvented the vertical stacking of room arrangement.

3

tion. The next floor down is given over to three more bedrooms—one a suite and two sharing a common bath—with a centralized laundry area. All room divisions and circulation paths follow the influence of the tartan grid's, two-directional, major-minor column bay spacing patterns. The ground floor is given over to mechanical space and a family room/emergency bedroom with its own full bath. All levels have view-addressing decks, and all spaces have the opportunity for relatively quick access to the outdoors.

Heather Cass realized that in order to appropriately frame the view and maximize its importance to those who use the house, it would be wisest to conspire a sense of suspense via the home's positioning and spatial interrelationships. A freestanding gateway of two pavilions with a deck spanning between greets the entrant at street level. One of the subordinate gatehouses accesses a 40-foot-long bridge to the top-level living room floor. Large-scale glazing at the backside of the house is sized to allow an indirect "tease" peek at the unlimited vista beyond, and once entry is gained to the home a cascading two-level stair interweaves with intervening "bridges" across its width falling away from the entry threshold. This kinetic sense is further heightened by the wood-capped, double-height space that grabs the entrant's attention and refocuses it from a window level out over the viewscape. This outsized space is controlled via the three-dimensional articulation of the aforementioned post-and-beam framing system of columns, mullions, and incidental beams, involving rhythmic architectural in-out gestures of voiding and filling the narrow bay spaces that flank this living room area. In so doing, the major axes of stairway and central common hall are cross-axially punctuated by the conspired alignments of doorways and subspaces that are formed by the grids employed.

From the exterior the most overtly dramatic feature is not the home's assertive vertical form. It is the innocently honest presence of the outsized structural support for the commodious deck. Rather than utilize spindly

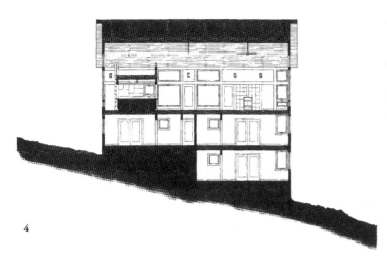

4

Figure 4 *Longitudinal section. The tartan-gridded plan has implications in elevation as well, as windows, light fixtures, and the kitchen (and a loft set above it) all work in cross referenced, gridded coordination with the rigorously organized plan grid.*

Figure 5 *Transverse section. The central public bay is revealed to have a butterfly truss roof spanning not only over the central living room but flanking intermediate bays as well. The master bedroom bay is revealed to be a simple shed. Note that the basement spaces have been "blacked out" in this view.*

columns up to three stories in height, Cass has utilized 9-foot-deep ganged dimensional lumber knee braces to gain extreme rigidity by their full-story depth. In registering these braces to the aforementioned three-dimensional structural grid that supports the central bay of the house, an abstract plan organization becomes three-dimensional structural expressionism, and the carefully considered steel angles tying the components together become a subordinate series of focal points, giving a potentially abstract system a sense of scale and craftsmanship.

From the exterior, the materials used reinforce the sense of a superstructural grid interacting with a simple gable form. It is the dialogue between the linear and the formal, the solidity of a proud gable mass form and the peek-a-boo quality of its perforations, which makes this home a delightful architectural exercise. Although this home alludes to a "shotgun shack" axially derived organization, it has more to say about intricate interweaving of space, structure, and form.

Although this is a vacation home—built for Ned and Carol Martin and their six children, ranging in age from preadolescent to postgraduate—it has full-sized bedrooms, three and half baths, and a "real" kitchen, as well as a separate informal living space. There is less storage than in a full-time residence, but the spatial and structural efficiencies evident are still applicable to any small-home design.

5

It is the clearheaded expressiveness of Heather Cass's design that overcomes the negative potentialities of the inhospitable hillside. An architectural event can be both inspiring and view focused and thereby provide a homing beacon for a large family. It is not often that the competing forces of view and architecture can be so elegantly coalesced, but small houses have a unique capacity to dominate a site with the presence of their condensed forms and at the same time rest lightly on the landscape via their diminished footprint and minimized mass.

6

Figure 6 *Entry. As the entry stair zooms down two flights to grade, a clear shot is seen through two spanning floor plan extensions, and then secondarily an angled prospect through the entire house is seen, and the fully realized three-dimensional tartan grid can be seen as its expression in both. Structural members and ornamental trim pieces provide an overarching order to a view-focused home.*

Figure 7 *(opposite) Living-dining room as seen from the kitchen-loft space. Once again, trim and structure combine to celebrate an overarching order of the grid.*

Modest Intentions, Vigorously Expressed

A diminutive house respects the landscape and provides exceptional accommodation for its occupants.

THIS home evidences many of the benefits of custom home design that are implicit for houses of any size but become almost miraculous when seen in the context of a relatively small building. There is an extraordinary quantity of spatial diversity, formal articulation, and intensity of detailing present given its modest aspirations and simple organizing principles. The design of this 3,200-square-foot, 4½-bedroom home is by Bohlin Cywinski Jackson Architects for Allan and Day Weitzman who are empty-nesters. This home, intended by the architects to be more cottage than mansion, achieves an amazing variety of spatial experiences in the context of a tight footprint. Essentially, a three-and-a-half-story structure rises from a 27- by 40-foot base perimeter and focuses upon the Severn River, north of Annapolis, Maryland.

The organization can be seen in two ways. First, the plan is a distinctly tripartite arrangement with a skewed entry "pseudo-pod" tethered to a dominant central "bar" flanked by a heavily articulated lean-to appendage set to the side opposite the entry. Vertical circulation is set cross-axially to the central axis straddling the three bays. Second, the house functions using these three bays to accommodate entry, living-sleeping-studio spaces, and wet spaces, respectively. Each element expresses its

---

S T A T S

PROJECT NAME AND LOCATION:
Weitzman House,
Annapolis, Maryland

ARCHITECT:
Bohlin Cywinski Jackson

COMPLETION DATE:
1986

TOTAL HEATED SQUARE FEET:
3,200

PERCEIVED SQUARE FOOTAGE:
3,860

CIRCULATION-TO-TOTAL-AREA RATIO:
10 percent

BEDROOM-SPACE-TO-TOTAL-AREA RATIO:
27 percent

GROSS COST:
$275,000

COST PER SQUARE FOOT:
$86

DURATION OF DESIGN PROCESS:
One year

DURATION OF CONSTRUCTION:
One year

Photos © Chris Barone.
Drawings by the architects.

---

identity in a cogent manner: The skewed entry wing is wrought as a shed tilted to greet those coming down the meandering entry path. The central bar nobly respects its own symmetry and aggressively expresses its verticality. The last bay, the saddlebag stacking of wet cores, uses an articulated window wall and outrageously aggrandized column to recognize the view of the river, all capped by a subordinate shed roof set in deference to the relatively grand intentions of the central bar. It should be noted that this home's four-level occupancy is now prohibited by most national building codes, although it was acceptable when the home was built in the mideighties.

Circulation makes every effort to be a grand linking element, ascending from the tilted entry pavilion up to the master bedroom and studio wing of the second floor and further to the topmost floor of guest bedroom suite and studio space, finally leading to a lofty perch that accommodates an oblique view to the water and an extraordinary perspective down through the first two levels.

It is almost surprising that the owners explicitly requested a "modest" home and that the architects describe elements of this home as "naive" and "toylike." The home's level of sophistication and thoughtfulness evidences an unrelenting sense that there should never be a

Figure 1 *Entry prospect. A seemingly simple three-story slab of a building spawns a relatively mute entry pavilion. Indications of the surprising interiors to come can be seen in the dancing glazed wall that joins the entry pavilion to the main home. Note the surrounding water views.*

Figure 2 *Floor plans. A semidetached entryway provides a focal point from afar while a central dominant bar harbors the major public spaces with a large-scale central fireplace addressing the living area. The secondary bay (right) harbors the large-scale kitchen and dining area, which in turn projects to form a terrace that descends to the water view. Wall and window systems thoroughly conspire to create readings between parts (ragged glazing walls, celebrational columns, effervescent stairs). On the second floor a large-sized master bedroom suite (top) is set to the rear of the building with a study set to address the view and the multiheight atrium set above the dining area. The uppermost level has a separate bedroom with a loft above it and a bathroom with another study-studio space set to address the view out to the water and down through the atrium. Unseen is a downstairs bedroom/family room.*

1

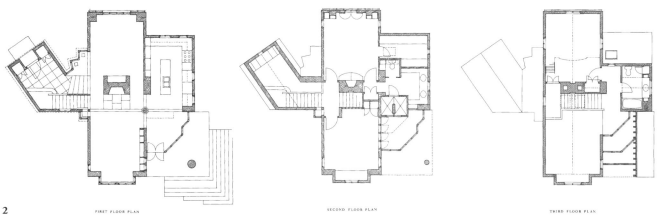

2

FIRST FLOOR PLAN   SECOND FLOOR PLAN   THIRD FLOOR PLAN

3

Figure 3 *Water side. Set to have a sweeping view out over the lake, the backside view of this home is radically different from its front where formerly stoic centered roofs are extended to form a shed, underneath which billowing window walls are barely contained.*

Figure 4 *Transverse section. An overtly vertical ascension from entry (left) up through to lofty study and bedroom spaces set at the top of the stairs. A central fireplace utilizes the stair underside with a mirrored ceiling-scape to provide for an inglenook while bathrooms and kitchen stack in the right-side bay and a "real" stair descends to a fully usable basement level.*

Figure 5 *Longitudinal section. Cut through the atrium, a celebrational roof (right) spawns a meandering glass wall that focuses upon an oblique view of the water, and serving spaces of bathrooms and kitchen are incidentally cut by this view. Note the coincidence of skylight and interior window set above the toilet in the second floor and the use of multiple ceiling articulations to allow many implicit structural and geometrical possibilities to be manifest. Note the repetition in glazing, cabinetry, and trim of an orthogonal gridded motif.*

missed opportunity even when designing a home of this size and scale. Trim is alternately semisymbolic of a cottage-style vernacular or elegantly expressive of simple structural shapes highlighted by color.

There are lessons to be learned beyond the aesthetic in this home as well. By reigning in the perimeter of this home, a fairly problematic subsoil condition was avoided, and the possibility for erosion was minimized. The heights attained by this vertically stacked structure allow for an extraordinary range of views and maintain a proud, if diminutive, presence in the natural world. By stacking all the wet cores and isolating the central chimney mass and HVAC ducting, this home evidences the ability to reduce costs and enhance efficiency by vertical alignment of service areas.

The structure of the home is also deceptively simple, utilizing very normative framing techniques, all designed with respect for simple framing dimensions. The tight bay spacing allows for easy accommodation of the meandering window walls at both the entry joint and the backside shed.

Additionally, a great amount of specialized functional integration is evident in the accommodation of two studio spaces (on the second and third floors) keyed to the owners' desire to keep their avocations separate from their socializing (and separate from each other). Similarly, a double shower is included in the master bath that is set

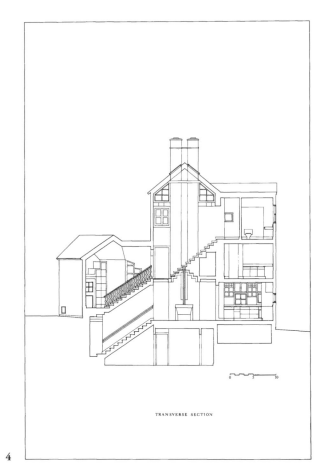

TRANSVERSE SECTION

4

LONGITUDINAL SECTION

5

within the context of a single space. Skylights are used to provide light for a basement guest bedroom and accentuate the impact and presence of the three-story chimney mass mentioned earlier, as well as to provide illumination for other interior spaces.

The unrelenting articulation of the wide variety of elements—spatial, structural, material, functional, formal, and experiential—evidences the spirit of innovation that can free a small home from the confines of preconceived limitation. Most importantly this is a home with modest underpinnings if elaborate realizations. Any home can benefit from the distillation and pungency that a small house affords, even one as interwoven and expressive as this. It is clear that a small home need not be a simple home as long as its intentions are well known. This home maintains its integrity by the use of consistent and obvious organizing principles, both inside and out. The rest is artful articulation on a grand scale.

Figure 6 *Third-floor bedroom. Overflow sleeping space is provided in a loft. The simple curvilinear lines are applied and color is carefully chosen to provide a sense of complete control over the design of all the elements imposed, underscoring a playful honesty that characterizes much of this house's detailing.*

Figure 7 *Entry, stair. A top-lit ascending vertical space creates an extraordinary beckoning axial sequence with flooring, balusters, and trim all conspiring to exhilarate those entering the building and promote a desire for further exploration. The central diagonally axial column can be seen in the slot of opening between the stair and the chimney mass in the left background.*

6

7

Figure 8 *Living/dining area. The column set at the crux of bearing conditions between the living area and dining area has its exterior counterpart in the superaggrandized column that supports the extended shed roof, which in turn contains the outsized and ever-articulating glazed wall that presents the sweetest prospect over the water.*

Figure 9 *(opposite) Top level of atrium. Doubled roof rafters span multiple layers of spaces and the great outdoors with multiple partial reflections creating a sense of orthogonally subdivided glazing in a kinetically ebullient dance.*

8

Multiple Personalities with a Single Focus

A professional-residential compound offers lessons for the future.

As the computer obviates the dictatorial power of urban centers to control the locus of our work-a-day worlds, it is becoming more and more common for people to work where they live or in close proximity to their living quarters.

Architects have often combined their studio and residential space. Charles Moore had an unprecedented ensemble of residences and offices strewn throughout the United States. There is little in his avowed polemic to evidence that Charles Moore was a didactic architect with a prescription for a "correct" mode of living, unlike Frank Lloyd Wright and his Taliesin. The very nature and design of this complex can be said to symbolize the potential for small houses to accommodate a variety of living arrangements and professional foci.

Essentially, this is an ensemble of three built parts: one house for Moore himself, one house for his partner in Texas, Arthur Andersson, and an architectural studio. Set on a hillside in Austin, Texas, this complex manifests a diversity of functions and forms interwoven with several unifying features.

Upon entry to a motor court, one wall of the combined complex forms a gateway—a threshold to an extraordinary axis that cascades to a linear lap pool that projects out into the landscape. This powerful and open-ended axis is received by a multitude

STATS

PROJECT NAME AND LOCATION:
"The Lazy O,"
Austin, Texas

ARCHITECT:
Moore/Andersson Architects

COMPLETION DATE:
1991

TOTAL HEATED SQUARE FEET:
5,000

PERCEIVED SQUARE FOOTAGE:
6,182

CIRCULATION-TO-TOTAL-AREA RATIO:
2 percent

BEDROOM-SPACE-TO-TOTAL-AREA RATIO:
9 percent

GROSS COST:
$400,000

COST PER SQUARE FOOT:
$80

DURATION OF DESIGN PROCESS:
Four months

DURATION OF CONSTRUCTION:
Four years

Photos © Tim Hursley.
Drawings by the architects.

of cross-axial relationships formed by some richly rendered landscape objects, building elements, and adjacencies—all set to the same orthogonal grid. This architectural activity has its permutations organized to allow for space to be "carved out," forming a series of interweaving courts, walks, built-in seating, and landscape elements. Almost invisibly, all three buildings relate to an outscaled oval overlay to all this rectilinear gridding. This lilting linear influence is the embodiment of counterpoint amid the heavily conspired and articulated architecture employed.

The occupancy accommodated is not a traditional one. It involves a two-bedroom, 2,400-square-foot, part-time residence for Moore, with two multipurpose loft spaces set on a second floor; a 900-square-foot, two-bedroom house with dense-packed storage for a full-time residence for Andersson; and 1,600-square feet of architectural studio space. Given the diversity of form, intensity of embellishment, and site development, the $80-a-square-foot price tag is absolutely remarkable. It is a tight price tag that has imposed the major structural elements to be coordinated in a rectilinear fashion and the palette of materials to be limited to those seen often in the Texas hill country.

This project uses materials to effect a classic "wolf in sheep's clothing"/"stealth" scheme that sneaks up

Figure 1 *Floor plans. An ensemble involving four basic components is axially and cross-axially linked as well as having a linear halo of an outsized ellipse traced throughout the large-scale composition. The office-studio is located in a controlled square seen at the lower left. Arthur Andersson's home is to the lower right, the late Charles Moore's home is to the upper left, and the interweaving and interwoven courtyard/lap pool is in a highly controlled yet naturally oriented common outdoor living area. The ellipsoidal influence is resonant but real in that it defines the edge between the private/serving spaces and the common spaces present within each house. In the case of the Andersson home, its arcing form subdivides a rectilinearly progressive corner home of several levels with a multitude of axial and cross-axial organizing features. For Andersson's home, the curvilinear imposition is a simple subdivision in a rectangular box. The clearly defined entry axis has an overt counteraxis that spans from the hearth of the Moore home through and across the lap pool. Each building has separate and unaligned entryways providing ample privacy for comings and goings. Dense-pack planning occurs to the outer edges of this compound with open and living areas addressing the courtyard and beyond.*

Figure 2 *Major axis looking back. Architectural forms and landscape elements, ornament, and furniture create a wondrously rich environment that allows multiple functions to co-exist without compromise! buildings combined within the complex.*

2

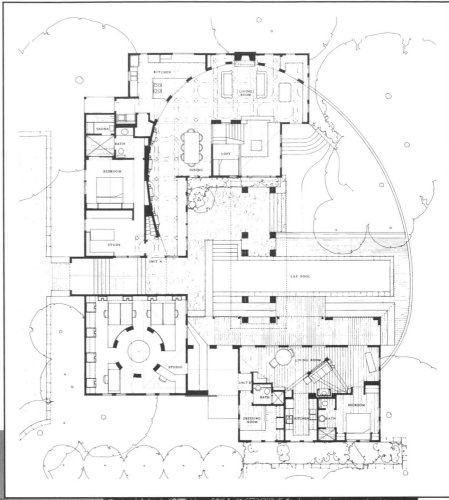

1

Figure 3 *Entry prospect. Once the gates are opened, a wonderland is revealed—a top-lit vaulted space and ever-descending ground plane, with views metered by batten siding and lighting fixtures and framed by a wide variety of landscape and architectural elements.*

Figure 4 *Entry section. A gateway from a common parking courtyard to the left allows for vertical descent and axial orientation to the lap pool (right) while the cross-axial trellis (center) orients to the Moore home's living area and hearth.*

Figure 5 *Axonometric. Simple gable roof constructions provide shelter while nonbearing (and often kinetically expressive) interior walls follow the ellipsoidal influence. A common architectural geometry is manipulated and houses a consistently kinetic interior event that transcends the limitations of the individual buildings combined within the complex.*

3

on you with prosaic materials and blank exterior forms and whose experiential impact explodes once the soft underbelly of the courtyard and the spaces that feed upon it are encountered. Subordinate and almost anonymously gray board-and-batten siding and corrugated-steel roofing give way to extreme color variations and overtly decorous detailing inside, first evidenced by a combination galvanized- and stainless-steel gateway and fully fleshed out in the extraordinarily ornamentalized living spaces of the two residences. The sense is one where a commonality of hyperactive mind-set is reached upon the piercing of this bland gray veil, and the mental musings within evidence an architectural scope and reach that is simply extraordinary given the "cheek-by-jowl" quality of this interwoven complex. Almost all materials employed are generic, and paint leverages an extreme impact at a minimal cost in the differentiation and articulation of the various elements. Architectural ornament is both aggrandized symbolically and trivialized comedically throughout all the spaces involved. Icons, both antique and newly minted, fleck the interior spaces, and a sense of wonder and delight can only be adequately described in pictures. Needless to say, the overlayed elliptical influence serves as a parade ground for this ongoing march of architectural expression.

ECTION THROUGH COURTYARD LOOKING NORTH

4

In these overt and subtle ways, this complex of buildings shows the unique potential of downsized dwellings. Small houses can be grouped to accommodate a wide variety of functions simply because of their diminutive stature. The typical American home accommodates multifunctional diversity via an ever-increasing airbag of space containing an ongoing litany of functional distinctions given to a seemingly endless array of rooms. Houses can be designed to maximize efficiency and thus accommodate diversity if the serving spaces of bathroom, kitchen, and storage can be dense-packed to a cabinetmaker's level of design definition, allowing the remaining common spaces to be freed up as they are in this project.

5

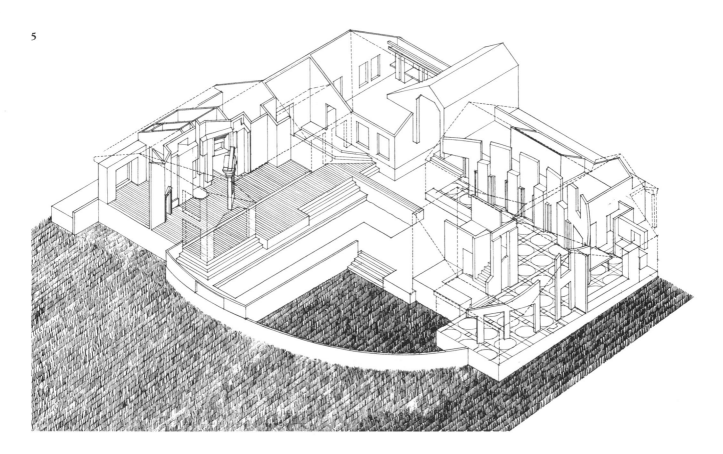

Figure 6 *Cross-axial section. The Andersson house (left) has its serving spaces set within a flat ceiling context and its public spaces addressing the courtyard having a vaulted ceiling-scape, while the Moore house (right) follows the contours of the land to provide a depressed floor-vaulted roof living room with a ascending look out over the courtyard. The trellis's column organization responds both to the primary entry axis and to the organizing aspects of the entire compound.*

SECTION THROUGH COURTYARD LOOKING WEST

6

It is only because this complex "takes care of business" via the careful insinuation of these serving spaces that the served spaces of living, dining, and courtyard can be fully liberated to afford the spatial and ornamental pyrotechnics that have been employed.

What makes this building all the more intriguing is that there are virtually no real working drawings for this project. This was a "design-as-you-go," ad hoc exercise with the intermittent presence of Moore and the ongoing presence of Andersson giving direction and focus. Despite this, the two residences are virtually microdesigned in their planning so they can be downsized to a point where a building form that might typically harbor a large Texas family can harbor two households and an office space.

It is perhaps the oxymoronic future of the American home that it will need to become more functionally efficient to facilitate the limitless variety of custom fits necessitated by our ever-fractionalized life-styles. By introducing the workplace into the context of home and hearth, a functional diversity is achieved that is both exhilarating and a little bit scary as well. In this particular case the architectural studio has only indirect functional and visual access to the central court with its almost diagrammatically square plan set as the blind cornerpost amid the pirouetting residences.

If the conceptual baggage of traditional housing sizes and types can be overcome, this sort of mutation in the American home can be allowed to proceed. Single-family homes set isolated from one another in a meandering grid of streets may be our present condition, but it is definitely tied more to precedent than to our cultural future. As families fracture and re-form and as careers explode from our central urban cores into the countryside, it is just this sort of residential-professional environment that will claim an ever-increasing share of the housing marketplace. Zoning codes will need to adapt, but the trend is unavoidable.

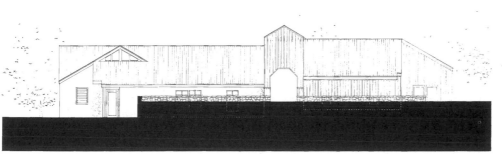

WEST ELEVATION

7

Figure 7 *Entry elevation. An ambiguously low eave line (facilitated by the drop off of the site beyond, and thus a lower floor level) and a celebratory tower-gateway amidships present an intriguing but stark public face.*

Figure 8 The Andersson living room. A tiny inglenook is framed by a semi-free-standing architectural centerpiece with a canted ceiling and icons as light fixtures, evidence of the latent and overt humor present throughout this work.

8

10

Cookie-cutter homes simply don't mesh with a culture that is redefining the word *family* at every turn. As these revisions to our social fabric continue to unravel its predictable weave, a crazy quilt of options and identities will begin to take over a certain portion of the future housing market. The Quarry Road house, dubbed "The Lazy O" by the late Charles Moore, evidences the best part of design/build innovation, where a goodly amount of functional experimentation is mixed with architectural zest and panache to form an image that has as much latent functional meaning as it has aesthetic rewards.

Now that Charles Moore has passed on, this home will be transformed into a memorial to his work, either as a hostel for young architects or a more museumlike reincarnation. Not only is this in the best spirit of small-house design and academic encouragement, but it is in the best spirit of one of this century's most accomplished and beloved practitioners.

Appendixes

The Concept of "Perceptual Space"

As noted in The Small House, and adapted for this book.

W HEN architects describe their projects to other architects, clients, or the media, they often use square footages to delineate the scale of their work.

The baseline square footages laid out in this book are based on standard practice of counting all heated space within perimeter walls, and the use of double-height space and other variations has been eschewed.

Sometimes architects cheat to increase the amount of reported square footage built to reduce the cost per square foot of the projects. The more they build for less, the more innovative and resourceful they appear in spending their clients' money.

In the presentation of these houses, the use of nominal figures alone would misrepresent the projects. I have therefore attempted to offer an alternative to nominal square footages. I have proposed that a secondary figure be presented, a figure ambiguously called "perceived square footage." Since most square-footage figures are interpretive products, it is important to acknowledge that a building is *perceived*, not *measured*.

Two essential elements unacknowledged in nominal-square-footage calculation are axes and double-height spaces. Since these elements are used in the recalculation, definitions are needed.

Axis. An axis is a linear space linked visually through other spaces, with a beginning and an end defined by incidence with an aligned element—door, window, stair, fireplace, and so on. Axes are often corridors, or subdividing, orienting alignments in larger rooms.

Double-height space. Double-height space is space that is 10 or more feet high, before any cathedralizing ceiling angling. Note that for ease of calculation, no recognition of ceiling peak height is considered in this formula.

In addition, small architecturally defined exterior spaces directly integrated into the house plan—decks, patios, porches—should be acknowledged, but unoccupiable space not visible from the interior of the house should not.

THE FORMULA

Axes

Since axes are often perceived and utilized, all axes, as separable plan elements, are counted twice.

Example: The original Dickinson house has one major axis, which is 3.5 by 38 feet, and three subaxes—kitchen, living room (fireplace and west window), and second-floor corridor—all assumed at 3 by 20 feet. The total added square feet would equal:

$$(3.5 \times 38) + (3 \times 20) = 313 \text{ square feet}$$

Double-Height Space

The second house-expanding perceived space does not increase usable floor area but should be counted. Since all space has its major impact upon entry and since vertically enhanced space relies on the diagonal perception along sight lines across rooms, all spaces with a wall height of 10 feet or more should be perceptually sized as the true cross dimension at entry times the perceived diagonal to the maximum wall height. The resultant square-foot count replaces the normal length times width measurement in nominal computation; hence, there is a net gain.

Example: In the original Dickinson house the living room and study area have two-story spaces. Normally, the living room would be calculated as 16 by 20 feet and the den as 13 by 12 feet for a total of 476 square feet. Figured as perceived square feet, the result is as follows:

Living room:

> 20 actual feet x 22 diagonal feet = 440 square feet

Study:

> Single-height portion = 7 x 12 feet = 84 square feet
> Double-height portion = 12 actual feet x 21 diagonal feet = 252 square feet

The total number of perceived square feet in these rooms is 776. This represents a net increase of 300 square feet, or 40 percent.

Defined Space

All spaces defined architecturally but unheated or necessarily enclosed that are directly perceived from within the house should be acknowledged in the computation of perceived space. Since these spaces are usable only during fair weather, they are counted as half their nominal square feet.

Example: In the original Dickinson house the entry deck (3.5 by 5 feet) and north deck (6.75 by 20 feet) would be counted as follows:

$$\frac{(3.5 \times 5) + (6.75 \times 20)}{2} = 76.25 \text{ square feet}$$

Unused Space

Carports and unheated utility spaces that have no functional utility save appliance storage and that are unperceived from the house should not be counted.

Example: In the original Dickinson house the 450-square-foot carport would not be counted.

The Whole-House Example

Here are the results all factored into the original Dickinson house:

Total nominal square feet, heated:	1,100
Added areas:	
Axes	313
Double-height space (net increase)	300
Defined, unheated space	76
Total perceived square feet:	± 1,789

It is hoped that as the perceived square footages are compared with the nominal figures for the projects presented, an enhanced sense of successful small-home design will be communicated.

Directory of Architects

ABACUS, Architects
 & Planners
186 South Street
Boston, MA 02111

Anderson/Schwartz Architects
180 Varick Street
New York, NY 10014

Robert S. Bast Architect
Silver Street
R.R. 1, Box 307
Hinesburg, VT 05461

Bohlin Cywinski Jackson
182 North Franklin Street
Wilkes-Barre, PA 18701-1499

Robert B. Reed of Bayliss Brand
 Wagner, Architects
10801 Main Street
Bellevue, WA 98004

Bumpzoid
260 Fifth Avenue
New York, NY 10001

Arne Bystrom Architect
1617 Post Alley
Seattle, WA 98101

Heather Cass
Cass & Associates, Architects, PC
1532 Sixteenth Street, NW
Washington, D.C. 20036

Mark Simon and Trip Wyeth
Architects & Planners
67 Main Street
Centerbrook, CT 06409

Walter F. Chatham Architect
225 LaFayette Street
New York, NY 10012

Cooper Johnson Smith Architects, Inc.
442 West Kennedy Boulevard, 320
Tampa, FL 33606

Duo Dickinson, Architect
94 Bradley Road
Madison, CT 06443

Jeremiah Eck Architects, Inc.
69 Canal Street
Boston, MA 02114

Garrett and Martha Finney
400 West Hortter Street
Philadelphia, PA 19819

Peter Forbes and Associates, Inc.
70 Long Wharf
Boston, MA 02110

Roderic M. Hartung Architect
8 Novelty Lane
Essex, CT 06426

Lyndon/Buchanan Associates
2604 Ninth Street
Berkeley, CA 94710

William Maclay, Architects & Planners
P.O. Box 335, Main Street
Warren, VT 05674

McInturff Architects
4220 Leeward Place
Bethesda, MD 20816

The Miller/Hull Partnership
Maritime Building, Room 220
911 Western Avenue
Seattle, WA 98104-1031

Moore/Andersson Architects
2102 Quarry Road
Austin, TX 78703

Nagle, Hartray & Associates Ltd
230 North Michigan Avenue
Chicago, IL 60601

Alex Riley and Associates
Box 153
Inverness, CA 94937

Shope Reno Wharton Associates
18 West Putnam Avenue
Greenwich, CT 06830

Stuart Silk Architects
1932 First Avenue East
Seattle, WA 98101

Tigerman McCurry Architects
444 North Wells Street
Chicago, ILL 60610

Richard S. Tremaglio, Architect
Five Story Street
Cambridge, MA 02138

William Turnbull Associates, Architects
  & Planners
Pier 1½, The Embarcadero
San Francisco, CA 94111

Dennis Wedlick
Suite 1220, 885 Third Avenue
New York, NY 10022

Yale Architectural School Building Project
Class of 1995
180 York Street
New Haven, CT 06510

Index

ABOUT THE AUTHOR

Duo Dickinson is a registered architect with his own practice in residential and light commercial design. The winner of a 1985 *Architectural Record* Record House Award, Mr. Dickinson is the author of *The Small House, Adding On,* and *Common Walls/Private Homes.* His work has been published in more than 40 magazines and has been featured on national television. He has taught at Yale University and Roger Williams College, and he has lectured at seminars and conferences throughout the United States.

Paul Bosman Architects
302 Main Street, Suite 201
Los Altos, CA   94022